Female Circumcision

PENNSYLVANIA STUDIES IN HUMAN RIGHTS

Bert B. Lockwood, Jr., Series Editor

A complete list of books in the series is available from the publisher.

Female Circumcision

Multicultural Perspectives

Edited by Rogaia Mustafa Abusharaf

PENN

University of Pennsylvania Press
Philadelphia

10   9   8   7   6   5   4   3   2   1

Published by
University of Pennsylvania Press
Philadelphia, Pennsylvania 19104-4112

Library of Congress Cataloging-in-Publication Data

Female circumcision : multicultural perspectives / edited by Rogaia Mustafa Abusharaf.
    p.   cm.—(Pennsylvania studies in human rights)
  ISBN-13 : 978-0-8122-3924-9
  ISBN-10 : 0-8122-3924-5 (cloth : alk. paper)
  Includes bibliographical references and index.
    1. Female circumcision—Africa.   2. Female circumcision—Moral and ethical aspects—Africa. 3. Female circumcision—Africa—Prevention.   I. Abusharaf, Rogaia Mustafa.
II. Series.
GN645.F43   2006
391.2096—dc22   2005042362

Contents

Chapter 1
Introduction: The Custom in Question

Rogaia Mustafa Abusharaf

I do not wish them to have power over men; but over themselves.
—Mary Wollstonecraft, A Vindication of the Rights of Woman, 1792

When the sign heralding the promising waters arrives—the sighting of flying fish beyond the prow of the boat—the crewman facing forward ought to be the first to see them.
—Toni Morrison, Playing in the Dark, 1992

Changing traditions and behaviors that have such long histories is not easy. When one does not understand a problem it is not easy to appreciate it. If you do not understand your health, you cannot appreciate the problems of female genital cutting, and if you do not continue to educate people they will not understand. All we are seeking is knowledge. Knowledge will change people's attitudes.
—Mansata, former female circumciser in the Gambia, 2000

Bolokoli, khifad, tahara, tahoor, qodiin, irua, bondo, kuruna, negekorsigin, and kene-kene are a few of the terms used in local African languages to denote a set of cultural practices collectively known as female circumcision. These practices, which are fervently adhered to by some ethnic and national groups, "are differentially embedded in specific institutional and social structures" (Kratz 1994: 346). In each context, there is marked variation in prevalence, in the type of surgery performed, and in the rituals associated with it. Even within the same geographic locality, the nature of the practice, its justifications, and the age at which it is performed differ vastly by ethnicity and class. For instance, among the Yoruba of southwestern Nigeria, 90 percent of adults remain determinedly committed to the perpetuation of female circumcision, whereas in another section of the same ethnic group, the Ijebus, this tradition, which was formerly widespread in the community, has been unreservedly rejected (WHO 1996).

Generations of supporters of these contested practices espouse a wide range of ideas about why female circumcision constitutes an important part of their cosmology and worldview. These practices, which others often contemplate with horror and trepidation, are exalted and sanctified through the very language used to refer to them. Most of the local terms translate as ritual purification. To followers, these operations are, first and foremost, important events constituting "a domain of cosmological fixity: the changes they encompass are a recalibration of local detail to the grand order of things" (Herzfeld 2001: 209).

No one has been able to identify the origin of female circumcision with any accuracy, and explanations of its genesis and growth remain highly speculative. One prevalent belief, which was widely held by some European travelers, saw the practice as an ancient Egyptian invention and explained its adoption in other localities as a product of cultural diffusion. For example, Karim and Ammar showed how "Aetius (A.D. 502–575) quoted with approval the Egyptian custom of the amputation of the clitoris before it grows large chiefly about the time when the girl is marriageable" (Karim and Ammar 1965: 3). However, the ascription of the practice to ancient Egypt remains highly controversial in historical scholarship.

An alternative, yet equally ubiquitous supposition on the question of origin has identified Islam as the incontestable source of the practice. This assumption is clear in David Gollaher's argument that "In the world of Islam, female circumcision has long been acknowledged as a rightful counterpart to male circumcision" (Gollaher 2000: 191). Linking female circumcision to Islamic philosophy and instruction has proven quite dubious. If Islam is indeed the foundation of female circumcision, how can we explain the persistence of the tradition among non-Muslim peoples who embrace it with equal ardor and enthusiasm? Conversely, how can we account for the fact that the great majority of adherents in some Muslim societies do not carry out any form of female genital excision? Contrary to the facile correlation of Islam and female circumcision evidenced in Esther K. Hicks's *Infibulation: Female Mutilation in Islamic Northeast Africa* (1996), extensive ethnographic studies and demographic reports have demonstrated that people across religious affiliations share the notion that female circumcision is an act of cleanliness and self-control. When the Islamic jurist Jamal Badawi was asked about the existence of authentic texts in the primary sources of Islam which require female circumcision for religious reasons, his reply was unequivocal:

"no mention of female circumcision is to be found in the Qur'an either directly or indirectly. There is no known Hadith which requires female circumcision" (Badawi 2000: 2). Since the Qur'an (the scripture believed to be revealed to the Prophet Muhammad) and the Hadith (the teachings of the Prophet) are the two most important sources for all aspects of jurisprudence and social regulation, the absence of female circumcision from these texts and teachings demonstrates that the various views surrounding the practice are matters of interpretation. These competing interpretations are not to be equated with incontrovertible religious edicts. Several leading Muslim jurists have confirmed that there should be no conjecture or speculation about the fact that these practices preceded Christianity and Islam, and that, whatever their origin may be, the call for ending these harmful operations should be loud and clear. The Religious Leaders' Symposium, held in Gambia in 1998, was a step in the direction of a public repudiation of the practice; the Arusha Declaration on Harmful Traditional Practices urged religious leaders to take concrete steps to strengthen their commitment to educating, sensitizing, and convincing their followers to end female circumcision by forming coalitions for this purpose (see IAC *Newsletter* 28, December 2000: 16).

While female circumcision is, for the most part, carried out in Africa, it exists among other ethnic communities in India, Malaysia, the Arabian Peninsula, and Indonesia (Aldeeb 2001). It is estimated that over 130 million girls and women have undergone genital excision and at least two million per year are expected to go through the practice (WHO 1999). Rising tides of migration have altered the geographical distribution of female circumcision dramatically and prompted momentous debates on tolerance, asylum-seeking and refugee-determination systems, and multiculturalism. Tom Hundley of the *Chicago Tribune* commented that until a few years ago, female circumcision was thought to be a Third World problem, but now, because of shifting immigration flows, the practice has appeared in Europe, especially in Italy, France, Britain, and the Scandinavian countries. Health authorities in Italy estimated that 40,000 women of African origin, mostly Somalis, have undergone the practice and 5000 young girls are currently at risk. The Centers for Disease Control and Prevention estimated that, in the United States alone, more than 150,000 women and girls of African origin have already been cut or might have the operation performed on them (Hundley 2002). On the medical front, health care providers are starting to learn about circumcised female bodies. An article featured in the *Philadelphia Inquirer* reported: "After years of unprecedented African immigration North American health professionals are seeing growing numbers of women who have undergone the controversial practice of female genital mutilation. Doctors have been confronting difficult births, unusual gynecologic problems and ethical quandaries, complicated by their own emotions as they try to relate to patients who consider ritual mutilation normal and proper" (McCullough 1999: 1). The rise of immigration from circumcision-practicing societies to the United States, Canada, Australia, and Western Europe led one observer to aver: "The custom of female circumcision could no longer be considered the possession of any people or continent" (Williams 1997: 498).

Local customs determine which kind of genital surgery girls undergo. The major types of surgical operations are grouped by the World Health Organization (WHO) into three categories (WHO 1998: 5–6). If the clitoris is entirely or partially removed, the operation is termed a clitoridectomy. In excision, the clitoris and part of or all of the labia minora, the inner lips of the vagina, are excised. The most drastic form of genital surgery is infibulation, in which the clitoris and labia minora are removed and then the labia majora, the outer lips of the vagina, are stitched together to cover the urethral and vaginal entrances and a new opening is created for the passage of urine and menstrual blood. Trained or untrained midwives, traditional healers, barbers, and occasionally doctors or nurses perform these surgeries. The consequences of these practices are unquestionably grave. In addition to the immediate risks of bleeding, shock, and sepsis and the longer-term risks of infertility, infection, and obstructed labor, there is an increasing concern in medical circles that unsterilized instruments may be spreading the AIDS virus, particularly when group circumcisions are performed. In her essay "Traditions Against Health: The Struggle for Change," the Sierra Leonian activist Olayinka Koso-Thomas wrote: "In most African countries, as well as in many other parts of the world, certain traditions, which have been kept intact for generations, have had serious effects on the health of the population. The continuation of one of these traditions remains baffling to those who understand its consequences, feel its impact on their lives, and suffer from its application" (Koso-Thomas 1995: 122).

Numerous groups in Africa today are grappling with these practices, which have proven harmful to women and girls, in an attempt to end them once and for all. Increasingly, female circumcision is becoming a focus of eradication programs throughout those African communities in which it is practiced. The well-informed efforts of African men and women to extirpate female circumcision are an obvious sign of significant social transformations that testify to new and emerging forms of internal self-criticism and cultural change. Organizations have adopted comprehensive strategies to persuade people to abandon the practice by articulating this initiative in culturally acceptable terminology and by employing legal, medical, political, and economic means to foster women's political representation and ability to partake in decision making processes. Today the Comité National de Lutte contre la Pratique de l'Excision in Burkina Faso, the National Association of Nigerian Nurses and Midwives, the Babiker Badri Scientific Association for Women's Studies in the Sudan, the National Research Network in Senegal, the National Union of Eritrean Youth, the Seventh Day Adventist Church in Kenya, the Egyptian Task Force, and the Maendeleo Ya Wanawake Organization in Kenya, in addition to 26 active branches of the Inter-African Committee on Traditional Practices Affecting the Health of Women and Children, are all addressing this highly sensitive issue. However, these organizations are well aware that female circumcision cannot be targeted for eradication in isolation from other equally pressing problems affecting the welfare of individuals and communities.

Perennial Debates

Language

Any meaningful discussion dealing with the question of female circumcision should heed the importance of terminology. As David Palmer argues, "language is the stage on which consciousness makes its historical entrance and politics is scripted" (Palmer 1990: 3). Attention to language is vital to understanding the political and ideological debates that surround the subject of circumcision. As the chapters in this volume make clear, the debates on what terms to use to describe these practices extend well beyond words. These practices, which have commanded the attention of Christian missionaries, colonial governments, human rights activists, health providers, and feminists, have come to be widely known as female genital mutilation (FGM). The joint statement issued in April 1997 by WHO, UNICEF, and UNFPA defined the practice as follows: "Female genital mutilation comprises all procedures involving partial or total removal of the external female genitalia or other injury to the female genital organs whether for cultural or other nontherapeutic reasons" (WHO/UNICEF/UNFPA 1997: 6). The Technical Working Group of the World Health Organization agreed that the adoption of Female Genital Mutilation (FGM) as a standard term for these practices is essential for research, training, planning, policy making, and formulating appropriate legislation at all levels (WHO 1996: 5). Participants stressed that the term FGM should include the physical, psychological, and human rights aspects of the practice (WHO 1998). Some nongovernmental organizations have chosen to adopt female genital cutting (FGC), a medical term which appears to be more neutral and sensitive to local beliefs.

Terminology cannot be isolated from the political discourse from which it emanates, or from devising suitable approaches to end the practice. In this collection, the contributors use the terms female circumcision, female genital mutilation, and/or female genital cutting, depending on their preferred practice. The term circumcision is used because it translates directly into African languages and because researchers have found that using FGM alienates those who still support the practice and must be persuaded to relinquish it. After all, these practitioners are the most important players in any effort aiming at obliterating the practice from society. Contributors who choose to use female genital mutilation explain how terminology figured in their particular experiences in the field with shifting attitudes within local communities; this matter is especially salient in Mohamud, Radney, and Ringheim's discussion of the Alternative Rites of Passage program in Kenya and Abdel Hadi's analysis of the abandonment of the practice in Deir El Barsha, a village in rural Egypt.

Beyond the diversity of terminology used in this volume, the question remains: Is female circumcision a vicious act of mutilation and injury, or a virtuous act of purity and rectitude? Two opposing views dominate current debates, one authorizing cultural accommodation and the other advocating the observance of universal standards of human rights. The former view has been widely vilified for sanctioning violence under the guise of culture, and the latter has been reproved for its ethnocentric stance toward cultural rights. The fundamental ideas embedded in these divergent viewpoints toward the practice deserve consideration.

Cultural Accommodation

Both practitioners and scholars endorsing accommodation of cultural difference and the "free exercise of culture" proclaim that reducing the ritual to a crime, as missionary, colonial, and feminist discourses have done, reflects the inability to "read and to see and to hear female genital mutilation as a series of complex social practices and signifiers which circulate in many other practices and signifiers to produce mutable and mutating and mutual social texts" (Fraser 1995: 338). Anthropologists have made significant contributions illuminating the motives for these rituals and the cultural contexts within which female circumcision is carried out (e.g., Boddy 1998; Gruenbaum 2001; Nhlaop 2000; Shweder 2002). Insofar as a culture is a "society's repertory of behavioral, cognitive, and emotional patterns" (Harris 1971: 137), it is self-evident that decisions affecting people's lives are not taken at random. In the words of Michael Ignatieff, "Increasing the freedom of people to exercise their rights depends on close cultural understandings of the frameworks that often constrain choice" (Ignatieff 2001: 72). Indeed, awareness of the body of knowledge, capabilities, and habits associated with female circumcision is key to the comprehension of its persistence across time and locales. Understanding the reasons behind these practices, however, does not imply that we should close our eyes to the effects of the practice on women's bodies. Rather, such knowledge helps us understand why this rite has met with the approval of its adherents for thousands of years.

In one of the touchstone studies on female circumcision, *Woman, Why Do You Weep?* the Sudanese physician Asma El Dareer began with these words: "I was circumcised in 1960, at the age of 11 years. I remember every detail of that operation, and that the worst part was when the wound became infected and I had to be given five injections of penicillin by the operator, a qualified nurse. From that time, I began to think, to wonder why girls are circumcised and to learn more about it" (El Dareer 1983: iii). The multiplicity of reasons advanced to explain why female circumcision is practiced all underscore the centrality of these practices in the formation of social identities across practicing communities. Why, then, do women subject themselves and their daughters to this unmistakably harmful tradition? To chart an episteme or a configurational interpretation of these practices, we must analyze the particular contexts within which such practices come to be accepted and upheld (Abusharaf 1998, 2001; Shweder 2002).

Many decades ago, Ruth Benedict argued that in all studies of social custom, the crux of the matter is that the behavior under consideration must pass through the needle's eye of social acceptance, and only viewing history in its widest sense can give an account of these acceptances and rejections (Benedict 1934: 232). Despite the austere nature of this ritual, its practitioners have attached important symbolic qualities to it. Not only have they come to accept the practice, but they also cling to it with conviction. From the standpoint of adherents, the performance of *tahara* invites an abundance of exultation, happiness, and joy. Such enthusiasm and devotion are rationalized on several grounds and supported by explanations that help spell out why this contested tradition continues to enjoy such a strong hold on people in many

societies today. Supporters attest to its significance in defining and reinforcing ethnicity. Because the justifications of the practice as a vehicle for making
ethnic boundaries are forcefully engraved in the consciousness of the community, few could acknowledge the legitimacy of anti-circumcision messages. In a study unraveling the magnitude of the practice and characteristics
of practitioners in West Africa, Diop et al. have unearthed complex factors
linking circumcision to ethnicity. The authors stated, "Consideration of numerous characteristics suggests that those that are most significant in Burkina Faso are Islamism and ethnicity (specifically the Mossi). The probability
of being circumcised is three times higher among the Mossi and twice as
high for Muslim girls. In Mali, the practice is nearly universal, but the probability of being circumcised is highest for the Bambara/Malinke ethnic group.
All ethnic groups in the Kassena-Nankana District of northern Ghana practice FGC" (Diop et al. 2001: 1–2).

Common rationalizations for the continuation of the practice include
its role in shaping and defining feminine sexuality and gender, aesthetics,
tradition, and religiosity, through which "cultural meanings are renewed and
recreated on a stage as wide as society itself"(Diamond 1989: 150). In spite of
the continued physical suffering that envelopes genital excision, it remains a
powerful celebration of, and homage to, what is desirable and considered be-
fitting in specific communities. As I have argued elsewhere (Abusharaf 2001),
not only have these supporters discounted the severe nature of the surgery,
but they also continue to stress its symbolism and metaphoricity. Suffering
and pain, they confirm, subside in the face of joy and pride, which form
emotional attachments among girls who undergo the practice together as
initiates, as well as between themselves and their sponsors and spectators.
This process, as several studies on ritual symbolism indicate, represents the
alphabet of gender conditioning. According to Audrey Richards, the importance of symbolism in ritual secures a kind of emotional compromise, which
satisfies the majority of the individuals who compose a society and support
its major institutions (Richards 1982: 169). Female circumcision, analogous
to other rites of initiation, can be seen as a way to metamorphose "the physical body into a sort of social filter able to contain within a social form, bio-
logical forces and libidinal energies that lie beneath" (Turner 1995: 168). It is
clear that this practice is entangled in an ideological web of social relations in
a given community of practitioners. This conception not only illuminates
the ways in which ideology shapes practices, but also contributes to comprehension of how emotional ties to specific rituals take hold and prosper. In

the course of the elaborate festivities and the rites associated with genital alterations, pain and suffering are appropriated and employed as techniques for creating social cohesion and gender solidarity. Following the ritual girls become adults, while those who are uncircumcised may not be vested with this rank whatever their age. As far as adherents of the practice are concerned, an uncircumcised female is not a woman. Because of the nature of this belief, its effects on consciousness cannot be underestimated. Not only do these rites initiate new roles and expectations for young women, but they also guarantee the strength of the group. Within this complex ideology, this ritual *tahara* provides a dramatic illustration of how emotions can play a critical role in cementing a practice that may otherwise seem detrimental and reprehensible.

One of the most fruitful approaches to persuading people to abandon this practice is to draw attention to these wide-ranging cultural views. Passing laws is a necessary but not sufficient measure if these laws do not take into account local views. As Geertz argues, "Like sailing, gardening, politics, and poetry, law and ethnography are crafts of place: they work by light of local knowledge" (Geertz 1983: 168). Understanding the complexity of local knowledge on the custom from a woman's standpoint is critical. A former circumciser in the Ivory Coast who became one of the most vocal opponents of the practice expressed concerns about bans or other coercive strategies that ignore the cultural context within which female circumcision is performed. Gueri Agnes Kone argued that there are major problems regarding the impact of a ban on a community: First, the mystical and spiritual elements associated with circumcision ceremonies, such as masks and masquerades accompanying the practice, represent spirits that are believed to protect both the practitioner and the circumcised girl. Banning the practice may therefore generate a sense of spiritual vulnerability (quoted in *Awaken* 1998: 10). In light of this set of cultural understandings, the practice is hardly thought of as a human rights issue, let alone as discrimination.

Universalism and Human Rights

Proponents of cultural accommodation have been taken to task for advancing culture at the expense of rights. For example, in his essay "Idols of Our Tribes? Relativism, Truth and Falsity in Ethnographic Fieldwork and Cross-cultural Interaction," Robert Shanafelt argues, "While it may be the diffusion of relativist methodology and ideals of tolerance that is anthropology's greatest contribution to cross-cultural understanding, this is only a temporary solution to the problem of evaluation whose weaknesses are revealed as the world increasingly globalizes" (Shanafelt 2002: 25).

From a universalistic standpoint, the reasons proposed by proponents of cultural rights are nothing but excuses for committing acts of violence against women. The universalist claims are strongly rendered in Ashley Montagu's "Mutilated Humanity": "I think it would be greatly to our advantage if instead of calling ourselves Homo Sapiens, we called ourselves Homo Mutilans, the mutilating species, the species that mutilates both mind and body, often in the name of reason, of religion, tradition, custom, morality, and law. Were we to adopt such a name for our species, it might focus our attention upon what is wrong with us and where we might begin setting ourselves right." Critics like Montagu portray practitioners as barbarians and savages who perpetuate "an archaic ritual mutilation that has no justification whatever and no place in a civilized society (Montagu 1991: 1).

From this standpoint, female circumcision is seen as a form of violence against women, indistinguishable from murder, rape, trafficking, forced prostitution, physical and emotional abuse, stalking, and sexual harassment. Proponents argue that female circumcision infringes upon human rights conventions that protect and defend women and children from violence and aggression. Seven conventions are cited in support of the argument that this constitutes a human rights violation: The Universal Declaration of Human Rights (1948); The United Nations Convention on the Rights of the Child (1959); The African Charter on the Rights and Welfare of the Child (1990); The United Nations Convention on the Elimination of All Forms of Discrimination Against Women (1992); The United Nations Declaration on Violence Against Women (1993); The World Conference on Human Rights Declaration and Programme of Action, Vienna (1993); and The United Nations High Commission on Refugees Statement Against Gender-Based Violence (1996). In light of the issues asserted at conventions, the practice is considered as a human rights violation because it transgresses three primary accepted protections: the right to heath, the rights of the child, and the right to bodily integrity (CRLP 2002: 69–80).

The Right to Health
The effects of circumcision hinge on the type of surgery, the proficiency of the circumciser, and the circumstances under which the operation was performed. According to Olayinka Koso-Thomas, negative effects occur at six stages: immediate, intermediate, late, at consummation of marriage, at

delivery of the firstborn child, and postnatal (1992: 25). According to Jones et al. (1999), there is a strong correlation between the type of cutting and the probability of health complications. This study, which focused on the practice as a reproductive health issue in clinics in Mali and Burkina Faso, concluded that most of the people are not acquainted with the harmful aspect of the practice, and thus both men and women accept the practice. The literature shows that more often than not, persons with no medical training or knowledge carry out these surgeries.

The Rights of the Child

Female circumcision is seen as a ghastly form of child abuse since children have no say whatsoever about the practice. Girls have no ability to speak against undergoing it; whether they wish their genitals to be cut or not is not important from the adults' point of view. In view of the absence of informed consent, female circumcision is seen as a violation of the Declaration of the Rights of the Child, which emphasizes "children must be guaranteed the opportunity to develop physically in a healthy and normal way" (Boulware-Miller, 1985: 164–65).

The Right to Corporeal and Sexual Integrity

Relying on liberal notions of autonomy and individuality, those who invoke the right to bodily integrity embrace a universalized discourse on sexuality, the body, and subjectivity. Consequently, female circumcision is seen as a form of castration that removes the women's organ of sexual pleasure and in so doing violates their fundamental rights. The argument that female circumcision curbs sexual gratification was advanced by the French urologic surgeon, Gérard Zwang: "Prior to first coitus, the clitoris is usually the only source of female orgasm. It has the obligatory role of activation-establishment of the epigenetic connection of orgasmic circuit. If this neutral reflex circuit is not active during childhood it will never be functional. In the months or years following first coition, intra-vaginal penetration cannot trigger an orgasm unless this circuit is functional. Ablation of the clitoris during the infancy prevents the establishment of the reflex circuit, and the woman will never be able to experience clitoral or vaginal pleasure" (Zwang 1996: 1). Karim and Ammar's study of female circumcision and sexual desire seems to bear out Zwang's analysis. The authors found that among Egyptian women, sexual desire, although not markedly decreased, was qualitatively affected, since orgasm relies on greater stimulation of all the sex organs (Karim and Ammar 1965). Some members from communities practicing female circumcision disagree; they affirm the notion that circumcision does not interfere with sexual desire or with their ability to experience pleasure in any way.

International Feminism

As Adrienne Rich, the American feminist poet, has remarked: "There is a danger today in feminist rhetoric, rigidified in reaction against the past, harping on the same old problems in the same old way, leaving unsaid what's really bothering women and men" (Rich 1993: 124).

Closely related to matters of terminology and universalistic human rights assumptions is the global feminist discourse on female circumcision. Feminists have portrayed the practice as a symptom of female victimization by male authority and an attempt to control women's sexuality (e.g., Eisler 1995; Hicks 1996; Hosken 1994; Lightfoot-Klein 2003; Okin 1999; Walker and Parmar 1993). This position betrays an unsettling propensity to homogenize representations of African women as helpless victims of patriarchal ideologies and norms. The practice has come to occupy an exceptional position in literary and nonfiction works relying heavily on a genre of horror and horrific imagery to highlight its gruesome, sadistic nature (Abusharaf 2002–2003: 127). Describing the performance of circumcision among the Bambara of Mali, Fran Hosken cites Pascal James Imperato's account: "Bambara girls are excised by the women of the blacksmith caste, who are also the pottery makers. The operation is performed on the outskirts of the village in the presence of the assembled adult female relatives of the candidates for the operations. In some villages, the operation is done at the site where the women make pottery. Each girl is seated on an earthen jar, which is turned upside down. Three adult female relatives stand behind her and hold her. With the legs spread apart, the operator takes hold of the clitoris and amputates it with a swift cut of a knife or razor. The amputated clitoris is buried or thrown into a rat hole" (Imperato, quoted in Hosken 1994: 219).

Such representations have undoubtedly shaped the feminist debate on the subject, evoking a discourse that questions the very cultural premises that poetize and legitimize the ritual among its devotees. Indeed, these representations and lacunae, which are so cogently established in the study of African women, have had devastating consequences. According to Richard Shweder, this global discourse "portrays African mothers as mutilators, murderers, and torturers of their children"; he suggests that "we should be dubious of representations that suggest African mothers are bad mothers, or that First World mothers have a better idea of what it means to be a good mother"

(Shweder 2002: 247). The depiction of Africans as cruel and uncivilized in feminist representational discourses created considerable disapproval and remonstration; these discourses are seen as a continuation of "imperial meaning-making" in which Africa and African women are constantly thought of in non-African terms.

Viewing African women primarily as victims of patriarchy, Hanny Lightfoot-Klein labeled them "prisoners of ritual" (Lightfoot-Klein 1989, 1992). This travelogue, which the *New York Times Book Review* praised as a "superb account of what Lightfoot-Klein discovered," has little to say about African adaptability or responsiveness to change. This notion has overwhelming consequences for sculpting the feminist discourse on female circumcision in the Western world (for recent critiques, see James and Robertson 2002; Chanock 2000).

Take, for example, the 1995 Beijing Decade of Women's Conference Platform of Action, which stated that women's rights are human rights. This declaration stresses the universality and indivisibility of human rights. It validates the philosophical line of reasoning that since human rights emanate from an essential human nature we all share, these rights are fundamentally universal, interconnected, and indivisible. Women's rights as human rights are founded on the central principle that men and women have equal rights by virtue of their humanity (CRLP 2005). As Machan acknowledges, the idea of human rights implies that "certain unifying principles of social conduct based on our understanding of what it is to be human, deserves systematic protection by legal enforcement" (Machan 1994: 479). No doubt, the notion of women's rights not only amplifies the possibilities of international law but also allows women the leeway to make international legal claims, as has been extensively examined by the legal scholar Hillary Charlesworth (1993). Indeed the idea of women's rights, human rights, and feminism as a proposition for change as well as a political movement that struggles to put an end to the subjugation of women has received significant support across geopolitical and cultural frontiers. However, there are critical divergences within feminism both as theory and praxis that need to be explored, especially those dealing with the representational discourses on female circumcision. A synopsis of critiques of mainstream feminists has special bearing on this matter. In the United States and Western Europe, mainstream feminism has come under considerable disapproval for discounting the existential realities that shape women's lives in less privileged circumstances (see Alexander and Mohanty 1997, Basu 1995, Mohanty 1988, Paravisin-Gerbert 1997). Mainstream feminists' focus on gender and male dominance at the expense of other forms of difference and hierarchy that weigh heavily in defining women's place in society has been the central point of criticism by feminists in developing countries. To steer clear of the predilection to "fetishize" African women, Sondra Hale urges "white feminists to self-interrogate, calling on us always to be suspicious of our ideas and beliefs, and to work on ways of being effective (invited) allies" (Hale 1994: 26).

Although many African women would recognize the influence of gender in shaping their lives, the common victimization narrative is often privileged at the expense of a thorough consideration of the systemic nature of oppression itself. Johnetta Cole cogently and correctly argues that "without denying the influence, and indeed the importance of tradition and culture, and without minimizing the pain that women can feel from bigoted attitudes and behavior, we can say with overwhelming evidence that the condition of women in society is fundamentally a reflection of economic structures and dependency" (Cole 1980: 162). Because of the critical consequence of class in the determination of women's lives, Gayle Rubin posited, "There is no theory which accounts for the oppression of women—in its endless variety and monotonous similarity, cross-culturally and throughout history—with anything like the explanatory power of the Marxist theory of class oppression" (Rubin 1975: 160). While gender and class are particularly decisive elements of women's experiences, no singular explanation can sufficiently explain the degradation of women's status cross-culturally (see O'Barr 1976). To escape reductionism, it is necessary to be aware of the various subject positions, or, to borrow Homi Bhabha's phrase, "strategies of selfhood," which qualifies race, gender, generation, institutional location, geopolitical locale, and sexual orientation (Bhabha 1994: 9). Disregarding these subject positions has led many women from non-Western societies to "feel foreign in feminism" (see Lam 1994: 865).

The feminist debate over women's rights as human rights poses complex questions surrounding the applicability of human rights laws under specific cultural, political, social, and economic conditions, particularly in the developing world. According to one Nigerian lawyer (quoted in Cook 1993: 5), "the rights discourse in Africa is not meaningful. The severity of socioeconomic problems faced by women in countries undergoing structural adjustment may require basic needs strategy rather than rights strategy." Leslye Amede Obiora put her finger on the pulse of a larger quandary when she argued: "To minimize the disparity between the rhetoric and the reality of human rights norms, those influenced by the liberal tradition can exercise the option of falling back on elaborate sets of infrastructure that is in place to actualize and sustain the rule of law. However, such reliance presupposes the availability of institutions that may not exist in viable forms across cultures" (Obiora 1998: 922).

The pressure to conform to cultural convictions is undoubtedly immense. Recognizing this overwhelming influence, African feminists and women's rights activists such as Nawal El Saadawi, Olayinka Koso-Thomas, Khalda Zahir, Nafisa Awad El Karim, Marie Assaad, Efua Dorkenoo, Fatima Ahmed Ibrahim, Raqiya Abdalla, Asma El Dareer, and Amna Mahgoub Osman have long recognized the gravity of the practice and attempted to engage in culturally acceptable dialogues with practitioners by taking into account their multiple views and concerns. For example, through persuasion and dialogue Amna Mahgoub Osman, a Sudanese feminist, succeeded in convincing tens of relatives to stop the practice; when she encountered tenacious opposition, she persuaded them to choose the mildest form of partial clitoridectomy. One of her relatives recounted the conversation she had had with Amna: "Amna convinced me that circumcision is a harmful practice and reminded me about the suffering of my two older daughters. She said to me 'Khadjia: are you going to be happy if one of your daughters dies in the surgery? You should instill good values in your daughters and help them be strong young women. Circumcision is not going to inculcate good values, only life-long injuries.' She said a lot of things and I am happy I listened. My older daughters are infibulated, the middle ones are excised, and the three young ones are uncircumcised. Amna was one of the closest people to me in this world. She helped me change my mind."

Similar cases across Africa demonstrate that those opposing female circumcision can act without offending believers' sensibilities. In Guinea-Bissau, Aja Tonnkara Diallo Fatimata, a female gynecologist, performs fake operations; her simulation has spared thousands of girls from the harm of surgery while satisfying the relatives who pressure them to undergo the procedure (*San Diego Union-Tribune*, 1 January 1997, quoted in *Awaken*). Such stories show that the "prisoners of ritual" are taking impressive steps towards ending the practice and are emerging as "subjects of their own history" (Magubane and Faris 1985: 91). It is therefore, imperative to heed Obiora's compelling proposal: "It behooves international campaigners to reconceptualize the affected population as subjects, not objects. All things being equal, they are best equipped to inspire critical attitudes and formulate efficient levels of change with more emphasis on grounding than upon attaining triumphs which are unsupported by the rest of the culture" (Obiora 1997: 360).

New Perspectives on Processes of Change

Recent years have witnessed a marked proliferation in the literature dealing with female circumcision across disciplinary boundaries. Anthropological literature on the subject has advanced our knowledge of the symbolic contexts within which female circumcision is performed and sustained. Although this knowledge is crucially important, little has been done to record how these symbolic systems change over time. In spite of the heavy weight that society places on individuals and communities to conform to its dictates and conventions, numerous examples of resistance demonstrate women's adaptability and receptivity to change—and even, happily, their ability to initiate and achieve social transformation in accordance with their own interests. As the studies in this volume demonstrate, cultural patterns do not continue in a static mode, as if frozen in time. Cultural traditions might come to be challenged in the name of the very principles and moralities to which they claim commitments and loyalties (Abul Fadl 1994).

In the light of these broader debates, this volume does not focus narrowly on female circumcision as a set of ritualized surgeries sanctioned by society. Instead, the contributors extend their attention to glaring gaps in current conceptualizations of the problem by exploring a concatenation of issues and processes through which female circumcision is being transformed in local and transnational contexts and by describing in detail the indefatigable attempts of grassroots activists to eradicate these practices in a variety of African societies. For this reason, and in response to the urgent need to illuminate local activism, several authors in this volume present highly descriptive accounts of campaigns against the practice in specific communities. These authors, most of whom are active members of NGOs, draw upon years of direct involvement with the communities in question. As these chapters so richly illustrate, people are not rigid beings unable to respond to the changing worldviews around them, and communities are not fixed, isolated, or immune to deliberate collective transformation. Forces of change within societies where female circumcision has traditionally been carried out have led courageous women and men to modify the practice or end it altogether, and the innovation has spread through multiple social channels until it is widely accepted. In this volume, considerable attention is devoted to systematic documentation of the shifting attitudes of African men and women towards these practices in Africa and among those of the African diaspora. The collection revolves around three substantive topics: the larger context within which female circumcision is performed and debated;

African efforts to end the practice; and current debates surrounding the practice in countries of immigration and asylum-seeking, specifically the United States and Canada.

Understanding local context is vitally important. As Rosalind Petchesky suggests, "Until we know more about the local contexts and ways of thinking in which women in their everyday lives negotiate reproductive health and sexual matters, we cannot assume that reproductive and sexual rights are a goal to seek and therefore one that has universal applicability" (Petchesky 1998: 1). Women's embodiment is configured by structural forces grounded in political economy and enacted on the terrain of intimacy and kinship. How women in specific sociocultural locations and generational positions understand their own situations is as important as what information and resources they have access to in articulating their interests and desires and envisioning alternatives for themselves.

The anthropologist Terence Turner has argued: "That the social body is produced as an ensemble of bodily activities implies that it must be understood as a pattern, or patterns of social appropriation of the real: specifically, the material reality of the body in action" (Turner 1995: 166). Providing a complex analysis of "the body in action" is the agenda of Fadwa El Guindi's pioneering ethnographic fieldwork. In contrast to most writings on female circumcision, which approach the subject from a personal, ideological and polemical, or feminist interventionist perspective, ethnography yields profound insights into the positions and perspectives of those who perform and undergo this ritual practice. In her chapter, "Had *this* been your face would you leave it as is? Female Circumcision Among the Nubians of Egypt," El Guindi contributes an ethnographic analysis of female circumcision as practiced by the Kenuz, Mettokki-speaking Egyptian Nubians who lived in Dahmit, a district that existed south of Aswan prior to the building of the High Dam. In recent decades, in a historical trajectory that parallels in more dramatic fashion the migration of many groups within Africa, the Kenuz Nubians were relocated to new rural communities in the south of Egypt, and men and whole families moved to cities for employment and education. El Guindi began her study with a three-year fieldwork project in Dahmit, Alexandria, and Cairo almost four decades ago, when she not only interviewed women and men on the subject of circumcision but also directly observed its performance. Later, during a research project on the Islamic Movement, she conducted interviews about the practice with college women *muhajjabat* (literally, headscarf-wearing, a sign of religious observance). El Guindi's chapter attends to the ways in which Nubian women have been changing the procedure even as they see continuing the ritual as a valuable way of enhancing and socially validating women's embodiment.

Explicating the multiple religious contexts within which female circumcision is discussed, Sami A. Aldeeb Abu-Sahlieh situates his analysis within a comparative framework and explores the parallels with male circumcision. Aldeeb argues that male and female circumcision are equivalent ritual procedures and that the rationales behind their performance are virtually the same. In examining the debates that surround both forms of surgical genital alteration, Aldeeb advances an argument that in principle any justification for infringing on the sanctity of the human body should be questioned. His conclusion is based on a rigorous analysis of religious arguments about circumcision in Judaism, Christianity, and Islam. He concludes that bodily integrity should be supported regardless of whether the excised person is male or female. While providing a textured comparative analysis of male and female circumcision in specific contexts, this chapter illuminates the possibilities for change across cultural and religious boundaries.

After exploring these contexts and debates surrounding the practice in Part I, the volume turns to examples of current campaigns in Africa to eradicate female circumcision. Although attempts to halt these practices in Africa are not new, globalization has brought this matter to the world's attention and stimulated intense international involvement in the issue. Today, national and international nongovernmental organizations (NGOs) and development agencies play active roles supporting programs initiated by women's groups. Asha Mohamud, Samson Radeny, and Karin Ringheim analyze community-based efforts to eliminate female circumcision in diverse districts in Kenya. Reporting their experiences, research, and evaluation of grassroots-oriented programs, the coauthors enhance our understanding of indigenous African activism.

The Alternative Rites of Passage program is one of the most successful strategies employed by the Maendeleo Ya Wanawake Organization (MYWO) to end the practice of cutting while preserving the ritual and enhancing the transmission of knowledge surrounding it. Although not every community considers circumcision a rite of passage, in those societies where female circumcision is embedded in a time-honored ritual joyfully celebrating the transition from girlhood to young womanhood, the entire process is a public enactment of themes associated with honor, maturity, and marriageability and, in some situations, courage. Whether the operation is carried out individually or with a group, the subject is secluded during the process, and the completion of the transition is celebrated by kinswomen and covillagers. The procedure is considered a vehicle for affirming the young woman's movement through the female life cycle and confirming her position in society. Mohamud, Radeny, and Ringheim show how, in communities where circumcision has been part of culturally valued rights of passage, the abolition of circumcision may be facilitated by the adoption of a viable alternative that replaces genital excision with other meaningful ceremonies. The chapter delineates in detail both community-based efforts and strategies for empowering individuals; most importantly, it shows how vitally women and families making new choices rely on social support from like-minded neighbors and kin. The strong commitment of MYWO to community outreach and mobilization has yielded remarkable success in raising awareness about the practice and enabling women to make effective decisions against continuing it.

In "A Community of Women Empowered: The Story of Deir El Barsha," Amal Abdel Hadi examines the significant shifts in attitudes that led a Christian village in Upper Egypt to abandon the practice without deliberate outside intervention. She argues that the experience of this community can best be understood as an example of economic and cultural change. The communal declaration against female circumcision was intricately linked to development efforts involving the Coptic Evangelical Organization for Social Services and local leaders. Abdel Hadi conducted field research to probe the factors that led villagers to change their thinking about female circumcision, sexuality, and bodily health. She concludes that development and education projects, coupled with substantial male labor migration, combined to produce transformations at the level of gender politics and the village society at large. Celebrating the tenth anniversary of the successful experiment, Deir Al Barsha today is hailed as a model for other communities to emulate. Both El Guindi's and Abdel Hadi's contributions illuminate the centrality of kinship networks in translating women's access to economic resources into decision making power over matters relating to their bodies.

A number of interventions to encourage individuals, families, and communities to abandon the practice of female genital cutting have been undertaken in West Africa over the past decade. Nafissatou J. Diop and Ian Askew provide detailed descriptions of programs conducted by national committees, NGOs, and grassroots activists which center on awareness-raising campaigns that highlight the health problems associated with the practice. Strategies aiming at converting traditional practitioners and formal health care providers who do the cutting have had limited positive results in several countries. More recently, organizations have developed and supported community-based behavior change strategies. Until recently, interventions were implemented without much attention to documenting how they work and evaluating their effects on knowledge, beliefs, attitudes, and behavior. Consequently, there was little empirical evidence of what strategies are most effective in inducing participants and communities to abandon female genital cutting. Since 1996, the Population Council has undertaken a series of operations research studies in the region to test and evaluate a range of strategies. Innovative research methods have been developed to generate quality information concerning anti-FGC campaigns.

Diop and Askew highlight significant findings of operations research studies undertaken in Senegal, Burkina Faso, and Mali. Their analysis deepens our understanding of the importance of including community perspectives on the practice, especially its negative health outcomes, as well as lessons learnt about the role of health providers and the conversion of traditional practitioners. Community interventions that use an integrated approach, including public declarations and social support for forgoing FGC, are exemplified by the Village Empowerment Program (VEP) conducted by Tostan, a Senegalese NGO. One of the most successful projects in Africa, Tostan's VEP mobilizes whole villages to sign on to plan their campaign "so that no one carried a stigma" by dissenting and abstaining from performing the ritual (see WHO 1999: 115). Diop and Askew's chapter not only provides empirical data about the effectiveness of common intervention strategies but also illuminates the social processes through which they work.

Local, national, and international NGOs have shouldered an enormous responsibility for eradicating practices that undermine the health and welfare of women and children. The Inter-African Committee on Traditional Practices Affecting the Health of Women and Children (IAC) has played an outstanding role in 26 African countries since its formation in 1984. With support from the World Health Organization (WHO) and other international agencies, the IAC facilitates networking among groups providing training for health providers, sensitizing policymakers and the public, and devising strategies to eradicate such harmful practices as early marriage and public defloration of brides, as well as female circumcision.

Hamid El Bashir systematically assesses the multifold activities of a national committee affiliated with the IAC in a country where female circumcision is widely practiced and has been explicitly defended. Making female genital mutilation (FGM) its highest priority, the Sudan National Committee on the Eradication of Harmful Traditional Practices Affecting the Health of Women and Children (SNCTP) has carried out a wide range of programs, often in conjunction with local NGOs and national government agencies, including a mass media campaign, training sessions and informational materials for health care providers and grassroots groups, and the training of trainers. El Bashir's research employed Participatory Rapid Assessment and Appraisal methods and was conducted through contacts with diverse actors in the field (e.g., community leaders; men, women, and children; health workers; and cooperating organizations) in both rural and urban areas. Reporting the critiques articulated by SNCTP's grassroots partners as well as its striking ability to mobilize nationally and its measurable successes in changing attitudes and behavior in some groups, El Bashir's chapter elucidates the strengths and limitations of national-level work.

Throughout the recent history of female circumcision in the Sudan, religious leaders, politicians, and feminists from a growing women's movement have taken on the challenge of addressing female circumcision in all its complexity. Nongovernmental and governmental organizations working at local, regional, and international levels have proposed diverse agendas ranging from supporting the medicalization of the practice to abolishing all forms of circumcision. The Babiker Badri Scientific Association for Women's Studies (BBSAWS), under the auspices of Ahfad University for Women in Khartoum, emerged as a leading force in calling for an integrated, unified campaign to end the practice. Over three decades, BBSAWS has launched and sustained a remarkably comprehensive effort to eradicate female circumcision in the Sudan. Shahira Ahmed discusses the BBSAWS pioneering initiatives to integrate health, legal, psychological, and religious debates regarding the practice. This holistic approach succeeded in breaking the silence on the harmful effects of female circumcision, not only in the Sudan but across Africa. Translating selections from awareness-raising booklets, interviews, and workshop proceedings, this chapter emphasizes the complexity of the issue and highlights some of the main hurdles to overcome as expressed by the local leaders and active citizens who are campaigning against female circumcision.

Raqiya D. Abdalla describes the struggle of Somali women to end female circumcision. Because of the pervasiveness of female circumcision in Somalia, the voices supporting it were loud and clear. Abdalla challenges widespread beliefs which correlate the practice with women's inferiority and subjection in Somali society by showing that resistance to circumcision is not new and that through grassroots activism, poetry, and storytelling women facilitated the exchange of ideas and dialogue that support behavioral changes in their communities. The chapter represents a unique contribution by allowing women's voices to come to the fore. I have argued that using personal narratives counteracts the pervasive tendency in literature on female circumcision to speak for the excised women (Abusharaf 2001). Abdalla's use of personal narratives is prompted by the need to comprehend women's viewpoints as seen through the lens of everyday experience.

Part III of this volume considers the debate in immigrant-receiving societies surrounding the question of whether female circumcision should be considered a criminal act imposed by parents on children and as a human rights violations serving as grounds for political asylum. Tiko Pkoye has warned against the "unmitigated pressure impinging on the average immigrant family unit in the United States" as an outcome of this reporting (Sudanet 2002: 1008052). On September 30, 1996, the U.S. Congress enacted a provision criminalizing the practice as part of the Illegal Immigration Reform and Responsibility Act of 1996. According to this provision, "Whoever knowingly circumcises, excises, or infibulates the whole or any part of the labia minora or labia majora or clitoris of another person who has not attained the age of 18 years, shall be fined under the title or imprisoned not more than 5 years or both. The statute exempts a surgical operation if such an operation is necessary to the health of the person on whom it is performed and is performed by a person licensed in the place of its performance as a medical practitioner" (CRLP 1997). A survey on national-level legal measures chronicled proposals in fifty countries worldwide to enact laws against the practice (Rahman and Toubia 2000). Although no one has yet been tried under these laws in the United States, in France Malian midwives were convicted along with two men and three women (Hosken 1999).

In the United States, Canada, and Australia, female circumcision has received the lion's share of media exposure. Sources of sensationalist coverage in the United States range from such popular magazines as *Marie Claire*, *Jet*, and *Ladies Home Journal* to talk shows such as Oprah Winfrey and *20-20*, television sitcoms such as NBC's *Law and Order*, and even the R-rated movie *Barber Shop*. Two incongruous factors account for the production of knowledge in host societies—using the term knowledge to encompass representations that may be vicarious and distorted, but nonetheless powerful in determining policy. The first factor is the widespread publicity of fears harbored by the dominant groups of host societies of the continuation of the practice by immigrants and refugees who seek to preserve it in the diaspora. Only a few organizations are bridging the gap between immigrant-sending and immigrant receiving societies (for an exemplary project, see Abdel Magied and Badri 2000.) Second, knowledge of female circumcision is produced through public discussion of several recent asylum cases brought on behalf of African women escaping female circumcision that received considerable media coverage. Since the famous 1996 case of Fauziya Kassindja, the Togolese woman who fled her country and sought refuge in the United States, the practice has been considered grounds for a well-founded fear of persecution sufficient for refugee status. Migration and asylum seeking contributed considerably to the enactment of legislative measures in the receiving societies of Western Europe and the North America. In Germany, the Green Party (Buendis '90/Die Gruenen) introduced a motion on the practice into Parliament in November 1997. This motion, which stressed genital excision as a violation of bodily integrity, announced support for nongovernmental organizations to provide training and accepted FGM as a ground for asylum (*Awaken* 1998, 2: 3–4).

Audrey Macklin's chapter on policy formation in Canadian law opens by shifting the question to which we should attend from whether or not immigrant-receiving nations should tolerate the practice of female genital mutilation to how FGM can be eradicated and then demonstrates that acknowledging the differences between this principled goal and a range of democratic means makes all the difference. Focusing on policies proposed, adopted, and implemented in Canada, Macklin explores the complex positioning of women within refugee communities in which FGM is prevalent and the sometimes unanticipated ways in which women's efforts to end it intersect in practice with the provisions of public policy, offering a probing case study involving Somali activist women who used the legal system of the host country to redress this particularly stark manifestation of gender inequality within their communities.

Finally, Charles Piot tracks the groundbreaking 1996 "Kasinga" clitoridectomy asylum case through the U.S. courts, the media, the Internet, the embassies, and the State Department, and through Kassindja's own autobiographical accounts. His chapter explores the way in which the case was discursively constructed in various global arenas; the question of her refugee status brought a Togoan issue into transnational circulation. By dissolving a complex West African reality into a series of binary oppositions between modernity and tradition, choice and coercion, autonomy and obligation, individual and community, the courts and the Western media selectively appropriated the "facts" of the case and demonized the local community in the process, which came to stand metaphorically for all of Africa. Reflecting on the role of anthropologists in the objectifying construction of African woman as victim, as well as on his reassessment of this subject's situation, Piot concluded that "Kassindja's travail is better understood as one about modernity than tradition, more about the state than the family, more about the entanglements of personal histories than the timeless traditions of an African community."

These essays provide insights into the everyday struggles of Africans to empower women at the grassroots in the process of social transformation. The dialogue about women's rights and human rights that has begun within these communities has reached from local to national and transnational forums, shifting the terms of the debate from the victimization of women to women becoming agents of change in the most intimate and collective dimensions of their lives.

PART I

Local Contexts and Current Debates

Chapter 2

"Had This *Been Your Face, Would You Leave It as Is?" Female Circumcision Among the Nubians of Egypt*

Fadwa El Guindi

An Egyptian woman with whom I was having a conversation about female circumcision asked me pointedly: "had *this* [referring to the female genitalia] been your face, would you leave it as is?" This question was startling; I had not previously connected a woman's genitalia with her face. Her remark implies an analogy that raises a host of questions about the cultural meanings of female circumcision. It suggests that female circumcision is a cosmetic procedure for beautification, with the implication that it enhances female sexuality. The significance of the comment lies in the notion that the appearance of two distinct parts of the female body—in one cultural setting, a woman's genitals, and in another, her face—can be subject to surgical alteration for the same purpose: beauty enhancement and sexual appeal. This notion alone flies in the face of the widely held Western assumption, which is made especially by activist feminists, that female circumcision is performed to reduce female sexuality.

The customs and traditions of female circumcision analyzed in this essay are based on ethnographic observations of the Kenuz Nubians of Egypt, people who had been moved from their original homeland, which now lies under the waters of the Nile River held back by the Aswan High Dam, to Kom-Ombo further north in Egypt. This essay draws upon empirical data gathered through intensive ethnographic fieldwork which I began conducting among Kenuz Nubians almost forty years ago. Conceptually and theoretically, it builds on observations and insights from a number of my other ethnographic research projects, especially on the Islamic Movement in the 1970s through the 1990s (El Guindi 1981, 1999), on Egyptian birth ceremonies (El Guindi 1986 film), and on Zapotec ritual (El Guindi 1986).

The people known as Nubians have populated villages stretching for a thousand miles along both banks of the Nile River from the First Cataract at Aswan south into the Sudan through the region known as Dongola, an area of broad, fertile lands and islands of rich soil situated south of the Third Cataract. Although this string of Nilotic villages and hamlets is geographically isolated and culturally distinct, the region has been continuously settled for millennia. Nubians today identify with the ancient kingdom that flourished in the cities of Kerma and Old Dongola, and they inhabit a landscape rich with the heritage of the past: spectacular temples and statues from Pharaonic times, and remnants of the Christian and early Muslim eras. Historically, Nubia has linked sub-Saharan Africa and Egypt. The border between Egypt and the Sudan now bisects the region, dividing the population into Egyptian Nubians and Sudanese Nubians. Within Nubia, groups are distinguished by language and dialect.

Egyptian Nubia has always been relatively isolated and poor in natural resources. The cataract at Aswan was a natural barrier to river traffic long before any dams were built, and the scorching deserts on either side of the narrow Nile riverbed discouraged contact with other groups. The arable land consisted of small amount of alluvial soil deposited annually by the Nile. Beyond the alluvium lay sterile sand and rock; the Nubians ventured into this barren are only to bury their dead and to gather the plants and grasses that sprang up there after an occasional rain. This environment restricted economic and population growth; its meager resources could provide a subsistence for no more a few hundred thousand people. Nubia's river traffic has always been discontinuous, its desert environment inhospitable, and its natural resources limited. The lack of economic opportunity discouraged colonial occupation of Nubia and allowed indigenous culture to develop.[1]

At the turn of the twentieth century, however, the first of a series of dams was constructed at Aswan. The already limited arable lands of the Nubian valley were progressively diminished by reservoirs rising behind higher and higher dams. This steady encroachment culminated with the building of the High Dam at Aswan, which finally flooded the entire region of Egyptian Nubia and part of the Sudan. In 1963, this development necessitated the resettlement of villagers to more livable regions and created an uninhabited zone between Egypt and the Sudan. Egyptian Nubians, who are comprised of three linguistic groups, were resettled by the Egyptian government in newly built villages and communities south of Aswan, near Kom-Ombo.[2] The Kenuz make up one-third of Egyptian Nubians south of Aswan. Their language, called Mettokki, is close to the one spoken by the people of Dongola in the Sudan more than a thousand miles to the south. Linguistic records suggest that the Mettokki language spoken by the Kenuz separated from the Dongolese ancestral language a few centuries ago, perhaps when the ancestors of the Kenuz moved north to trade at Aswan.[3] Many Kenuz Nubians now speak Arabic as well as Mettokki.

Contemporary Egyptian Nubians are overwhelmingly Muslim, but the region has a complex religious history. In the sixth century Nubia became a Christian land. However, Islam became an influential force in the lives of Nubians long before the final collapse of the Christian states and the eventual conversion of the entire population. Egypt, Nubia's powerful neighbor to the north, was Muslim; so were the nomadic Arab groups who surrounded Nubia on all sides. There is no historical evidence of coerced mass conversions to Islam. Rather, the historical record suggests that the Kenuz Nubians gradually became Muslim through intermarriage with Muslim Arabs who settled in the region around Aswan.[4]

Throughout the Kenuz Nubians' history of migration, intermarriage, displacement and resettlement, their cultural tradition was reproduced from generation to generation and continues to shape the lives of Nubians today. How did Nubian culture remain strong, persisting through all these social-historical changes? The answer lies in the influence of women, who in a matrilineal system are responsible for the transmission of tradition and the preservation of the Nubian way of life.[5]

Before delving further into the particular cultural meanings surrounding the practice of female circumcision among the Kenuz Nubians of Egypt, however, we must note that female circumcision can be found in many parts of the world. Although it has deep historical roots, it is not of Arab or Islamic origin. Indeed, it was practiced for medical and punitive reasons in Europe and the United States during the nineteenth and early twentieth centuries. In regions where female circumcision is prevalent, the practice is found across religious and ethnolinguistic lines. In the Arabic-speaking Nile Valley region, Christian men, like Muslim men, all undergo ritual circumcision, and Christian women, like Muslim women, are ritually circumcised where female circumcision is also practiced (see Abdel Hadi, in this volume). Islam accepts male circumcision and deals with it as a non-religious custom, but is almost silent on female circumcision. The Qur'an, which is regarded as divinely revealed, says nothing about the practice. The Hadith or teachings, historical literature that is regarded as having secondary or interpretive authority, makes only a few indirect and ambiguous references to it (see Aldeeb Abu-Sahlieh, in this volume).[6]

In one of the earliest anthropological studies carried out among the Kenuz Nubians which examined the ritual of female circumcision (El Guindi 1966, 1978; Callender and El Guindi 1971; cf. Kennedy 1970), my colleague Charles Callender and I used the term circumcision for the male procedure and called the female procedure excision. The Kenuz Nubians considered the two practices culturally equivalent and used the same term for both. This cultural and linguistic equivalence is made throughout Egypt. The standard Arabic term is dual-gendered: the Arabic root t-h-r, derivatives of which mean purification, takes the gendered forms *tahara* (f) and *tuhur* (m). Two other Arabic terms applied to female circumcision, *khitan* and *khifad,* also presume a parallel with male circumcision. I prefer to avoid the surgical classifications that are often used in Western, medically oriented literature and terminology such as female genital mutilation that is popularly used by outsiders advocating intervention. Here, following local terminology, I use the most common term, female circumcision, and explore its significance to those who practice it.

Over forty years ago, after intensive fieldwork among the Kenuz Nubians, Callender and I argued for the significance of the notion of the cultural equivalence of male and female circumcision (El Guindi and Callender 1962–1963; Callender and El Guindi 1971). I argue now that this cultural equivalence extends analytically as a structural equivalence: that is, the two gendered rituals play equivalent roles in the transition of male and female children to adulthood. After the Nubian project, I conducted research on rites of passage in other Islamic and non-Islamic settings, which led me to reexamine the role that ritualized circumcision plays in negotiating life crises. In the cycle of life in Africa and the Arab East, male and female circumcision practices have a structural processual role, mediating between the gendering rite of passage, the birth ritual (see El Guindi 1986 film; also 1998: 489–97; 1999: 62–66), and the maturational rite of passage, the wedding.

In rituals of circumcision one can find elements from the rituals of birth, celebrated on the seventh day, and of marriage, celebrated in weddings. By combining properties from both rituals, circumcision links them in a mediating process. Ritually, it becomes a sexualizing point that marks a transitional phase between birth and marriage. At his or her wedding, the gendered individual becomes mature and complete. Unmarried Muslim men in particular are considered religiously half complete (*nos din,* in Arabic). Circumcision transforms the girl or boy into an appropriately sexual young woman or man who will be fit for marriage. Birth rituals, circumcision rituals, and weddings mark not static points in the individual's life but rather a processual cycle of cultural life.

In my long-term research in Nubia, I not only interviewed women and men about the practice of circumcision but also observed the practice. In my research on the Islamic Movement during the 1970s and 1980s in urban Egypt (1981, 1999), I discussed the practice with *muhajjabat* (headscarf-wearing) women attending college in Cairo. In this chapter I pull together those widely cast empirical threads to weave them into a descriptive and analytical account of female circumcision.

The analysis delineates four dimensions of this ritual, which I describe as (1) beautification for sexual pleasure; (2) the women's world; (3) demasculinization; and (4) the Islamic rationale. Each dimension is introduced by a vignette or story, drawn from an ethnographic encounter, which epitomizes what is involved for people who practice this ritual in cultural context. I also compare the practice of female circumcision with past and present practices of bodily alteration among women in the West, in order to elucidate the salience of cultural meanings in shaping these rituals. Finally, I emphasize that women in Nubia have been changing this ritual of sexualization on their own accord, as a result of the circulation of new ideas and interpretations among themselves, rather than in response to outside intervention.

Beautification for Sexual Pleasure

The aesthetic and sexual significance of surgically altering women's genitals is close to the surface of Nubian women's comments about female circumcision, although this rationale is often presumed rather than articulated. The startling question with which this essay begins illuminates the meaning of female circumcision as an aesthetic enhancement of what is perceived in this culture as central to female sexuality. The remark invites us to compare circumcision with "nose jobs," "facelifts," and "breast enlargement," which are commercially available in the United States. These cosmetic surgeries mutilate the body, yet Americans who express concern about female circumcision in other places do not campaign against these practices with equal fervor despite the known health risks involved. Surely these painful and dangerous cosmetic surgeries, like female circumcision, signify something about the sexual meanings of women's bodies in the culture (Sault 1994).

The sexual meanings of female circumcision are highlighted by another intriguing ethnographic encounter that occurred during my fieldwork among the Kenuz Nubians during the 1960s. While I was discussing circumcision, defloration, and pleasure in sex with a small group of women, one woman looked at me and crisply said: "circumcision makes a woman nice and tight. The man finds great pleasure in tight women, unlike Cairo women whose vaginas are wide enough for four men to enter together." Skeptics might dismiss the argument that narrowing the vagina increases the husband's pleasure as a male-oriented rationale for the practice, but it deserves serious consideration. In order to understand this remark, we must acknowledge the antagonism that many Nubian women expressed toward women in Cairo, whom they regard as sexually loose in more than a literal sense. Nubian men who migrated to the city to work were increasingly marrying additional wives there, despite the strong objections of many Nubians who uphold endogamy—the practice of choosing husbands and wives from within the group. Women disapproved of the tendency of migrant men to take non-Nubian wives and spoke disparagingly of the children of such mixed marriages. But the increasing prevalence of marriage to non-Nubian women cannot be used to refute the argument that men derive pleasure from tight vaginas. Other factors account for the polygyny that occurs when men are away, such as men's sexual and domestic needs during long absences from their wives, the temptation of the forbidden but available fruit, the seduction of difference, and various personal situations. Clearly the same option is not available to the women waiting in the village for their husbands' conjugal visits.

This woman's comment about vaginal tightness, which represents a belief that is widely held among Kenuz Nubians, suggests a cultural awareness of sexual pleasure and a concern with the factors producing it. In Nubia, as throughout the Arab region, the cultural assumption is that a man's arousal and pleasure give much pleasure to the woman. This understanding is quite different from contemporary Western notions of individualized sexual pleasure as experienced by a heterosexual couple, in which each seeks pleasure and "performs"[7] so as to obtain or produce it. These sex behaviors and the associated manners can give a robotic quality to the experience and often result in disappointment at the lack of mutual, simultaneous orgasm. The Nubian and Arab view of sex is a more complementary than individualist one, based on an internalized sex culture that encourages erotic body movements and elaborate bed language to create an ambience conducive to mutual arousal. For example, men perfume their bodies prior to sex (El Guindi 1999: 8). The woman has the greater responsibility for producing this environment, but the sex experience is integrative and mutual, rather than a matter of individualized pleasure-seeking.

Popular culture cultivates much lore, which is freely passed from older women to younger ones, regarding how to deal with husbands, techniques to arouse them during sex, and foods that enhance their sex drive. Medications developed in the United States such as Viagra, designed to enable men to achieve and sustain erection and women to achieve single or multiple orgasms, are being aggressively marketed internationally by the multinational pharmaceutical corporations and are now penetrating Arab markets.[8] In Egypt these drugs are the subject of humor in cartoons and movies. The cultural emphasis, however, continues to be on natural foods and beverages as means of enhancing the sex drive. A popular rhyming Arabic expression, "hotti el-gargir taht el-serir," advises women to "place *gargir* under the bed." *Gargir*, the herb arugula, is a standard ingredient in green salads in the region. The idea is to give the husband a large quantity of arugula, which is considered an aphrodisiac. When a woman objects to the priority and preference in quality and quantity of food given to a husband, other women's response to her would be: "How silly, it all comes back to you in the end." One implication is that semen carries all the nutrients back to the woman; another is that nutrients for the man will result in pleasure for the woman. Whether this return is understood in literal or metaphorical terms, the goal is an increase in sex activity and enhancement of pleasure, which is conceived as mutual.

On public transportation and other public spaces within the hearing of many who awkwardly stretch to listen in, an older *baladi* woman (for an explanation of the traditional urban women and men known as *baladi*, see Early 1993 and El-Messiri 1978), most likely a maternal aunt, advises, or even admonishes a young newlywed: "Have I not told you many times before? Move under him with passion. The aroused man gives pleasure to the woman." This advice recognizes the interactive dimension of the sex experience. Open, woman-to-woman socialization cultivates the desired sex experience.

Female circumcision in Nubia can appropriately be compared with breast enlargement in America. In the American context, cultural analysts maintain, this practice of surgical bodily alteration is promoted primarily through popular culture, which socializes women to feel good about themselves and increase their value by displaying their breasts as objects for male viewing and manipulation. The phenomenon deceptively called "breast enhancement" could well be called "breast mutilation."[9] Culturally, it amounts to substituting men's sex pleasure in women's breasts for their maternal function. The symbolic significance of breasts is deeply rooted in Western

European culture, as the historical record of hostility toward breasts in witch hunts demonstrates (Barstow 1994: 148–50). The notion that women become impure or polluted from sex finds one point of origin in the separation of sex from maternity that was symbolized by the virginity of Mary and asexuality of Jesus and extends through much of Christian history. The dominant view from the early nineteenth to the early twentieth centuries, derived from certain Christian ideologies and intensified by a strand of Protestant and Victorian thinking, socialized women to shun sex in order to be morally pure, while emergent modern critiques of this sexual regime lamented that "ladies" were frigid and nonorgasmic. The American feminist movement of the late 1960s sought to liberate women from the dominant ideologies that restricted their sexualities, as well as from clothing and cosmetics that restricted or altered their natural and healthy bodily form.

Having internalized the view that breasts are for men's pleasure, some American women reveal their breasts by wearing low-cut or clingy clothing in order to attract attention, provoke arousal, and promote seduction. Undergoing breast mutilation in order to enhance men's erotic pleasure involves accepting the negative consequences of such a surgical procedure for women's own health and sexuality, which are well known. In addition to the potentially serious deleterious effects of breast implants on women's general health, the operation produces a loss of sensation in the nipples. Here is the ultimate irony, since women have learned to learn to feel sexual pleasure from nipple stimulation. Embracing breast surgery to please men while giving up return stimulation stresses the lack of mutuality and self-objectification inherent in this mode of sex pleasure. Nevertheless, it brings dividends, especially in the sex trade, and its continuing practice in a post-feminist era is worthy of further exploration.

In contrast, Arab women consider breasts important for two purposes: feeding offspring for extended periods (Islam recommends two years) and as a manifestation of femininity in a strongly dual-gendered culture. The cultivation of heterosexual pleasure is focused more on the woman's genitals and her eyes, as well as the cultivated ambiance surrounding sexual relations.

The cultural importance given to a female body part—breasts in American culture, and genitals in Arab culture—leads to certain rationalized "improvements" through surgical procedures. This view, which works across cultural lines, challenges the ethnocentric view which presumes that the practice of adolescent female circumcision diminishes or controls a mature woman's sexuality. While surgical alteration of the female genitals might have that result in some cases, cultural factors are central to the experience and interpretation of women's sexual pleasure.

In Arab culture, women derive their sense of feminine sensuality not only from heterosexual relationships but also from the cultural support and the validation provided by non-sexualized bonding with women. The cultural meanings of women's embodiment and sensuality are generated within the women's world, which is a core dimension of Arab and African culture.

The Women's World

"I will not permit you to circumcise my daughter or pierce her ears—both practices alter the natural body and are decadent," said a father to the women in his upper-middle-class family in Cairo during the 1940s. Female relatives were pressuring a mother in the city to circumcise her daughter. Upon finding out about it, the father strongly expressed his disapproval. By linking ear piercing and female circumcision, the father was opposing any alteration of the female body. He rejected its association with the enhancement of feminine beauty. The women, on the other hand, were concerned about the curtailment of sexual energy in adolescence. In their view, unchecked sexual energy might drain a growing girl, damaging her health and making her weak and skinny.

Female circumcision belongs to the women's world, and ordinarily men know little about it or how it is performed—a fact that is widely confirmed in ethnographic studies. Many men neither encourage nor condemn it. There are individual cases when a man, possibly influenced by his mother, insists on a circumcised bride, just as there are cases when a father does not support the practice. Overall, however, the sexualizing ritual of female circumcision is neither initiated by nor intended to appeal to men; it is the women's concern.

The element of choice is worth considering in this context, since Western discussions of the practice focus on circumcised girls' lack of freedom of choice in the matter. In the Arab world, the decision to circumcise is made by women for their daughters. In the case in which a father objected to his daughter being circumcised, which some might consider progressive or enlightened, the girl still had no say in the decision; not being circumcised and not having her ears pierced was not her choice, but was imposed on her by her father. In America, the male infant who is routinely circumcised in the hospital when he is three days old also has no choice. Moreover, the medical circumcision of non-Jewish male infants is devoid of any ritual that might provide cultural support to him, the family, and society at large. Cross-cultural discussions about these matters should employ a single standard, not apply different standards to boys and girls or to Americans and Arabs or Africans. In many debates, choice is not used consistently and tends to bias discussion about circumcision. The notion of choice is also individualistic, tending to isolate a practice from its cultural meanings.

The 1978 conference on the position of women and girls in Africa held in Khartoum, the Sudanese capital, included a session on female circumcision which presented detailed accounts of the procedure and showed ethnographic films documenting the ritual surrounding it.[10] Many male participants stood up and confessed to the audience their total ignorance of the practice and how shocked they were to learn about it. These male participants in the workshop vowed to make sure that their daughters would not be circumcised. As the encounter in Cairo during the 1940s demonstrates, however, some men in the past also had strong feelings against the practice when they were informed about it.

Demasculinization

The prevalent view in Africa is that male circumcision defeminizes men and female circumcision demasculinizes women. Female circumcision is seen as removing maleness through the cutting of the phallic clitoris and thus enhancing femaleness (see Brunet and Vidal's 1986 film, *Garçons et filles*). Removal or reduction of this masculine appearance is the way to feminize women. From this perspective, female circumcision is about altering the female body to confirm its femininity.

Anthropologists should examine female circumcision in Africa in terms of female sexuality as defined by women as well as men, rather than as a matter of male control of women. Its cultural meanings in those contexts differ from the use of clitoridectomy in the Anglo-American past, which was a mode of punishment for women who were regarded as inappropriately sexual, whether excessively or insufficiently so. According to Wallerstein, "clitoridectomy was performed in England and the United States from the 1860s to about 1920 to treat . . . 'emotional' problems," including promiscuity, and "to enhance orgasmic response" (1984: 735). Basic contradictions pervaded the Anglo-American version of female circumcision. Above all, it was punitive.

Unmarried adolescent girls were diagnosed as deviant for expressing an active interest in sex and might be "treated" with a surgical operation when confinement and other measures of control failed. Married women were subjected to the surgery to remedy what were seen as sexual or emotional problems inhibiting their satisfaction or even interest in heterosexual intercourse. The contradiction between clitoridectomy's sex-suppressing purposes in adolescent girls and its sex-enhancing purposes in adult women demonstrates that cultural meanings, rather than medical criteria, were central to this practice.

However, the aspect of control is not entirely absent from the African and Arab practice. Women who support the circumcision of young women are concerned about the sexual energy expended as a girl is growing and her body is maturing into womanhood. Being slim is usually seen as evidence of sexual energy wasting the body. This view assumes that girls' sexuality is strong and recognizes the sensitivity of the clitoris in the sexual maturation process. The women of the family bear a heavy responsibility to protect the virginity of girls until they are married in order to prevent a possible crisis for the family and the community.

In addition to beautification and feminization, circumcision is intended to control the sexual energy of a virgin until marriage. It is not considered a mechanism for the permanent reduction of the woman's sexuality. Rather, this purpose of circumcision pertains only to the period of sexual maturation prior to marriage; the procedure is supposed to promote sexual pleasure within marriage. There is no cultural suggestion that the surgical procedure performed on a young girl permanently diminishes her sexuality. There is evidence that this can and does happen, however, and some Arab women are concerned about this unintended consequence of the procedure. Some girls find the experience traumatic, and some young women construct the memory of their particular childhood circumcision experience in this fashion. Perhaps, when cultural support is withdrawn and the procedure is performed without rituals outside the context of the women's world, the experience is more likely to be remembered in such a way. In some instances, strong girls who resist the surgery physically may be cut more extensively than those who comply quietly.

In Egyptian culture, whether Arab or Kenuz Nubian, three distinct rituals mark the male and female life cycle: gendering the sexes is ritualized on the seventh day after birth; sexualizing individuals occurs through rituals of circumcision; and maturity is reached through rituals of marriage. A strong, active, and gendered sexuality in marriage is regarded as highly desirable and is culturally cultivated by socialization among women, who learn elaborate erotic bed talk, behaviors during sex, and which foods enhance sex. The nuanced difference between the intent of diminishing women's sexuality and a temporary reduction of a virgin's sexual energy is significant, especially when seen in the context of a culture that attaches positive value to sexual enjoyment and realistically accepts its natural role in human life.

The Islamic Rationale

Unlike certain Western and Christian traditions that deny sexuality in favor of purity from pollution, Islam does not separate piety from sexuality either in doctrinal ideology or daily life (El Guindi 1999). Sexual fulfillment is stressed in Islam and is even considered a woman's right; for example, absence of fulfillment is an acceptable ground for married women to initiate divorce. Islam realistically recognizes the sexual needs and desires of both women and men.

Islamic rationales for this practice have recently been advanced as part of the Islamic Movement in Egypt and elsewhere. When I asked a *muhajjaba* (headscarf-wearing) Cairo University student in the late 1970s whether she would circumcise her future daughter, she said she would because the practice was Islamic. When I asked her for the specific Islamic source that supported this practice, she thought intently for a while and then calmly said that she would explore and research the matter, and if she found no legitimate religious foundation she would not circumcise her daughter. To this *muhajjaba,* and for many other Muslims whose frame of reference is religious, religious support is primary. This encounter clearly points to the importance of Islamic authority as the basis for female circumcision—or for regarding it as merely customary, and therefore questionable.

In the Sudan, as among the Nubians of Egypt, the milder form of the procedure, which is categorized medically as excision, is referred to as *sunna.* The word *sunna* is used in several ways. Technically, sunna means the "path of the Prophet," the sayings and practices of the Prophet Muhammad which stand as an ideal standard and model for Muslim behavior. These are recorded in compendia of hadith, Islamic narratives recorded by the Prophet's students, which are considered an important authority for Islamic teaching but, unlike the Qur'an, not divinely revealed. As historical texts, hadith give voice to differences and are open to interpretation. In the Sudanese context, the term *sunna* refers to a form of circumcision that is less severe than infibulation, but its usage suggests Islamic sanction for the practice. Although it does not assert that the procedure is required, the term validates the practice for most Muslims in the Sudan. Without exploring the etymology of the terms used to describe the practice, the label *sunna* itself suggests an Islamic basis, and this legitimacy is usually not questioned or challenged. The Islamic basis of female circumcision is now under scrutiny, and if Muslims were to conclude that there is no religious authority for it, then the practice might be changed or given up entirely.

If the practice were persuasively presented as Islamic, on the other hand, female circumcision would spread widely and rapidly among Muslims living in regions where it has not been customary in the past. This has not happened in Egypt, and I doubt that it will occur elsewhere, because the religious evidence that can be mustered in support of female circumcision is considered weak. Women advocates against female circumcision use the absence of an authoritative basis for the practice in Islam to support their activist programs to stop the practice. Interestingly, both those who are pro-circumcision and those who are anti-circumcision resort to Islam for support for their position.

In order to fully understand the practice of female circumcision, we must examine it in cultural context, as all these dimensions come into play in the enactment of the ritual. Next I present an ethnographic description and analysis of female circumcision as I observed and recorded it in the field during the early 1960s. This case study highlights not only the embeddedness of this ritual in an entire culture but also the ways in which the procedure of female circumcision has been changed by women themselves over time.

Changing Ritual Practices Among the Kenuz Nubians

The Mettokki-speaking Kenuz Nubians lived in Dahmit, a district that existed until 1963 in the south of Aswan, Egypt, until the building of the High Dam, which resulted in the inundation of much of the region. The Nubians of this area were successfully, although not happily, relocated by the government, in one of the largest planned relocations of a population in the world, to the district of Kom-Ombo just north of Aswan. They left Old Nubia behind, and with it their homes, their dead, and their collective and individual memories. The elders among them found displacement especially distressing. The Nubian Ethnographic Survey, a three-year fieldwork project, documented their culture during that crucial period of change.[11] This account is based on data and observations collected during that project, which our research team analyzed at the time and I have reanalyzed recently.

The Kenuz Nubians have two procedures of female circumcision. The older procedure, called infibulation in Western medical terminology, involves extensive removal of all the external genitalia and the suturing of the vaginal opening, leaving only small openings for urination and menstruation. The Kenuz call it "Pharaonic circumcision." A new, less severe form seems to have been introduced in the late 1950s or early 1960s. They call this "nylon circumcision," indicating an innovative form of circumcision, as the term "nylon" was used to refer to any object or activity that was modern and fashionable. This form of excision is, however, more extensive than the form more commonly practiced in Lower Egypt, which involves cutting off the tip of the skin or hood over the clitoris and thus bears a greater resemblance to the practice of cutting off the foreskin of the penis. Nylon circumcision replaced Pharaonic circumcision during the course of normal change in customs and resulted from a variety of influences. This dramatic shift was not planned; there was no organized, self-conscious movement, and no foreign individual or group intervened to bring it about. Kenuz Nubian women initiated change on their own, presumably from the acculturation of their migrants. Women who had migrated to the big cities of Cairo and Alexandria brought back the knowledge of alternative forms of procedure. Some women explained the shift as a response to the severity of the older form, which required the assistance of a midwife at marriage "either to cut the scar tissue before consummation could occur, or—if defloration preceded consummation as a distinct act—to instruct the husband in the proper technique" (Callender and El Guindi 1971: 31).

At the time of our initial fieldwork during the 1960s, the proper form of female circumcision was a matter of debate, with considerable tension between those who adopted nylon circumcision and those who insisted that the older form is better. I recall how one mother who had lived in Cairo was convinced by the women in Dahmit to redo the procedure for her daughter, who had been circumcised in the city. I was squatting on the ground visiting with a group of women when the daughter moved a little further away from us, but remained in full view, and proceeded to urinate. A woman watching her pointed out to the mother that the urine was shooting far forward like that of a man. Discussion ensued about the operation having been improperly performed. In this instance, it is clear that the masculine anatomical form is what was being rejected. When a properly circumcised woman urinates, they believed, the urine falls straight beneath her. The thrusting forward of the daughter's urine meant that she had not been sufficiently demasculinized, demonstrating the inadequacy of her first circumcision. The Pharaonic form removes any parts that resemble the masculine anatomy. These women judged the new form by this criterion, which underlines the centrality of feminization to the cultural meaning of female circumcision.

Despite these tensions between proponents of nylon circumcision and practitioners of Pharaonic circumcision, change was taking place. The midwives I interviewed gave 1961 as the year in which the newer form was adopted by everyone. The midwives said they supported this change because they had found infibulation to be a cause of complications when brides were deflowered and babies were delivered. The midwives saw a clear shift in the attitudes of the women: they were requesting the less drastic form of circumcision for their daughters because it caused less pain and prevented complications. Change came about mostly from the women themselves who, having experienced the operation, were thoroughly aware of the pain involved. They explicitly described the older procedure as severe. Mothers often avoided watching the procedure for their own daughters, finding the pain unbearable to watch. Ironically, however, this form survived for hundreds if not thousands of years because women insisted on it.

Some Kenuz men looked at the practice from the perspective of their long absences from the village when they worked in the cities for months or years at a time. They saw the older form as a way to control women's sexuality so they could tolerate waiting for extended periods until their husbands visited. Women rejected this rationale, saying that neither form of circumcision resulted in any reduction in sexual desire. Exercising discipline and self-control, women wait patiently for their husbands. The moral reputation of a woman is a corporate matter, bound up with the entire group. Maintaining family and group reputation is the responsibility of every individual—men and women (El Guindi 1999). Tarnishing group reputation is severely dealt with. In such close-knit community, concealing love affairs with resident men was next to impossible. Becoming pregnant when her husband was absent was catastrophic for the woman and the whole community. I followed developments surrounding one case during my fieldwork from its beginning until the mysterious death of the pregnant woman (El Guindi 1962–1965). Social pressure, rather than female circumcision, was the primary means of moral regulation.

Looking at this ritual practice from the point of view of those who practice it is crucial to interpreting its significance and a necessary step before making any evaluation. Here we must recognize that Kenuz Nubian women made a choice to end some procedures and to continue or adopt others. The girls socialized in the system will go through it because their mothers went through it and their mothers support having their daughters circumcised. Some arguments made by feminist activists against female circumcision make this matter of choice central but employ it inconsistently, imposing a double standard. Choice is not brought up in relation to men who undergo very severe circumcision in various parts of the world, or the male babies in America who are operated on involuntarily. I find the cruelty of American male infant circumcision to lie in two dimensions: the absence of choice, and the absence of ritual. The operation is rendered coercive and meaningless. Why do not activist feminists care about men's circumcision? Their agenda is narrowly focused on women in Africa and the Middle East, who can be presented as inferior, less advanced, or more oppressed than Western women. This explanation is consistent with the disproportional energy they devote to the veiling of women, which cannot be considered mutilating, or imposed on women without choice. Most interventionist debate is polemical and uniformed about context and culture. It assumes that women in non-Western societies are childlike and helpless, passive victims of their men, who must be saved by Western missionaries and feminists. This stance is arrogant and ethnocentric. When Nubian women decided to switch from a severe form of circumcision to a form they considered more humane, the older practice ended. In most cases local men were indifferent. Only a few men defended the continuation of the older custom; some objected to it for humanitarian reasons, and some considered it against the teachings of Islam.

These observations should end discussions of female circumcision as a ritual imposed on women by men as a means of supporting their patriarchal power and transform the nature of feminist intervention. If such intervention is needed and requested, feminists should engage in collaborative projects that are conducted under the leadership of local women, draw on their expertise, and are fully informed by reliable studies of the local community and cultural context.

Circumcision Observed

During my fieldwork in Nubia, I was invited to attend the excision procedure and ritual celebrations for a girl who was the daughter of a migrant woman who had returned to visit her relatives in Dahmit. The ceremony took place in the mid-afternoon in the courtyard of the house in which the family was staying during their visit to the home village. The ritual was held on the 28th day of *Shawwal*, the tenth month in the Islamic calendar, which was a propitious time in the lunar cycle. The phases of the moon mark many sacred beginnings as well as thresholds of endangerment. This day was chosen to reduce the risk of harm during the period of *mushahra*, a liminal state that lasts from the waning of the old moon until the appearance of the new moon. Celebrating a ritual on the 28th of the month reduces the *mushahra* period to two days before the beginning of the next month.

Several women and unmarried girls of the neighborhood gathered in the courtyard, including children of both sexes. The mother stayed in one of the rooms around the courtyard, away from the area where the procedure took place. She explained that she could not bear to watch the operation. Several women seated the girl on an overturned basin, high enough for the midwife to reach her comfortably. The women held the girl firmly. The midwife squatted on the ground facing the girl with a pot of charcoal beside her. The girl started squirming and had an expression of fear on her face. When the midwife was ready to operate, another woman pulled the girl's dress up over her face so she wouldn't see the operation and exposed her genitals so the procedure could begin. The midwife held a lancet and spread the girl's legs apart. The women held the girl tightly as she began to twist to free herself from the women's grasp; uncontrolled movements would have endangered her during the surgery. The midwife dipped her left hand in the charcoal to ensure that it would not slip and grasped the girl's genitals while using the lancet in her right hand to make a series of small cuts. No anesthetic was applied.

This procedure manifested all the properties that anthropologists identify as pertaining to initiation rituals, including the endurance of pain. Girls are not taught or expected to refrain from crying in such situations. The girl was screaming and bleeding. When the midwife had finished the surgical procedure, she called out for water and used it to wash off the blood in the genital area. There was no stitching. She asked for an egg and henna leaves. She broke the egg, separated out the white, and carefully smeared the egg yolk over the wound; then she put on the henna leaves. Finally the midwife pressed the girl's legs together and bound them with strips of cloth at the thighs and ankles.

In many cases the pieces of skin and flesh that are surgically removed are placed along with some grains and other medicinal ingredients in a *hegab*,[12] or protective pouch, and worn on the girl's body. An equivalent practice occurs in a boy's circumcision, in which the removed foreskin is kept in a protective *hegab*. In this case, the acculturated migrant mother did not want anything special done with the pieces of the girl's clitoral and labial tissue, so the midwife buried them. The operation lasted about 15 minutes.

At that point the women in the courtyard began to give *zaghareet* (joy-cries) as in a wedding, calling out: "yalla, you are a woman now," "you are now a bride," "bring her a groom," "bring her a cock, she is now ready for intercourse." One woman wrapped the girl in a *shogga*, a white cloak women wrap around their waist that reaches to the ground. The girl's mother came out into the courtyard and adorned her daughter with two necklaces, one silver and one gold. I was told that the silver necklace was a gift from a *shaykh*, which would protect the girl from any harm caused by the evil eye, and the gold was to guard her against *mushahra*, which can be caused by gold worn by any visiting woman—gold is countered by gold. Whatever the local symbolic interpretation, the gift of silver and gold that the mother bestows on her newly circumcised daughter, personally placing them around her daughter's neck, has other implications. In this culture, jewelry is women's personal wealth; it is owned entirely by women and represents the major form of wealth they possess. Nubian women proudly wear their precious jewelry on public occasions and during their migrant husband's visits. The gift of jewelry is a rite of mother-daughter bonding which is ritually and publicly celebrated. The girl is publicly celebrated for her transition into sexuality, which makes her ready for the next phase in woman's life cycle, namely marriage.

After dressing her daughter with jewelry, the mother picked her daughter up in her arms and carried her out through the courtyard gate, crossing the household threshold. She stood holding her daughter as onlookers watched and then reentered into the courtyard, still proudly carrying her daughter. This particular rite is explained as the way to avert *mushahra*, which occurs when visitors cross the household threshold and encounter a vulnerable individual who recovering from circumcision or childbirth. The woman's body is vulnerable because she is in a state of liminality. If the vulnerable individual steps over the threshold first, before a visitor enters and encounters her, any possible effects of entry are neutralized and harm is averted. In anthropological terms, the ritualized crossing of the threshold has broader implications. It is a public announcement to the community that the daughter is now successfully circumcised and had passed from one phase of her life into another.

The joycries, comments about the young woman, gifts of jewelry, and passage over threshold, surrounded by the celebratory ambience in the courtyard, are all a way to celebrate the young woman's sexuality. The mother gently placed her daughter on a straw mat in the *sabil*, a cool, covered section of the courtyard, for leisurely sitting and visiting. (Ordinarily *sabil* refers to the Arabic custom of having water in a container placed outside the residence along the road that is made available to any passerby.) As no anesthetic is applied, the daughter is visibly in pain. The child guests gather around the girl and try to coax her into eating boiled eggs the women brought, which are considered beneficial for healing and compensate for lost blood.

In the meantime, the mother went around the courtyard proudly giving all the guests perfume and candy. Later she served everyone lentil soup. Some women told me that this was a *karama*, an offering she had vowed to make on the occasion of her daughter's circumcision. Other women claimed that offering lentil soup is customary. During the meal, other women came to the house to offer their congratulations. They walked into the courtyard and joined the meal and festivities. Cautious women, or those who considered themselves in a state which might bring harm upon the girl, called their congratulations over the courtyard wall from outside. The fear comes from the understanding that a person in a state of liminality is vulnerable to possible effects of *mushahra*. A few days after the circumcision I witnessed, the new crescent moon appeared, marking the beginning of a new Islamic month and the end of her state of liminality. Guests could then enter the household to visit her.

In the courtyard, a woman guest began making a *hegab* for the newly circumcised young woman to wear on her body. In a square piece of white cloth she put *baraka* seeds and ground coffee. The mother sewed the cloth together with the ingredients inside. Before leaving, each guest gave the mother *no'ut*, money gifts ranging from 5 to 10 Egyptian *piastres*. The midwife received a fee of thirty *piastres*. In addition, she was given cigarettes, dates, soap, and *gargush*, a local sweet cracker eaten with tea and offered to guests. Women told me that this payment was relatively high by local standards. Women in the village could not afford to pay the midwife that much. This migrant woman from the city was relatively wealthier, which raised others' expectations; paying the midwife well was a way for the woman to display her status.

Conclusion

Examining the ritual practice of female circumcision in the context of rural Nubia in relation to contemporary practices in urban Egypt and in comparison to prevalent practices of bodily alteration in American culture lends important insights into how this controversial matter can best be approached. The analytic framework developed in this chapter defines female circumcision not as an isolated moment or an independent rite of passage but rather as it is grounded in a cultural tradition that shapes the trajectory of women's lives through a succession of rituals. Circumcision is best understood as ritual of sexualization that mediates between two other significant rites of passage, the gendering that follows birth and the adulthood that is attained at marriage.

Placing female circumcision in cultural context and examining it in comparative perspective enables us to get beyond polemical observations and interventionist postures toward the practice and puts an end to unidimensional arguments that frame it in relation to "patriarchy" and other forms of male domination of women. This essay demonstrates the value of a more ethnographically balanced approach that includes male circumcision and compares the African and Arab practice of female circumcision with other modes of bodily alteration practiced now and in the past in American and European culture. This approach transcends the artificial boundaries between what are phrased as subjective and objective positions and between what are defined as theoretical and activist or engaged anthropology (El Guindi 2001; Bourdieu 1990).

Finally, the Nubian case demonstrates that the form of female circumcision has been changing in response not to external interventionist pressures but rather as a result of local women's individual and collective choices. Women in communities that practice female circumcision make their own decisions about the ritual procedure based on cultural considerations that are important to them and in response to the dynamic conditions of their own lives. In considering circumcision, we must include male and female forms in the same discussion, become acquainted with the rich local knowledge on the practice and region that exists in the local language, embed the practice in wide cultural and cross-cultural context, humbly recognize local debates, and acknowledge internal action for change. Engaging with female circumcision should be collaborative and respectful of local knowledge and choices.

Chapter 3

Male and Female Circumcision:
The Myth of the Difference

Sami A. Aldeeb Abu-Sahlieh

International and national organizations working to abolish female circumcision generally assume that male and female circumcision are
two distinct practices and that only female genital excision should be abolished. They base this distinction on the presupposition that male circumcision is founded on religious beliefs and confers health benefits, while asserting
that female circumcision is not an essential part of any major religious tradition and has deleterious effects on health.

Two examples illustrate this attitude. The seminar on traditional practices organized by the UN Commission on Human Rights in Ouagadougou,
Burkina Faso, on April 29–May 3, 1991, recommended that states pass "legislation forbidding these harmful practices to the health of women and children,
notably the excision" (UN Economic and Social Council 1991, 12.6, par. 136).
The report of the seminar explains: "According to the opinion of the majority
of the participants, the explanations drawn from cosmogony and those based
on religion must be regarded as superstition and denounced as such. Neither
the Bible nor the Qur'an prescribes to women to be excised. In terms of the
strategy to struggle against excision, it has been recommended to do this in
such a way to dissociate, in the mind of people, male circumcision that has a
hygienic function, from excision that is a serious breach of the woman's physical integrity" (UN Economic and Social Council 1991, 12.6, par. 27). I addressed a series of questions to Mrs. Halimah Al-Warzazi, special rapporteur
of the UN on traditional practices: "Are you fighting against male and female
circumcision or only against one of them? If you fight against one of them,
which one? Why do you neglect the other one?" She answered: "On the level
of the UN, only female circumcision is considered a harmful practice that it is
necessary to abolish. The question of the circumcision of the male child is excluded therefore from the preoccupations of the UN. I consider that this

practice, apart from the fact that it is religious for the Jews and the Muslims, is a hygienic element that American physicians perform at the time of child-birth to all, be they Jews, Muslims, Catholics or other. Therefore, it doesn't seem to me appropriate to amalgamate female circumcision that is considered dangerous for health and male circumcision that, on the contrary, is beneficial."[1] This opinion prevails among most advocates for the abolition of female circumcision at all levels, locally and internationally.

This essay calls this set of assumptions into question and seeks to demonstrate two important points: those who are opposed to female circumcision should also be opposed to male circumcision, for the same reasons; and the two major sets of justifications that are repeatedly offered to distinguish between male and female circumcision—religion and health—are not supported by the facts. The essay takes up the religious and medical rationales for accepting or opposing male circumcision in turn. First, it shows that male circumcision, like female circumcision, has been debated within the religious traditions that are seen as justifying it absolutely. Second, it considers the arguments made for its health benefits, demonstrating that many such claims have proven entirely spurious and that the medical evidence for its health effects is, at the very least, quite mixed. The discussion of the health effects of male circumcision is especially important at this moment because circumcision is being seriously considered by international agencies as a technique for preventing the spread of HIV/AIDS. There are many other reasons why male and/or female circumcision is practiced that relate to culture rather than religion or health and are not addressed here; readers interested in more details should refer to my book, *Male and Female Circumcision Among Jews, Christians and Muslims: Religious, Medical, Social and Legal Debate* (Aldeeb 2001).

Religious Justifications for the Distinction

Contrary to the opinion of those who maintain that male circumcision is justified by religious norms, these norms have historically served to either legitimize or to condemn both male and female circumcision.

Debates Among Jews

Ancient Texts: The Torah and Prophets
The Torah (the Hebrew Bible, or, in Christian terms, the Old Testament) contains no rule establishing female circumcision, while it constitutes the

basis for the practice of male circumcision among Jews, Muslims, and Christians. Two texts govern this practice:

When Abram was ninety-nine years old, God appeared to him and said to him: "I am *El Shaddai* [God Almighty]; walk before me and become complete. I wish to set My covenant between Me and you, and to multiply you exceedingly." And Abram fell upon his face; and God talked with him. "As for Me, lo! My covenant is now with you, and you shall be the ancestor of a multitude of nations. And no longer shall you be called Abram, but your name shall be Abraham, for I have appointed you the ancestor of a multitude of nations. And I will make you exceedingly fruitful; I will make you yourself into nations of you, and kings shall come forth from you. And I will establish My covenant between Myself and you and to your descendants after you, throughout their generations as an everlasting covenant, to be God to you and to your descendants after you. And I will give to you and to your descendants after you the land where you are now an alien, all the land of Canaan as a perpetual holding; and I shall be God to them." And God said to Abraham: "As for you, you too must keep My covenant, you and your descendants after you throughout their generations. This is My covenant which you shall keep between Myself and you and your descendants after you: Every male among you shall be circumcised, you shall circumcise the flesh of your foreskin, and this shall become as a sign of the covenant between Myself and you. And at the age of eight days every male among you shall be circumcised throughout your generations, he that is born in the house or acquired with money from any stranger who is not of your descendants. He that is born in your house and he that is acquired with your money must be circumcised, and My covenant shall be upon your flesh an everlasting covenant. An uncircumcised male who is not circumcised upon the flesh of his foreskin, his soul shall be cut off from his people; he has broken My covenant." (Genesis 17:1–14)[2]

God spoke to Moses (saying): "Speak to the children of Israel (saying): If a woman conceives and gives birth to a male (child), she shall be ritually unclean for seven days, just as in the days of her separation during her menstruation shall she be unclean. And on the eighth day the flesh of his foreskin shall be circumcised. She shall remain in the blood of purification for thirty-three days; she shall touch no sanctified thing and not come into the sanctuary until the days of her purifying are complete. If she gives birth to a female (child), she shall be ritually unclean for two weeks, just as at her time of separation, and remain in the blood of purification for sixty-six days." (Leviticus 12:1–5)

In the first text, male circumcision is sign of a covenant between God and Abraham and his descendants; therefore, ritual circumcision in Hebrew is called *B'rit Milah*, literally the covenant of the cut. The second text situates circumcision in relation to the ritual purification of the mother after childbirth. In many subsequent texts, the Torah distinguishes between the circumcised and the uncircumcised, marking the uncircumcised as ritually impure and therefore forbidden to engage in certain holy acts. Circumcision is also presented as a marker distinguishing Jews from foreigners; several texts stipulate that any adult male who joins the Jewish people must be ritually circumcised. In the later prophetic writings, significantly, the physical circumcision of the foreskin is sometimes treated as a mere metaphor for spiritual holiness rather than as a bodily sign of the covenant; thus Isaiah, Deutero-Isaiah, and Jeremiah speak of the circumcision of the heart, the lips or tongue, and the ears.

Jews have practiced female circumcision in some places and at some times in the past (see Strabon 1909, 3: 367, 465), and Ethiopian Jews (Falashas) continued to perform it until recently (Leslau 1957: 93; Davis 1972: 155; Bruce 1790, 3: 341–42.) But it seems there is no religious debate around this practice. Many Jews oppose female circumcision among other groups while refusing to question the practice of male circumcision within their own group. Such was the case for Edmond Kaiser, founder of "Terre des Hommes" and "Sentinelles," who advocated the abolition of female circumcision in Africa.[3] This stance, which is also common among non-Jewish American opponents of female circumcision, is hypocritical and bespeaks cultural imperialism.

Male circumcision continues to be practiced by the vast majority of Jews, even though they have abandoned many other biblical norms and ritual observances. However, opposition to the practice is evident in Jewish texts ever since ancient times. Historical sources indicate that some Jews dropped the practice, and a few men even restored their foreskins (I Maccabees 1:15; Ginzberg, 1937, 5: 273). Jewish religious authorities took active measures against those who were not circumcised (I Maccabees 2:45–46). Today, some orthodox rabbis honor those who sacrificed their lives to resist the abolition of circumcision as Jewish heroes (Cohen 1984: 4–5).

Recent Debates

The modern Jewish debate over male circumcision began after the French Revolution of 1789, which aimed to create a secular society where national citizenship replaced affiliation with particular religious communities. The spread of this idea across Europe, coupled with the extension of civil rights to Jews, prompted Jewish leaders to question many practices that set them apart from their fellows. A proposal to suppress male circumcision and to substitute an egalitarian ceremony for both boys and girls entering the covenant, enacted symbolically without the drawing of blood, came as early as 1842 in Frankfort (Barth 1990: 141–44). In 1866, sixty-six Jewish physicians in Vienna signed a petition against the practice of circumcision. By the late nineteenth century, the practice was evidently on the decline in Western Europe. In some places where the Haskalah (Enlightenment) predominated, rabbinical councils decided that uncircumcised sons of Jewish mothers were to be recognized as Jews, shifting from a ritual to an ethnic definition of identity (Barth 1990: 146). Theodore Herzl, the leading Zionist, did not circumcise his son; he was circumcised later, as an adolescent, at the insistence of his father's followers (Wallerstein 1980: 250, n. 15).

This debate over circumcision was brought to the United States with Jewish immigrants from Western Europe. In this country, Reform rabbis decided in 1892 not to impose circumcision on male converts. However, at the turn of the twentieth century the rise in immigration from Jewish communities in Central and Eastern Europe, where the ritual was still largely unquestioned by religious Jews, muted the debate. The trend toward hospital rather than home births and the medical practice of circumcising all male infants within the first three days, which became universal by mid-century, confronted Jews with a dilemma: should they accept circumcision that does not conform to Jewish ritual? Rabbis tried to remedy this situation by training Jewish physicians as ritual circumcisers and by requiring symbolic ritual circumcision before performing marriages. In 1979, the American Congress of Reform Rabbis decided that circumcision was mandatory and that it had to be performed according to Jewish norms with the prescribed religious ritual (Barth 1990: 146–48).

Currently, the critique of circumcision has been renewed in progressive Jewish American circles, in part because of its exclusion of female children and in part because of its questionable medical effects (Mark 2003; Pollack 1995; Goldman 1995, 1997). Because in recent years pediatricians have become increasingly opposed to routine circumcision and because the prevalence of circumcision among non-Jews is declining, Jews find themselves once more alone to decide. Those who are not religiously observant have little motivation to continue the practice. A significant number have in fact refused to have their sons circumcised, although most are reluctant to discuss their decisions in Jewish circles. Faced with this situation, some Jewish authors have suggested that the physical form of circumcision be modified, that the ritual precede the operation, and that women become ritual circumcisers (Hoffman 1996: 219). Others advocate the complete suppression of the physical operation, substituting an entirely symbolic ritual through which sons and daughters alike are brought into the covenant. Finally, still others reject the ritual as well as the physical operation.[4]

This debate is also taking place in Israel. In 1997, human rights activists founded an organization to fight against sexual mutilation. Despite the opposition of their relatives, parents refuse to circumcise their sons because they consider the practice abusive to children and thus contrary to Israeli law. This group argues that the medical risks of circumcision far outweigh its potential health benefits and that circumcision reduces sexual pleasure. The head rabbi of Israel, Eliahu Bakshi Doron, has defended the ritual not for its possible medical benefits or its effects on sexuality but on the simple ground that this an ancient and God-given practice.[5]

Debates Among Christians

New Testament Texts
Jesus attacked the religious authorities of his time on many questions of ritual and ethical practice, but there is no record of his taking a position concerning circumcision. Of the four Gospels, only Luke states that Jesus was circumcised when he was eight days old (Luke 2:21). Another reference to circumcision occurs in John:

> Jesus answered them: I performed one work, and all of you are astonished. Moses gave you circumcision—it is, of course, not from Moses, but from the patriarchs—and you circumcise a man on the Sabbath. If a man receives the circumcision on the Sabbath in order that the Law of Moses may not be broken, are you angry with me because I healed a man's whole body on the Sabbath? Do not judge by appearances, but judge with right judgment. (John 7:20–24)[6]

The Acts of the Apostles reports that, when non-Jews began to become Christian, the question of circumcision was widely debated. After Peter had converted an uncircumcised Roman centurion, circumcised Christians of Jewish origin criticized him for associating with the unclean. Peter explained his action by recounting a vision in which he had heard a voice telling him three times: "What God has made clean, you must not call profane" (Acts 10:15–16, 11:8–10). The position that circumcision was not necessary for Christian salvation was not immediately accepted. The question was addressed in a meeting of apostles and elders in Jerusalem, which decided that it is not necessary for pagans who convert to be circumcised. They must "abstain from things polluted by idols and from fornication and from whatever has been strangled and from blood" (Acts 15:2, 15:19–20), observing only a few basic Jewish laws.

Paul, who was responsible for converting pagans whose laws forbade circumcision, returned repeatedly to this question. Two passages summarize his position:

Let every one lead the life which the Lord has assigned to him and in which God has called him. This is my rule on all the churches. Was any one at the time of his call already circumcised? Let him not seek to remove the mark of the circumcision. Was any one at the time of his call uncircumcised? Let him not seek circumcision. For neither circumcision counts for anything nor uncircumcision, but keeping the commandments of God. (1 Corinthians 7:17–20)

You have put off the old nature with its practices and have put on the new nature, which is being renewed in knowledge after the image of his creator. Here there cannot be Greek and Jew, circumcised and uncircumcised, barbarian, Scythian, slave, free man, but Christ is all, and in all. (Colossians 3:10–11)

Circumcision among Christians was not mandatory but optional, and Paul set the distinction between circumcised and uncircumcised men aside entirely.

The debate about male circumcision continued among early Christians. Origen (d. 254 C.E.) argued that the physical circumcision required of Abraham had been superseded by a spiritual circumcision, the circumcision of the heart rather than the foreskin. Origen described physical circumcision as a shameful, even obscene practice, which made the body appear hideous and repulsive. Cyril, Patriarch of Alexandria (d. 444), also interpreted circumcision symbolically, criticizing Jews for taking biblical laws literally.[7] Mentioning Paul, he wrote: "The real meaning of circumcision reaches its fullness not in what the flesh feels, but in the will to do what God has prescribed" (373–75). To this religious argument, Cyril added another that has figured prominently in historical and contemporary debates: the perfection of human nature.

You consider . . . the circumcision of the flesh as something of importance and as the most suitable element of the cult. . . . Let us examine the use of circumcision and what favors the Legislator [God] will bring us through it. Indeed, to inflict circumcision on the parts of the body which nature uses to beget, unless you have one of the most beautiful reasons to do so, is not without ridicule; furthermore, it amounts to blaming the art of the Creator, as if he had overloaded the shape of the body with useless growths. However, if . . . we interpret what has been said in this way, does it not amount to judging that the divine intelligence is mistaken in what is fitting? Because if circumcision is the best way to shape physical nature, why was it not better and preferable from the beginning? Tell me then, if someone says that the infallible and intact nature is mistaken, does it not look like unreason? (365)

the God that is above all things created thousands of races of living beings devoid of reason. However it appears that in their constitution, oriented toward the most exact beauty, there is nothing either imperfect or superfluous. They are quite free of these two lies and escaped this double accusation. How could God, the artist by excellence, who gave such attention to the smallest things, make a mistake in the most precious of all? And when he introduced in the world the one that is after his image, would he have made him uglier than the beings devoid of reason, if it is true that in them there is no mistake, whereas there is one here? (367)

Recent Debates

Circumcision continues to be practiced in certain Christian communities in the Middle East that are in contact with Muslims. The Copts of Egypt, Sudan, and Ethiopia practice both male and female circumcision. In my discussions with the Copts of Egypt, I noted that they use the same arguments as Muslims: the circumcision of Abraham and Jesus. They are not informed of the view of Acts of the Apostles or Epistles of St. Paul. Coptic religious leaders say that baptism replaced circumcision for Christians. Referring to St. Paul, Anba Gregorius repeats that circumcision is nothing; he sees it as a custom or an optional hygienic measure (Gregorius 1988: 20–27). Maurice As'ad, Director of the Ecumenical Council of the Oriental Churches, says that God created man and woman in a splendid form, and no one has the right to cut a part of his or her body. For As'ad, female circumcision is forbidden because it consists of cutting a part of the sexual organ, whereas the male circumcision is optional because it touches the sexual organ only superficially (As'ad n.d.: 6) Therefore, he considers only female circumcision as mutilating.

In the late twentieth century, religious debate about male circumcision resumed in earnest among Christians, notably Protestant fundamentalists in the United States. Books by Christian physicians as well as ministers tout the purported medical benefits of circumcision, as well as proclaiming it to be a divine commandment that is still incumbent on Christians. In these texts, circumcision is justified as a means of maintaining purity by curtailing sexuality and by fending off numerous illnesses; those who disobey the divine orders must expect to suffer from the consequences (McMillen 1995; Gayman 1991). The TV evangelist Pat Robertson, who ran for president in 1988, said: "If God gave instructions for His people to be circumcised, it certainly would be in good judgment as God is perfect in wisdom and knowledge" (quoted in Bigelow 1995: 84–85).

Other Protestant fundamentalists question this interpretation of the Bible. Pastor Jim Bigelow argues that if circumcision prescribed by God to the Jews is good, then all biblical prescriptions must also be worthy of obser-vance, such as keeping kosher and purifying women after menstruation and childbirth. He discounts the health reasons often adduced in support of cir-cumcision and notes that the medical procedure practiced today differs sig-nificantly from the ritual prescribed in the Bible. He further asks why, if it is so beneficial, God did not make circumcision universal. Bigelow argues that the New Testament texts that dismiss circumcision were inspired by the Holy Spirit. He concludes: "Logically, you cannot pick and choose at will. Old Tes-tament law handed down by an all-wise God is either all good medicine or it is altogether something else! In looking over . . . those ordinances . . . , it seems quite justifiable to conclude that God's intent and purpose was not to reveal medical knowledge in the law but to fashion a unique people upon the earth" (Bigelow 1995: 86–87).

Rosemary Romberg, a Christian nurse married to a Jew and author of *Circumcision, the Painful Dilemma* (Romberg 1985), explains that Christian parents who are aware that there is no valid medical reason for circumcision figure that circumcision must be good since it is prescribed by the Bible. To counter this way of thinking, she wrote a short pamphlet (Romberg n.d.). Like Jim Bigelow, Romberg argues that many other practices that are also prescribed by the Bible are not accepted nowadays. For Christians, the ques-tion of circumcision has been decided by the New Testament, which consid-ers it as nothing or as a metaphor for inner holiness. Following early Christian theologians, Romberg maintains that, since humanity has been redeemed by the suffering of Christ, there is no need to draw blood by circumcision. Fi-nally, by making children suffer, circumcision violates the key principles of the New Testament, especially loving kindness toward others.

Debates Among Muslims

The Qur'an and the Tradition of Muhammad
The Qur'an, the primary source of Muslim law, mentions neither male nor female circumcision. Some Muslim authors find a justification for male cir-cumcision in the verse 2:124: "Recall that Abraham was put to the test by his Lord, through certain commands (*kalimat*), and he fulfilled them. [God] said, "I am appointing you an *imam* for the people."[8] Referring to certain sayings of Muhammad, classic and modern Muslim authors interpret the term *kalimat* as referring to the commandment of circumcision given to Abraham as reported by the Bible. As Abraham is a model for the Muslims, they must act as he acted: "Then we inspired you [*Muhammad*] to follow the

religion of Abraham, the monotheist; he never was an idol worshipper "
(16:123).

Given the lack of a Qur'an text directly prescribing male or female circumcision, Muslim authors base their opinions on interpretations of Muhammad's recorded sayings. Here are some examples of writings supporting
circumcision by contemporary Arabic authors:

Muhammad asked a circumciser woman if she continued to practice her profession.
She answered in the affirmative while adding: "Unless it is forbidden and that you order me to quit this practice." Muhammad replied to her: "But yes, it is permitted.
Come closer to me so that I can teach you: If you cut, don't go too far because it gives
more glow to the face and it is more pleasant for the husband." (Jad-al-Haq 1983, 9:
3121; Al-Sukkari 1988: 84)

Muhammad said: "Circumcision is sunnah for men and makrumah for women." (Al-
Sukkari 1988: 59)

The term *sunnah* means that it is accommodating to the tradition of Muhammad or simply a custom in the days of Muhammad. The term *makrumah*
means "meritorious action or noble deed," which implies that it is preferable
to practice female circumcision.

The Shiites mention Imam Al-Sadiq: "Female circumcision is a makrumah; is there
anything better than a makrumah?" (Al-Jamri 1986: 170–71)

Muhammad said: "The one who becomes a Muslim must let himself be circumcised
even though he is older." (Al-Sukkari 1988: 50)

One asked Muhammad if an uncircumcised could make the pilgrimage to Mecca. He
answered: "No, as long as he is not circumcised." (Abd-al-Raziq 1989: 71)

Muhammad says: "Five [norms] belong to the fitrah: the shaving of the pubis, the
circumcision, the cut of moustaches, the shaving of armpits and the size of nails."
(Al-Sukkari 1988: 55)

The term *fitrah* indicates practices that God taught his creature. The one
who seeks perfection must conform himself to these practices. These are not
mandatory practices, but simply advised (Al-Sukkari 1988: 55–56).

Classic Muslim authors relate that Sarah, who was jealous of Hagar, argued with her and swore to maim her, but Abraham protested. Sarah answered that she could not recant a vow. Then Abraham told Sarah to
circumcise her, so that circumcision became a norm among women (Ibn

Abd Al-Hakim 1922: 11–12; Al-Tabari 1992, 1: 130). Muslims see themselves as descended from Abraham and Hagar through their son Ishmael, so this practice is incumbent upon them.

Debates Concerning Male Circumcision

Male circumcision has not always been practiced by Muslims. Classic authors are not unanimous about the circumcision of Muhammad. Some think that he was born circumcised, and others believe that he was circumcised by an angel or by his grandfather (Al-Asbahani 1988: 99–105; Al-Sukkari 1988: 67–68). These contradictory speculations around an important fact of his life suggest that Muhammad was not circumcised. This inference is strengthened by the fact that neither Ibn-Ishaq (d. 767 C.E.) nor Ibn-Hisham (d. 828), the two famous biographers of Muhammad, speaks of his circumcision. After learning of the death of old men who were ordered to undergo circumcision after their conversion, Hasan Al-Basri indignantly protested that many people belonging to different races became Muslim in the days of Muhammad; no one looked under their clothes to see if they were circumcised, and they were not circumcised (Ibn-Qudamah n.d., 1: 85). Ibn-Hanbal recounts in his compilation, *Al-musnad*: "Uthman Ibn Abi-al-As was invited to a circumcision, but he declined the invitation. Asked why, he answered: in the days of Mohammed we didn't practice circumcision and we were not invited" (Ibn-Hanbal 1998, 4: 217). Al-Tabari says that the Caliph Umar Ibn Abd-al-Aziz (d. 720) wrote to the general of his army, Al-Jarrah Ibn Abd-Allah (d. 730), who had conquered the region of Kharassan: "Those who pray before you toward Mecca, excuse them from the payment of tribute." People then hurried to convert to Islam. One told the general that people converted not out of conviction but to avoid paying the tribute and that he needed to submit them to the test of circumcision. The general consulted the Caliph, who answered him: "God sent Muhammad to call people to Islam, not to circumcise them" (Al-Tabari 1992, 3: 592).

In recent decades, some Muslims have rejected the interpretation of the Qur'an verse 2:124 as supporting circumcision (Abduh 1980, 1: 373–74). Imam Mahmoud Shaltout, relying on the authority of Imam Al-Shawkani, argues that texts regarding male and female circumcision are neither clear nor authentic (Shaltout 1980: 331–32). Yet the overwhelming majority of modern Muslim authors maintain that male circumcision is mandatory.

According to Saudi religious authorities, a man who converts to Islam must be circumcised, but if he refuses to enter Islam for fear of this operation, this requirement can be delayed until the faith is consolidated in his heart.[9]

Ahmad Amin reports that a Sudanese tribe wanted to adhere to Islam. The chief wrote to Al-Azhar in Egypt to ask what it was necessary to do. Al-Azhar sent him a list of requirements, placing circumcision at the top. The tribe then refused to become Muslim (Amin 1992: 187). Al-Sukkari grants the woman the right to dissolve a marriage if the husband is not circumcised, because the foreskin could be a vector of disease and cause disgust that would interfere with the goals of the marriage, love and good understanding between the couple. Since Islam is a religion of cleanliness and purity, the woman has the right to marry someone beautiful and clean (Al-Sukkari 1988: 70–77).

At least five modern Muslim authors dispute the practice of male circumcision, however. In 1971, the Egyptian thinker Issam-al-Dine Hafni Nassif translated the work of Joseph Lewis, *In the Name of Humanity* (1956), under the title "Circumcision is a harmful Jewish mistake" (Nassif 1971). In the foreword, which is longer than the text itself, Nassif asks Muslims to put an end to male circumcision, which he considers a barbaric practice introduced by Jews into Muslim society. The sarcastic journalist Muhammad Afifi published a long review of this work in the Cairo magazine, *Al-Hilal*, expressing open hostility to male circumcision. The Libyan judge Mustafa Kamal Al-Mahdawi, currently charged with apostasy, similarly regards male circumcision as a Jewish custom. Al-Mahdawi adds that God did not create the foreskin solely as a superficial object to be cut (Al-Mahdawi 1990, 1: 348–50). Jamal Al-Banna, the younger brother of Imam Hassan Al-Banna (founder of the Muslim Brotherhood movement), invoking the verse "Yes, we created Man in the most perfect form" (95:4), says that neither male nor female circumcision is part of the Muslim religion since neither is present in the Qur'an (quoted in Aldeeb Abu-Sahlieh 2000, annex 23). Finally, the Turkish author, Edip Yuksel, the representative of a Muslim group in the United States founded by the Egyptian Rashad Khalifa, who rejects all reference to the traditional teachings (Hadith) of Muhammad, said in a release on the Internet: "One must ask how a merciful God could command such pain and injustice to children. . . . For all true savants of the Qur'an, the answer is clear. God, in his infinite mercy, cannot accept such a cruel ritual. This act is not mentioned at all in the Qur'an. It is only in recent inventions (hadith), human work, that one can find such laws and cruel rituals. . . . Let us put an end to this old crime against our children dating back many centuries."[10]

The Qur'an is the only holy book of these three faiths that omits the term *circumcision* and insists, in ten verses, on the perfection of human nature.[11] One of these verses pronounces any alteration of God's creation by cutting off body parts to be an act of obedience to Satan, not to God.[12] The silence of the Qur'an in regard to male circumcision may—indeed, in my opinion, must—be interpreted as signifying opposition to this practice.

Debates Concerning Female Circumcision

Although numerous Muslim authors condemn female circumcision, the majority maintain that it is a *makrumah*, a meritorious act rather than a mere custom, basing their opinion on Muhammad's words. The debate has been especially furious in Egypt since the mid-twentieth century. The Egyptian Commission of Fatwa (which issues advisory religious decisions) gave three somewhat contradictory rulings. The fatwa of May 28, 1949, declared that the abandonment of female circumcision does not constitute a sin (Makhlouf 1981, 2: 449). The fatwa of June 23, 1951, considers female circumcision desirable because it restrains nature—that is, sexual passion. It does not allow consideration of the opinions of physicians regarding its detriments (Nassar 1982, 6: 1986). The fatwa of January 29, 1981, whose author is Jad-al-Haq (who later became the Sheik of Al-Azhar), affirms that it is not possible to abandon the teachings of Muhammad in favor of the teaching of another, even a physician, because medicine evolves. Responsibility for a girl's circumcision falls on the parents and those in charge of her. He adds: "If the people of a region refuse to practice male and female circumcision, the chief of the state can declare war on them" (Jad-al-Haq 1983: 3119–25).[13]

Those Muslims who practice female circumcision think that it is part of their religion. The decision not to circumcise a daughter has serious social consequences. In certain countries, an uncircumcised girl is not able to marry, and people speak of her as of a person of bad moral conduct, sexually promiscuous, or possessed by the devil. In the Egyptian countryside, the matron who practices female circumcision delivers a certificate for the marriage (Zenie-Ziegler 1985: 66–67). El-Masry relates the words of an Egyptian midwife who had circumcised more than 1000 girls. According to her, fathers who oppose the excision of their daughters should be lynched because in effect they accept the girls becoming prostitutes, which she sees as the only recourse for unmarriageable women (El-Masry 1962: 3).

Numerous organizations in Muslim countries where female circumcision is practiced oppose it by offering religious reasons for this position. They assert that the Qur'an affirms the perfection of God's creatures. Nawal El Saadawi, the famous Egyptian physician and writer who was herself excised, asks: "If religion comes from God, how can it order man to cut off an organ created by Him as long as that organ is not diseased or deformed?

God does not create the organs of the body haphazardly without a plan. It is not possible that He should have created the clitoris in a woman's body only in order that it be cut off at an early stage in life" (El Saadawi 1980: 42). Opponents of female circumcision add that texts assigned to Muhammad are of little credibility. Imam Shaltout (1980: 331) and Sheik Mohammad Al-Tantawi[14] argue that, in the absence of any certain basis in the Qur'an and teachings of Muhammad, the opinion of physicians should determine the law.

Medical Justifications for the Distinction Between Male and Female Circumcision

Contrary to the opinion of those who invoke medical arguments to oppose female circumcision and to promote male circumcision, medical arguments have served to legitimize or to condemn both practices. There are no sound medical grounds for the distinction between male and female circumcision. The health effects of these procedures are at best questionable, and at worst deleterious, for both males and females.

The assumption that female circumcision is much more harmful than male circumcision is ubiquitous and often unquestioned. For example, in September 2000 UNICEF-Switzerland distributed a flyer titled "Excision: Mutilation or Ritual?" that states: "The term excision is not explicit. It recalls the circumcision of boys that consists in removing a part of the foreskin: this practice has some hygienic advantages without hindering in any way the normal function of the penis. On the contrary, excision is a mutilation of the female genital organ with lasting consequences for the health of the woman concerned and for the children whom she will bring into the world." Such an affirmation is incorrect because it does not take into consideration the different forms of each practice and their health effects on males and females.

There are four major forms of male circumcision:

1. Cutting away, in part or in its entirety, the skin of the penis that goes beyond the glans, which is called the foreskin or prepuce.

2. An extension of the first type, which involves cutting the mucous membrane under the foreskin. This procedure is practiced mainly by Jews, although it is far from universal among them. The *mohel* (ritual circumciser) grips the foreskin firmly with his left hand. After determining the amount to

be removed, he clamps a shield on it to protect the glans from injury. He then takes the knife in his right hand and amputates the foreskin with one sweep along the shield. This part of the operation is called the *milah*. It reveals the mucous membrane which lines the foreskin. The *mohel* then grasps the edge of the membrane firmly between his thumbnail and index finger and tears it down the center as far as the corona. This second part of the operation is called *periah*.[15] This operation was introduced by rabbis in the second century to make restoration of the foreskin more difficult.

3. Completely peeling the skin of the penis and sometimes the skin of the scrotum and pubis. Called *salkh* in Arabic and flaying or decutition in English, it existed (and may continue to exist) among some tribes of South Arabia. This practice was described and documented in various Western sources (Henninger 1989: 393–433; Chabukswar 1921: 48–49; Koriech 1987: 77). It has often been condemned by Muslim authorities. Thesiger affirms that the King Ibn-Sa'ud forbade it, considering it a pagan custom (Thesinger 1959: 91–93). A fatwa issued by Ibn-Baz (d. 1999), the highest Saudi religious authority, condemned it (Ibn-Baz 1995, 4: 30).

4. Slitting open the urinary tube from the scrotum to the glans, creating an opening that looks like the female vagina. Called subincision, this type of circumcision is still performed by Australian aborigines (Bryk 1943: 128–34; Annand 2000).

There are also four forms of female circumcision (WHO 1997: 3):

1. Excision of the prepuce, with or without excision of part or all of the clitoris.

2. Excision of the clitoris with partial or total excision of the labia minora, clinically called clitoridectomy.

3. Excision of part or all of the external genitalia and stitching or narrowing of the vaginal opening, conventionally called infibulation.

4. All other types, including pricking, piercing, or incising the clitoris and/or labia; stretching the clitoris and/or labia; cauterizing the clitoris and surrounding tissue by burning; scraping off tissue surrounding the vaginal orifice (*angurya* cuts) or cutting the vagina (*gishiri* cuts); the introduction of corrosive substances or herbs into the vagina to cause bleeding or for the purpose of tightening or narrowing it; and any other procedure that falls under the definition of female genital mutilation.

It is clear from this classification that, before considering which is more harmful, male or female circumcision, we must determine which type of circumcision we are speaking about.

Sexual Consequences of Male and Female Circumcision

There is a tendency to exaggerate the harmful sexual effects of female circumcision and to underestimate those of male circumcision. According to
Dorkenoo, who is responsible for WHO policy on sexual mutilation: "Clitoridectomy, which is the most common form of FGM, is analogous to peni-
sectomy rather than to circumcision. Male circumcision involves cutting the
tip of the protective hood of skin that covers the penis but does not damage
the penis, the organ for sexual pleasure. Clitoridectomy damages or destroys
the organ for sexual pleasure in the female" (Dorkenoo 1994: 52). Ancient
sources do not trivialize the sexual effects of male circumcision in this way.
Some Jewish religious authorities from the Hellenistic period on regarded
male circumcision as a proper means of reducing the sexual pleasure of the
man and his partner in order to control lust, an opinion based on their negative perception of sexuality. In his treatise on law, Philo (d. 54 C.E.) wrote:

I consider the circumcision to be a symbol of two things most necessary to our well-
being. One is the excision of pleasure [that] bewitches the mind. For since among the
love-lures of pleasures the palm is held by the mating of man and woman, the legislators thought [it] good to dock the organ which ministers to such intercourse, thus
making circumcision the figure of the excision of excessive and superfluous pleasure,
not only of one pleasure but of all the other pleasures signified by one, and that the
most imperious. (Philo 1984, Book I: 105)

The divine legislator ordained circumcision for males alone for many reasons. The
first of these is that the male has more pleasure in, and desire for, mating than does
the female, and he is more ready for it. Therefore He rightly leaves out the female,
and suppresses the undue impulses of the male by the sign of circumcision. (Philo
1979, III: 47)

Maimonides (d. 1204 in Cairo), a rabbi, physician, and philosopher who was
regarded as among the most trustworthy authorities on Jewish law, wrote in
his *Guide for the Perplexed*:

As regards circumcision, I think that one of its objects is to limit sexual intercourse,
and to weaken the organ of generation as far as possible, and thus cause man to be
moderate. Some people believe that circumcision is to remove a defect in man's formation; but everyone can easily reply: How can products of nature be deficient so as
to require external completion, especially as the use of the foreskin to that organ is
evident. This commandment has not been enjoined as a complement to a deficient
physical creation, but as a means for perfecting man's moral shortcomings. The bodily injury caused to that organ is exactly that which is desired; it does not interrupt

any vital function, nor does it destroy the power of generation. Circumcision simply counteracts excessive lust; for there is no doubt that circumcision weakens the power of sexual excitement, and sometimes lessens the natural enjoyment; the organ necessarily becomes weak when it loses blood and is deprived of its covering from the beginning. Our Sages . . . say distinctly: It is hard for a woman, with whom an uncircumcised [man] had sexual intercourse, to separate from him. This is, as I believe, the best reason for the commandment concerning circumcision. And who was the first to perform this commandment? Abraham our father, of whom it is well known how he feared sin. . . . We must keep in everything the golden mean; we must not be excessive in love, but must not suppress it entirely; for the Law commands: "Be fruitful, and multiply" (Genesis 1:22). The organ is weakened by circumcision, but not destroyed by the operation. The natural faculty is left in full force, but is guarded against excess. (Section III, chapter 49)

The Egyptian Coptic theologian Ibn-al-Assal (d. c. 1265) echoed Maimonides' opinion regarding the utility of circumcision: "Some physicians and distinguished philosophers say that circumcision weakens the tool of pleasure, and this is unanimously desirable" (Ibn-al-Assal 1908, 2: 418–21). Thomas Aquinas (d. 1274) also referred to Maimonides, writing that circumcision is a means "to weaken concupiscence in the interested organ."[16]

This idea is also expressed by classic Muslim jurists. Ibn-Qayyim Al-Jawziyyah (d. 1351) wrote that male and female circumcision curbs concupiscence. "If it [lust] is exaggerated, makes the man an animal; and if it is annihilated, makes him an inanimate thing. So circumcision curbs this concupiscence. For this reason, you never find uncircumcised men and women satiated by mating" (quoted in Aldeeb Abu-Sahlieh 2000, 1, annex 1). Al-Mannawi (d. 1622) reported that the imam Al-Razi taught: "The glans is very sensitive. If it remains hidden in the foreskin, it intensifies pleasure during mating. If the foreskin is cut, the glans hardens and pleasure becomes weak. This fits our law better: to reduce pleasure without suppressing it completely, a just medium between excess and carelessness" (Al-Mannawi 1995, 3: 503). As these quotations demonstrate, the notion that male circumcision is beneficial because it diminishes sexual pleasure is found in all three major religious traditions.

Contemporary opponents of male circumcision agree with these ancient authors that circumcision reduces sexual pleasure, and they have found scientific explanations to affirm this view. Unlike the ancient authors, they take a positive view of sexuality and consider full sexual enjoyment an individual right. Opponents say that sexual pleasure is obtained not from the glans alone, but by the corona of the glans, fraenulum, and foreskin. The glans penis is neurologically ill-equipped for fine sensations. When the foreskin is removed, the glans and its coronal crown lose their protection, harden with age, and become drier. So, they maintain, circumcision causes the progressive loss of sensitivity in the glans and its corona. Also, in eliminating a large proportion of the penile skin, circumcision eliminates many nerves and destroys foreskin muscles, glands, mucous membranes, and epithelial tissue. Circumcision also injures the fraenulum (Fleiss 1997: 41; Cold and Taylor 1999: 37–38; Laumann et al. 1997). Although circumcision does not prevent erection, the reduction of skin makes it tenser, less elastic, and less mobile.

These alterations in the penis affect sexual acts. In preparing for intercourse, the man caresses the woman's clitoris, prepuce, and labia. She caresses the man's penis, slipping the skin back and forth over the glans in order to maintain the erection until she is ready for penetration. This gesture is uncomfortable when the foreskin has been removed and the penile skin has been shortened. Circumcision also destroys or damages the glands that secrete lubricating smegma. To compensate for this, women may use a lubricant, which can be harmful, or resort to fellatio. Foreplay is shortened, depriving the man and woman of pleasure before penetration. The absence of the foreskin and the lack of penile lubricant also make sexual intercourse irritating or painful for both parties by increasing friction. In this respect, the sexual relation of the intact man defers from the sexual relation of the circumcised man. The circumcised man penetrates the woman more quickly and violently, in search of an excitation that the intact man enjoys naturally (Ritter 1992: 12-4, 15-1; Romberg 1985: 173; Warren 1997: 89; Zwang 1997: 71; O'Hara and O'Hara 1999: 79–84; Hammond 1999: 87). The negative sexual effects of circumcision have been remarked by American physicians. Some circumcised men in the United States are restoring the foreskin to remedy problems created by circumcision.

Supposed Health Benefits of Male and Female Circumcision

Health effects are regularly cited to distinguish between male and female circumcision, but the history of male and female circumcision shows that demonstrably false claims of health benefits have served to legitimize both practices. I take up the most commonly touted pseudo-benefits in turn.

Promotion of Cleanliness and Prevention of Masturbation

Over time, circumcision has been advertised as a remedy or preventative for a wide array of physical and mental conditions, ranging from baldness to lunacy. Cleanliness constituted, and still constitutes, one of the main arguments of the proponents of male circumcision. They claim that the lack of cleanliness causes numerous sexually transmitted diseases and cancers of the penis and prostate. Opponents refute such arguments on medical grounds, and they contend that these claims demonstrate the medical profession's propensity to conform to the dominant culture's attitudes despite their lack of scientific basis. In the 1950s, one American physician invoked the cleanliness argument to advocate female circumcision, assuming that women were unable to maintain proper hygiene and concluding that the result would be frequent vaginal infection, painful intercourse, and frigidity (quoted in Romberg 1985: 23). Today, physicians and laymen alike contend that teaching proper genital hygiene to boys and girls is simple (Wallerstein 1980: 75; Ritter 1992: 8-1).

In the past, prevention of masturbation was often invoked in Western cultures to justify both male and female circumcision. Although it was never mentioned in the classic Arabic sources, this justification is now repeated by contemporary writers for the practice of both male and female circumcision (Rashid, quoted in Aldeeb Abu-Sahlieh 2000: vol. 1, annex 13; Al-Ghawwabi 1951: 62; Ammar 1979: 47; Al-Jamal 1995: 2). The first sign of the widespread phobia about masturbation was the 1715 London publication of a booklet descriptively titled "Onania, or the heinous sin of self-pollution, and all its frightful consequences in both sexes considered, with spiritual and physical advice to those who have already injured themselves by this abominable practice." Panic over masturbation spread rapidly across Europe and the United States and was promoted by numerous medical writers (Stengers and Van Neck 1984: 72–89). John Harvey Kellogg, father of the popular breakfast cereal, played a prominent role in the campaign against masturbation and made a fortune from selling books persuading people that masturbation was a disease; he blamed masturbation for thirty-one different ailments (Goldman 1997: 58–59). Many methods and mechanical devices for suppressing masturbation were recommended by physicians, including, for extreme cases, such surgical operations as infibulation, castration, cauterization, and circumcision (Wallerstein 1980: 36). At the turn of the twentieth century, several Jewish American physicians promoted circumcision as a means of preventing masturbation and the horrible diseases that resulted from the presence of the foreskin. Relying on theories of eugenics, some extremists even suggested that chronic adult masturbators be sterilized and forbidden to marry. The absurdity of such views makes it obvious that medical opinion followed the common social and cultural prejudices of the day.

When masturbation phobia receded, American physicians stopped recommending circumcision on those grounds, but some shifted to new rationales for the practice. For example, in 1942 the popular "baby doctor," Dr. Benjamin Spock, concluded that "circumcision or other operative procedures should . . . be avoided at almost all costs in the treatment of masturbation" (quoted in Wallerstein 1980: 125). However, he remained in favor of the circumcision of male infants for hygienic reasons, abandoning that position only in 1976 (Spock 1976: 12).

Prevention of Venereal Disease, Penile and Cervical Cancer, Phimosis, and Urinary Tract Infections

Before the discovery of microbes, venereal diseases such as syphilis provoked terror in the West, much as HIV/AIDS has done in recent decades. Syphilis was viewed as God's punishment for evildoers, and a few physicians even refused to treat patients (Wallerstein 1980: 37). Circumcision was often proposed as a preventive measure, despite the lack of scientific evidence regarding the mechanisms of transmission in circumcised and uncircumcised penises. From the early twentieth century on, some physicians cited aggregate differences in the prevalence of venereal diseases among Jews, Gentiles, and Negroes as evidence that circumcision had a prophylactic effect. The racist assumptions that lay behind such arguments are apparent in a paper presented to the American Medical Association in 1947 by Dr. Eugene A. Hand: "Circumcision is not common among Negroes. . . . Many Negroes are promiscuous. In Negroes there is little circumcision, little knowledge or fear of venereal disease and promiscuity in almost a hornet's nest of infection. Thus the venereal rate in Negroes has remained high. Between these two extremes there is the gentile, with a venereal disease rate higher than that of Jews but much lower than that of Negroes" (Hand 1949, quoted in Hodges 1997: 8).

As late as the early 1970s, amid rising concern over premarital sexual activity among young people, some physicians suggested circumcision as an effective measure against epidemics of sexually transmitted disease (Ravich 1973: 45–46; Wallerstein 1980: 19–20). Criticizing such approaches from a medical perspective, Wallerstein concluded that overemphasizing the relationship of circumcision to venereal disease tends to limit consideration of the problem to males, but venereal infections may be more serious in women. In men, venereal disease is usually symptomatic, and the male genitalia are easily examined. Female genitalia are more hidden, and infections are often asymptomatic. A woman may be seriously ill, and also infect her sexual partner, without her condition being obvious. Therefore, Wallerstein asks, should the external genitalia of women be removed simply because they can be sites of venereal infection? It makes as much sense to do this as it does to remove the male foreskin to prevent venereal disease (Wallerstein 1980: 87). After reviewing the literature on this topic published from 1855 to 1997, Dr. Van Howe concluded: "Until recently, no studies have examined the impact of circumcision on overall STD incidence. The data indicate that a circumcised man may be at higher risk for an STD. This is consistent with the trends seen in the USA. As routine neonatal circumcision has been implemented, the rate of STDs has increased rather than fallen. Among first-world nations, the USA has one of the highest rates of STDs, HIV infection and male circumcision" (Van Howe 1997: 58).

Claims about the role of circumcision in the prevention of penile and cervical cancer appeared in the early twentieth century. In 1932, the Jewish American physician Dr. Abraham Wolbarst published an article asserting that circumcision prevents cancer. Based on his contention that Jews were immune to penile cancer, he theorized that penile cancer was caused by "the accumulation of pathogenic products in the preputial cavity" (Wolbarst 1932, quoted in Wallerstein 1980: 108). In 1942, expanding upon Wolbarst's theory of smegma as a carcinogen and repeating the myth of Jewish immunity to the disease, Dr. Abraham Ravich postulated a causal link between the foreskin and prostate cancer and restated the theory that female cervical cancer was caused by male smegma (Ravich 1942: 298–99). This claim was circulated by the popular magazine, *Newsweek*.[17] Ravich advocated the compulsory circumcision of male infants as "an important public health measure" (Ravich 1951: 1519–20; see also Hodges 1997: 27). This theory is based on the hypotheses that smegma is a carcinogen and that any observed differences in rates of penile and cervical cancer among Jews, Muslims, and Christians are explained by their varying practices of circumcision (Fleiss 1999: 396–97). The theory that circumcision prevents penile and cervical cancer was officially rejected by the American Academy of Pediatrics in 1975 (see American Academy of Pediatrics Report 1999) and by the American Cancer Society in 1996 (cited in Junos 1998: 27). Even if circumcision has some slight prophylactic effect, its risks far outweigh the possible benefits (Denniston 1997: 106; Wallerstein 1980: 109).

Phimosis is a condition in which the foreskin is too narrow to slip behind the glans. *Paraphimosis* is the condition in which the narrow foreskin is lodged behind the glans and cannot be pulled forward to recover the glans.

Both conditions may be painful, but they are localized. In the nineteenth and early twentieth centuries, some American physicians blamed phimosis and paraphimosis for a whole range of maladies, including paralysis, hip-joint disease, hernia, indigestion, constipation, inflammation and paralysis of the bladder, nocturnal enuresis, clumsiness, epilepsy, hysteria, neurasthenia, and clubfoot to cancer, syphilis, chancre, chancroid, and, of course, frequent nocturnal seminal emissions and masturbation. Circumcision was recommended as a cure for all of these conditions. If a male infant's foreskin would not retract, he was diagnosed as having a phimosis requiring circumcision (Hodges 2001: 40–51). This view also predominated in Britain until 1949, when Dr. Douglas Gairdner proved that this condition was in the great majority of cases a natural rather than a pathological phenomenon. Reviewing all the claims made for circumcision, Gairdner rejected them as unconvincing and concluded that the prepuce of the male infant should be left in its natural state (Gairdner 1949). In most cases, paraphimosis for which physicians recommend circumcision results not from disease but by forcibly retracting the foreskin and trapping it in the sulcus behind the glans. In pediatric practice the complaint is seen in infants whose parents have been instructed by a misguided doctor or nurse to retract the prepuce but not to pull it forward thereafter, and sometimes in older boys as the outcome of a bet or dare. Retraction under general aesthetic is almost always possible; circumcision should be considered only for the exceptional case of recurrent episodes (Warren 1997: 91; Rickwood 1999: 49).

In the mid-1980s, as other medical rationales for male circumcision were being disproved, some physicians turned to the prevention of urinary tract infections (UTI) as a new excuse to perform the procedure. Dr. Thomas Wiswell conducted an epidemiological study of children born in American military hospitals and suggested that circumcision might slightly reduce the rate of UTIs (Wiswell and Bass 1985). Proponents promoted Wiswell's research as indicating a medical need for circumcision. Opponents of male circumcision counter that, even if Wiswell's figures were correct, this benefit of circumcision is small and far outweighed by the risks. Furthermore, such infections can be treated and prevented without resorting to the scalpel (Warren 1997: 97; Denniston 1997: 105; Prescott 1989: 14; Rickwood 1999: 49). Opponents also note that females have higher rates of urinary tract infection than males, yet no doctor advocates routine and universal genital surgery to reduce the prevalence of UTIs; antibiotic treatment is endorsed by the usual and customary Standard of Care that prevails in the United States (Goldman 1997: 30–31). Finally, they argue that the maintenance of the intact child, coupled with proper hygiene, should protect him from urinary tract infections (Ritter 1992: 32-1). Circumcised men develop urinary tract infections at the same rates as intact men.

HIV/AIDS

The theory that circumcision prevents or significantly inhibits the transmission of HIV and thus constitutes an effective prophylactic measure against AIDS is the latest invention of the proponents of male and female circumcision. Without entering into scientific detail, the idea requires comment.

First, we must recognize that some Arab sources say that female circumcision, as well as male circumcision, prevents AIDS. An article titled "A witness of the bride's house says: Circumcision protects against AIDS" appeared in the Egyptian newspaper *Aqidati* on September 5, 1995. The author, Dr. Shafiq, stated: "A European medical organization confessed that circumcision protects against AIDS, this pestilence of the modern time"; and added: "This confession on behalf of a medical organization is probably the most strong and most eloquent answer against the ferocious campaign of CNN aiming to attack Islam which insists on circumcision." The campaign to which this article refers was a movie shown on CNN on September 7, 1994, concerning the circumcision of a girl in Cairo. On September 9, 1995, the Egyptian newspaper *Sawt al-ummah* echoed these claims and quoted Izzat Al-Sawi, an obstetrician: "If the Western medical organizations concluded that circumcision protects against AIDS and penile cancer, it must not astonish us because female circumcision doesn't present any problem and one doesn't have anything to fear from it." Sheik Al-Badri, who on June 24, 1997, obtained an annulment by a Cairo court of the decree of the Egyptian minister of health forbidding female circumcision, declared: "It is our religion. We pray, we fast and we circumcise. For 14 centuries our mothers and our grandmothers performed circumcision. Those that are not circumcised get AIDS more easily."[18]

The Egyptian press and sheik Al-Badri seek to convince the Egyptian public that female circumcision is not only a religious commandment but protects against AIDS. In citing the testimony of the European medical establishment to support this claim, they commit a serious falsification. The medical study they cited concerned male circumcision, not female circumcision. Opponents of female circumcision argue that it contributes to the propagation of HIV because unsterilized tools are used and infections commonly follow (Salim 1994: 50; Rizq 1994: 29). Furthermore, the more severe types of female circumcision, especially infibulation, make the woman highly vulnerable to injury and thus at increased risk of HIV transmission during sexual intercourse.

Second, the purported prophylactic benefits of male circumcision relative to HIV transmission are not founded on scientific evidence. The theory that AIDS can be prevented by circumcision started in the late 1980s, when some African studies suggested a link exists between the propagation of HIV virus and the uncircumcised penis. Proponents of male circumcision in the United States drew on this questionable data to defend this practice against rising criticism. However, when confronted by informed journalists,[19] even those doctors who promoted this theory had to admit that it has not been proven (Fink 1985 and 1986; Hodges 1997: 35). The reasoning upon which this theory is based is fundamentally flawed. Proponents make inferences from aggregate-level observational data across continents, focus on the foreskin as a vector of infection, and fail to take into account other epidemiological and social factors that affect HIV prevalence rates, such as the number of sexual partners and the frequency with which men engage in sexual relations with prostitutes (Van Howe 2001: 99–100).

Opponents of male circumcision criticize these studies because they are based on African data instead of data from the United States, where HIV infection is also prevalent (Kreiss and Hopkins 1993). The United States has a much higher rate of HIV infection than the non-circumcising nations of Europe. Within Europe, countries with higher rates of HIV infection are also those with higher numbers of circumcised Muslim immigrants and guest workers. Commenting on these figures, Fleiss wrote: "The unchecked myth that circumcision can prevent AIDS is not only false, but also dangerous. It may lead circumcised Americans to consider themselves immune to HIV and, therefore, free to practice unsafe sex with HIV-infected individuals. This will only cause more deaths and further the spread of HIV and AIDS" (Fleiss 1999: 393–94).

Opponents of male circumcision maintain that circumcision, instead of preventing AIDS, can increase the risk of HIV transmission. They mention a number of possible factors: the dryness of the circumcised penis, which exposes it to injury during sexual intercourse; the propensity of circumcised men to perform anal and oral sex; higher rates of homosexuality among circumcised men; the tendency of circumcised men to change sexual partners more often; the reluctance of circumcised men to use condoms; and the tendency of circumcised men to penetrate without much foreplay (Ritter 1992: 35-1). Finally, the false belief that circumcision protects men from HIV/AIDS can lead men to have unsafe sex and elevate their risk of contracting the disease. Even if circumcision did reduce the risk of HIV transmission in some measurable way, adopting circumcision as a prophylactic measure would be more expensive for a society than AIDS itself (Van Howe 2001: 119). As Dr. Ritter put it: "Obviously, it is contact with specific organisms that causes specific diseases, and it is education about safe sex, not amputation of healthy body parts of newborns, that is sane preventive medicine for sexually transmitted diseases" (Ritter 1992: 33-2).

Conclusion

The distinction between male and female circumcision continues to be made in the face of the ample historical and medical evidence to the contrary because of political reasons. Orthodox clerics and their supporters in the Jewish and Muslim traditions continue to insist that these practices are divinely ordained and therefore cannot be harmful. Even discussing the subject is taboo in some international forums, as it is within some religious institutions. Jews and Muslims are quite defensive about any suggestion that ritual practices they regard as part of their sacred traditions and core identities are medically harmful and not founded on a solid scriptural basis.

International experts and organizations working on the problem of female circumcision are very cautious about alienating these groups by criticizing male circumcision on the same grounds, since this might undermine their campaigns. WHO has published many documents and organized many conferences on female circumcision, but it has never taken up male circumcision. The term female circumcision was changed to Female Genital Mutilation in part to avoid offending Jews and Muslims by drawing an analogy between the two practices, as well as to emphasize the violence against women this practice entails. I found myself criticized in the 1997 Anti-Semitism World Report for comparing male and female circumcision in a paper presented to the Third International Symposium on Sexual Mutilations in 1994.[20] Open discussion of this subject is inhibited by accusations of anti-Semitism (Pollack 1997: 171). Christians as well as Jews make such accusations, and they are directed against both Jews and non-Jews. Betty Katz Sperlich, a Jewish nurse who founded an association called "Nurses for the Rights of the Child," says: "I've been called anti-Semitic by non-Jewish people. We are touching a deep nerve. But as a Jew how could I not speak up against Jewish circumcision? I would be letting Jewish babies down" (Sperlich 1997: 2).

The laws of all nation-states mention the right to physical integrity and impose penal sanctions and civil remedies against its violation, But the right to bodily integrity is not included in the Universal Declaration of Human Rights, the Covenant on Civil Rights, the Convention on the Rights of the Child, and the European Convention on Human Rights. This omission is certainly not accidental. The only two international documents that mention this right are the American Convention on Human Rights of 1969 and the African Charter on Human and Peoples' Rights of 1981.[21]

In conclusion, it is not logically possible to oppose female circumcision and to support male circumcision, unless you want to convince us that your culture or religion is better than that of others, or that girls are entitled to protection but boys are not. The right to physical integrity is a principle. We must accept or reject genital cutting in totality. If we accept this principle, we must refrain from cutting of children's genitals regardless of their sex, their religion, or their culture.

PART II

African Campaigns to Eradicate Female Circumcision

Chapter 4
Community-Based Efforts to End Female Genital Mutilation in Kenya: Raising Awareness and Organizing Alternative Rites of Passage

Asha Mohamud, Samson Radeny, and Karin Ringheim

The tradition of female circumcision is so deeply entrenched in the culture and decisions regarding the practices are not made by individuals. In addition to the father, the mother and the girl, we have the community and the extended family system. This makes it difficult for one individual or family to decide on its own without pressure from others.
—Leah Muuya, 1995

Ending the harmful practice of female genital mutilation can be accomplished by concerted efforts at the grassroots level that involve the entire community. In Kenya, the women and girls who are most directly affected by the practice, with support from the men in their families and communities, have cooperated to eliminate cutting from rites of passage guiding young women into sexual maturity. Mobilizing support among educators and religious leaders and addressing those who perform the operation, national and international nongovernmental organizations (NGOs) have offered resources and coordination to these grassroots campaigns. This essay explains what we have learned about the cultural meanings of this ritual procedure and the process of social change that women have initiated in Kenya.

The Maendeleo Ya Wanawake Organization (MYWO), a national grassroots organization dedicated to improving the health and well-being of women in Kenya, made abandoning the practice of female genital mutilation (FGM) an important priority in 1991.[1] The first step was to conduct a survey of traditional practices affecting the health of women and children.[2] Focusing on four rural districts of Kenya where the practice was common (Kisii, Meru, Narok, and Samburu), the 1992–1993 survey found that nine out of ten women had undergone various types of circumcision, some as young as 8 and most by the age of 15. FGM was typically performed in the village or the bush by traditional practitioners using unsterilized instruments. The survey confirmed that FGM is perceived to be an important aspect of a girl's social, moral, and physical development, allowing passage from girlhood to womanhood, bestowing respectability on her, and preparing her for marriage. Because FGM has negative consequences for the physical and psychological health of women and acts as a barrier to women's rights and advancement, MYWO decided to undertake a campaign to eliminate it. The organization conducted advocacy at the national level, with political leaders, policy makers, and journalists, and at the grassroots level, with programs designed to raise awareness that FGM harms women's health and violates their human rights and to mobilize these communities to end the practice.

With technical assistance from the Program for Appropriate Technology in Health (PATH),[3] MYWO began working in these four districts of Kenya, where FGM remained nearly universal. The community-based approach aimed to raise awareness of the human rights and health implications of FGM and to involve peer educators, teachers, and religious and community leaders in mobilizing for social change. The program was conceived to place those most directly involved with the practice of female genital mutilation at the center of its activities, so it was fully aligned with the expressed needs and perspectives of mothers, daughters, fathers, prospective husbands, and others within particular cultural communities. One important element in the program's success was the development of a culturally appropriate Alternative Rite of Passage (ARP). In several ethnic groups in Kenya, circumcision has been part of a ritualized, communally organized process to mark a girl's coming of age and prepare her for marriage. We realized that the cutting itself is only a physical symbol of this transition, so PATH and MYWO designed a program that preserved the social meaning of the ritual while eliminating the genital mutilation. The ARP program built on the existing rite of passage, promoting the positive aspects of this cultural practice and passing on traditional wisdom while educating girls about sexuality, HIV/AIDS, relationships, and family life. It culminates in a celebration of the girl's altered social status as a young woman. For girls and their families who have decided against FGM, the ARP provides social support to offset the stigmatization that commonly afflicts those who do not follow conventional norms. Beyond that circle, the ARP program celebrates a new, healthier social norm in a traditional manner, helping to persuade others that this innovation is compatible with important cultural values. The first ARP ceremony was held in 1996, and within six years 7,000 girls had participated in an alternative rite of passage.

The collaborative effort between PATH and MYWO is one of the few anti-FGM projects in Africa that has been able to document a social transition in the making.[4] The project focused deliberately on four districts where rates of female circumcision were high relative to the nation as a whole. In 1992–1993, at the beginning of the anti-FGM campaign, 78 percent of women under the age of 20 in those districts had been circumcised; by 1999, after five years of work, the proportion had fallen to 56 percent. Most citizens in the project areas now recognize that FGM is a violation of girls' human rights, a key intervention message. Less than half (47 percent) of women now favor continuation of the practice, as compared to nearly two-thirds (63 percent) at the beginning of the project. The shift away from FGM is not yet complete, but movement in this direction gathers momentum over time. Changing the attitudes of prospective husbands is an essential prerequisite for girls and their families to abandon the practice, since in the past young men have regarded circumcision as making young women fit for marriage. In the project areas, a majority of young boys now say they would be willing to marry an uncut girl. With a growing awareness of girls' human rights, the efforts to change this practice will trigger changes in social norms that will ultimately benefit not only girls but also their families, communities, and the larger society. Addressing the issue of female genital mutilation advances positive social norms that recognize girls and women as full human beings endowed with rights to bodily integrity and freedom from harm.

The practice of FGM in Kenya typically takes place in early adolescence and marks the transition of a young girl into sexual maturity. Here as elsewhere, female genital mutilation has its roots in the regulation of female sexuality and is seen as a way to prevent promiscuity, preserve virginity, and promote cleanliness. It is also widely believed to improve fertility, thereby making a woman more attractive for marriage. Enforced by the rituals surrounding it, FGM promotes social cohesion and is viewed by custodians of the culture as an essential traditional practice that must be protected from the onslaught of misguided modernizing influences. Those who would abandon the practice can therefore be subject to extreme social pressure and ostracism if they fail to uphold this social norm.

The prevalence of FGM in Kenya varies widely. The 1998 Kenya Demographic and Health Survey (DHS) estimated that the national prevalence rate among women ages fifteen to forty-nine was 38 percent (Carr 1997).[5] But this average conceals wide variations between ethnic groups and regions. Kenya is a mosaic of culturally diverse ethnic and linguistic groups; there are seven major linguistic groups and at least forty distinct ethnocultural groups. Many groups are concentrated in particular districts, while others are more dispersed within a region. Cities attract migrants from many different groups; the population of the capital, Nairobi, is culturally quite diverse. Swahili was adopted as a national language in order to generate a sense of national identity and belonging, and most Kenyans speak a mothertongue as well. FGM is practiced by more than three-quarters of the country's ethnocultural groups. Marked differences occur within regions. For example, MYWO's baseline survey found that in Kisii, a district in the far west inhabited by Kisii and Gusii speakers, 97 percent of women over age fifteen had been circumcised, while the Luos and Luhyas, the two largest ethnolinguistic groups in the far west, did not circumcise women at all. Prevalence rates also vary between groups that practice FGM. For example, the 1998 DHS found that among the Maasai 87 percent of adult women had been circumcised, while among the Kikuyu the rate was only 43 percent.

A brief discussion of the ethnolinguistic composition of the districts where MYWO and PATH worked is essential to understanding the projects conducted there, as an in-depth understanding of these distinct cultures informed the projects' design. Kisii, a district where the Kisii/Gusii ethnocultural group predominates,[6] is located in Nyanza province about 50 kilometers west of Lake Victoria. The district of Meru, which takes its name from the linguistic group that predominates there, is located in the eastern region, just to the northeast of Mount Kenya.[7] Narok, a district in the southcentral Rift Valley, is the home of the Maa-speaking Maasai, a distinctive ethnocultural group. Samburu, a district to the north of Narok in the eastcentral Rift Valley, is inhabited mainly by Samburu speakers.[8] In contrast to most people in Kisii and Meru, who live in agricultural villages, most people in Narok and Samburu raise livestock and migrate in kin-based groups as they herd their cattle. The MYWO/PATH project found somewhat different patterns of FGM in these four districts, and the programs designed by community activists there differed accordingly. Nonetheless, some major factors underlying the practice of FGM and key strategies that proved effective in facilitating its elimination can be identified. Indeed, the diversity of these districts is one of the strengths of this project; since these strategies worked in such different sociocultural contexts, they are probably more broadly applicable throughout Kenya, and they are worth considering in other regions across Africa where FGM is prevalent.

Redefining a Cultural Practice

Families practicing female genital mutilation believe that they are helping rather than harming their daughters. Prompting families to reevaluate this tradition required sensitivity to their culture and deeply held beliefs. All local terms used by Kenyan communities that practice FGM translate to "female circumcision"—as if it were the feminine equivalent of male circumcision, which is also prevalent in these groups. When we began working against FGM, it was more effective for us to use a term that was acceptable and culturally appropriate to these communities. We encountered a problem more basic than terminology, however: at that time it was taboo to discuss female circumcision openly. Circumcised girls and women were taught to keep their experiences secret. They would discuss them during seclusion, the period of healing and teaching following the cut, but after that, it was a cultural offense to talk about circumcision.

Our initial community mobilization activities sought to encourage circumcised girls and women to speak about their experiences. It was extremely difficult to initiate open discussion. Over time, a few women began to speak in public meetings about their own personal experiences or those of their daughters. To build support in the communities where we worked, we began with the few women who were already convinced that female circumcision was harmful. Soon activists emerged from these groups who would not be stopped by the cultural barriers against speaking about this matter publicly. Some were elected leaders of MYWO whom we trained in communication strategies. Pictures and anatomical models of the various types of FGM were introduced, and women were asked to tell us if what they saw could be referred to merely as circumcision. Many of them understood the difference between circumcision—cutting around the genitals—and mutilation—complete removal of the external genitalia. They concluded that what happened to many girls in Kenya was indeed mutilation, not circumcision.

This first group of activists took advantage of community meetings to talk about female genital cutting but was careful not to use the term FGM in public. The women introduced this terminology in the smaller group meetings they organized. At first it was difficult to convince women that what they and their daughters had experienced was mutilation. A number of women complained that the term "mutilation" was so negative. "Sisi hatu-fanyi hivyo," they protested; "we don't do that [mutilation] in my community." As the project continued, more women could see the difference between circumcision and mutilation, especially when our activists explained the distinction between male circumcision and female genital cutting. In our efforts to eradicate the practice, we have always corrected the impression that what was called female circumcision was equivalent to male circumcision. Many women began to realize that what had happened to them and their daughters was nothing short of mutilation.

As the debate heated up, men began to participate. At this point, more than a year after the project had begun, we started working with men to reach other men. The men's involvement helped a great deal to bring the issue into the open. Female circumcision was discussed in many meetings, and after members of the provincial administration had been exposed to these advocacy efforts they began to discourage female genital cutting in their areas. Soon the terms "female circumcision" and "female genital mutilation" were being used interchangeably. Today, in the places where we are working, the term FGM is more commonly used than female circumcision.

Understanding Cultural Meanings and Social Contexts

Selecting districts where the high prevalence of FGM had been documented, MYWO and its partner, PATH, gathered additional data about current practices and used the formative research to guide in program planning. The baseline survey conducted among a representative sample of 1,365 women ages fourteen to sixty in 1992–1993 showed that over 90 percent of women in the four project districts had been subjected to FGM. This study used the categories defined by WHO to classify the procedure into three types: clitoridectomy, excision, and infibulation. The most common procedure was excision, which 56 percent of the women had undergone; 36 percent had undergone clitoridectomy, which in Kenya is commonly called sunna; and 7 percent had been infibulated. Infibulation was most common in the northeast of the country; one-fifth of circumcised women in Samburu had been infibulated. This form of FGM is prevalent among groups who immigrated to Kenya from neighboring Somalia, where the procedure is customary. The mean age of circumcision was approximately fourteen years in three of the districts, but less than ten years in Kisii.

The great majority (80 percent) of genital cuttings had taken place in group settings. In most (71 percent) of these ritualized group procedures, a single blade had been used, increasing the likelihood of blood-borne infection. Traditional practitioners performed most cuttings, but some were performed by health practitioners, most notably in Kisii. The cuttings took place during school holidays and at harvest time, in the village, the initiate's home, or the bush. Medical problems caused by the procedure included infection and hemorrhage. Later complications commonly associated with FGM included urine retention, painful intercourse, and obstructed labor. Less than 20 percent of women surveyed said they had "no complaint," yet women who had experienced these complications rarely associated their problems with the procedure. Both men and women attributed health problems that are actually complications of FGM to other causes, including witchcraft, curses, and other disturbances in interpersonal relationships. Before being educated about the harmful effects of FGM, the vast majority believed that the procedure was beneficial to women's health. Nearly two-thirds (63 percent) of the respondents favored continuing the practice and planned to circumcise their daughters, citing the perceived health and social benefits. Even those who did associate health problems with FGM often favored continuing the practice to preserve their culture and to improve their daughters' prospects for marriage.

Circumcised girls were believed to make better, more obedient wives, to behave more respectfully to parents and elders, and to be more mature. Indeed, the rites of passage associated with circumcision were central to the transition from girlhood to adult womanhood. In focus group discussions, men said that uncircumcised women were oversexed, unclean, rude, bossy, and disrespectful. For girls, in addition to enhancing their chances of marriage, being circumcised was an opportunity to show their bravery, respect for their parents, and willingness to do anything their elders ask of them. The celebration following circumcision is an important opportunity for the family to display social status and entertain family and friends. Girls are enticed by the prospect of receiving gifts and the feasting, music, dancing, and special privileges they enjoy at the end of the healing period.

The baseline survey, as well as qualitative research conducted within the communities where the project was active, deepened our understanding of people's perceptions, beliefs, and behaviors with regard to FGM. Understanding the cultural significance and social context of the practice was essential for designing an appropriate intervention. Project staff realized that to instigate change required us to engage each community in a thorough examination of its values, norms, practices, and fears. PATH and MYWO planned to achieve these objectives through a phased implementation of interpersonal communication and community mobilization strategies that would facilitate social change. We envisioned an alternative to the existing coming-of-age ceremony following circumcision that would be acceptable to the community and would continue the valuable tradition of providing girls with education about family life and relationships. But first the project needed to raise awareness among local policy makers, community leaders, parents, and girls themselves of the harmful health and social effects of female genital mutilation.

Interpersonal Communication and Community Mobilization Strategies

PATH and MYWO built a communication strategy based on the present state of knowledge and attitudes in the four districts. We garnered the support of elders, teachers, and religious and community leaders to oppose FGM. Most importantly, we raised awareness about human rights and the harmful health effects of FGM and promoted a positive image of uncircumcised girls to counteract the negative stereotypes about them.

In each district, as well as at the national level, MYWO staff organized workshops to review findings from community studies and to initiate an intergenerational dialogue with religious leaders, village chiefs, elders, government officials, health care providers, local volunteers, and women leaders. Part of the challenge was overcoming the claim that the campaign was driven by foreign interference; we sought to promote understanding that this was an initiative by and for Kenyans. Other critics questioned the priority given to eradicating FGM in light of other prevalent health problems, such as malaria. Staff explained the health repercussions of FGM using detailed anatomical models, which had removable parts that enabled staff to show the normal genitalia, the different types of FGM, and the complications associated with these procedures. At first, one anatomical model per district was carted from place to place; then replicas were carved in wood for broader distribution. Through these models and group discussion, women began to make links between the procedure and their own experiences, for example, of excessive bleeding after genital cutting, perineal tears during delivery, and sexual problems. This process of making connections helped to open the discourse on health and human rights issues. Nevertheless, in some ethnic groups, circumcision was such an integral part of cultural identity that the idea of an uncircumcised girl was unfathomable and brought discomfort, disbelief, and embarrassed giggles from participants.

Community volunteers and artists were invited to participate in workshops that developed educational materials about FGM based on the formative research. The key messages developed to address perceptions and myths were: (1) FGM does not prevent infertility, but can cause difficult childbirth and infertility; (2) there is no difference between the behavior of circumcised and uncircumcised girls; (3) FGM has negative effects on women's sexuality; (4) educated girls can support themselves and their parents without being circumcised; and (5) FGM has nothing in common with male circumcision.

People who recognized the practice was harmful were trained to raise awareness among others. These change agents mobilized their communities to reflect on the value of their traditions, to recognize the differences between male and female circumcision, and to abandon the harmful practice of FGM. With the leadership of these advocates, chiefs and district government officials were persuaded to support community-wide education programs. One notable example of conversion was a parliamentarian from Narok who initially was opposed to the project entering his community. As a custodian of the culture, he believed that the initiative would undermine "strong Maasai traditions." MYWO persevered in reaching out to him, and the parliamentarian eventually appeared in a project video, *Secret and Sacred*, as a role model who did not circumcise his own daughters.

Peer educators, most of whom were women recruited through MYWO, were central to the project's community mobilization strategy. They included members of religious groups, teachers, health workers, and other volunteers. They were trained about the health and human rights issues surrounding FGM, as well as in interpersonal communication and counseling, decision making, conflict mediation, and peer outreach. Later, boys and men were also included as peer educators. In each district, the audiences to be reached were prioritized according to the prevailing pattern of decision making about circumcision, the age at which it occurs, and the level of opposition to eradication efforts from the community. For example, in the Kisii district, where 98 percent of circumcised girls have undergone the procedure before age twelve, both parents were implicated in the decision while the girl herself was too young to advocate for change on her own behalf, so the project addressed adults. In Meru, where the average age of circumcision is about fourteen, girls may have some say in the decision, and therefore the project reached out to both parents and girls. Girls in school were an important audience, especially since the peak seasons for FGM coincide with school holidays to allow time for healing and passing on of traditional wisdom during seclusion. The project reached students through several schools in each district. Teachers were trained to address FGM in the classroom, to stress the importance of girls' education, and to instruct students in how to communicate with parents and how to withstand social pressure. Schools embraced the project and developed skits and dramas supporting girls' rights, and students wrote songs and poems with anti-FGM messages. In some cases, schools even remained open during holidays to house girls who were trying to avoid being cut.

Religious leaders, along with educators, played an important role in mobilizing for change. At the turn of the twentieth century, Christian missionaries in this region discovered that the practice of FGM was widespread and had severe health consequences. Many decades later, when MYWO and PATH began to confront the issue, the early allies in these efforts were religious leaders, particularly Protestant ministers, who had been discouraging the practice among their congregants but making little headway, especially in rural areas. In Kenya, the practice of female circumcision cuts across religious affiliations: those ethnocultural groups that perform the ritual do so regardless of what religious tradition they follow. Nationally, about one-tenth of Kenyans are Muslim, and one-tenth follow indigenous beliefs. In the project districts, Muslim clerics were not involved, and the interpretation of Islamic teachings was not at issue. In Kisii and Meru, between 80 and 90 percent of the people are Christians, and the rest practice indigenous religions; in Samburu and Narok, most people practice indigenous religions, while between 10 and 25 percent are Christians. Christian clergy became the backbone of MYWO's community education and outreach activities in Kisii and Meru. Staff conducted workshops with religious leaders in all four districts that addressed the health and human rights dimensions of FGM. Together they developed theological arguments to use within their congregations: for example, that no sacred or authoritative religious texts promote FGM and that FGM violates girls' rights to bodily integrity. Facilitators encouraged these leaders not to impose FGM on their own daughters and to oppose FGM within their extended families and communities. During the materials development workshop, religious leaders advised the project to develop a poster that shows a little girl kneeling and praying: "God, give my parents the wisdom to protect me from circumcision."

Reaching out to health care providers and persuading them not to practice FGM and to oppose its performance in any setting was an important but problematic aspect of the community-level work. Many health care providers in the project districts were privately opposed to FGM, but when asked by parents to perform the procedure or to prescribe pain medication and antibiotics, some were convinced that the parents would carry out the procedure with or without the benefit of hygienic practices and therefore agreed to perform the procedure themselves, either in health care settings or in homes. In workshops with health providers, project staff helped them examine the conflicts in their roles as parents, community leaders, and providers of care. A training curriculum was developed to persuade health care providers that FGM violates the international human rights agreements that Kenya has signed affirming the rights of the girl child, as well as the Hippocratic Oath: "first do no harm." As a result of the workshops, some health care providers made a personal decision not to perform the procedure, while a few took a more public stand to oppose FGM when performed by their coworkers and colleagues. With advice from health providers, the project developed a poster showing a nurse refusing money from a mother. The message reads: "I am a health provider. I do not earn from circumcision—I do not circumcise girls."

Utilizing the Media and Persuading Policy Makers

The media played an important role in the campaign coordinated by MYWO and PATH. The first step was a media advocacy program to build national and community awareness of FGM. The report of baseline findings from both the qualitative and quantitative studies, which provided the first information of its kind in Kenya, was disseminated nationally and reported in the *Nation* and the *Standard*, the two main national newspapers. Media representatives were trained to broaden their understanding that FGM is a violation of the human rights of women and girls, as well as a cause of health problems for women. Members of the media were encouraged to report accurately on the practice. The media were invited to all project workshops and activities, and press releases were issued about the project's accomplishments and key events.

These efforts to engage the media bore fruit. A qualitative analysis of media coverage documented that between 1994 and 1999, 68 articles on FGM appeared in five national Kenyan newspapers. The media reported on FGM workshops, seminars, and conferences conducted by MYWO. Thirty percent of the articles on FGM specifically concerned MYWO's eradication efforts or mentioned MYWO events or MYWO spokespersons, indicating MYWO's prominent place in the national discourse. In addition to the press, television and radio programs covered FGM topics. Two videos, one on the practice and one on the alternative rite of passage ceremony, were produced by the project and widely distributed and viewed.

MYWO recognized the importance of strengthening public support for the eradication of FGM. The issue had been a matter of political controversy since 1989, when then-President Moi made the first of several public promulgations denouncing the practice and promising that those who performed it would face serious consequences. The results were predictably disastrous; many parents saw this pronouncement as an attack on their culture, so they chose either to have the rite performed in secret or to resort to health personnel in places where the nature of the girl's visit could be concealed. The decline in the age of circumcision that is visible in Kisii is largely related to parents' fears that the government would ban FGM before they had an opportunity to perform the rite. MYWO therefore adopted an approach that was not coercive or punitive, but based on education and advocacy. They trained staff from the Ministry of Health (MOH) and other government ministries and worked with women parliamentarians, the Kenyan Medical Association, and other nongovernmental organizations (NGOs) in Kenya. MYWO and PATH broadened the reach of their own activities through collaboration with international agencies and donors. As the public debate heated up in 1996, a Parliamentary Motion to legislate against FGM was introduced but failed to pass. In 1998, a national symposium on FGM led to recommendations calling for deliberate efforts to eradicate the practice in Kenya. In 1999, the MOH issued a "National Plan of Action for the Elimination of Female Genital Mutilation in Kenya, 1999–2019" which set out the goal, broad objectives, strategies, targets, and indicators for eradicating FGM. In December 2001, the government passed the Children's Bill, which made FGM a criminal offense. Although there is considerable discussion over whether this measure has driven FGM underground, the bill indicates the extent to which the issue reached a national level.

Addressing Underlying Reasons for the Practice of FGM

MYWO emerged as a national leader in the FGM debate. However, the project staff noted that those who were persuaded not to practice it often lacked the courage and skills to take a public stand against it. A young man asked, "What if my father and ancestors curse me?" The project staff realized that it had addressed the health and human rights implications of FGM and debunked some of the myths about uncircumcised girls, but it had not directly addressed the complex set of beliefs that compelled communities to continue the practice because of their fears about uncircumcised females. These concerns, rooted in the belief that control of female sexuality was essential for the overall health and survival of the community, formed a mindset that needed to be dismantled through new outreach efforts for particular audiences. The key messages developed included: (1) the desire to have sex is controlled by the brain and not by the genitals; (2) uncircumcised women are married in Kenya every day; (3) although our community intended to circumcise girls, the result is genital mutilation; (4) when a tradition outlives its usefulness, it has to be discarded; and (5) FGM violates the rights of Kenyan girls to health, gender equity, and freedom from torture and degrading practices.

Audience-specific strategies and comprehensive training packages were developed to mobilize communities, conduct peer education, do district- and national-level advocacy, build support in institutions including the legal system, and initiate alternative rites of passage. Making a public commitment to stand against FGM can reinforce the resolve of community members not to engage in the practice and to dissuade others from engaging in it. Pledges were developed to enable boys, girls, and parents to commit themselves publicly to refuse the practice. The commitment messages were: for boys, "I will not require circumcision as a prerequisite for marriage"; for parents. "I will not circumcise my daughters"; and for all, "I will educate my peers, family, and community about the ill effects of the practice."

Developing Alternative Rites of Passage

Families who were motivated to abandon the practice faced considerable social pressure, and uncircumcised girls were subjected to ostracism from their peers. Early on, project planners envisioned that an alternative rite of passage program would be a key strategy to provide social support to those girls and families who were willing to go against social norms. This ceremony, which incorporated positive social aspects of the customary procedure, would also address the concerns of community members who wanted to keep cultural traditions intact.

The vast majority of FGM procedures in Kenya take place in group settings, so change must also be carried out at the group level. Traditional rites of passage marking the transition to adulthood typically include five to seven days of seclusion during which groups of girls are provided with family life education by their mothers and other female relatives as they recover from the cutting. In designing the alternative rites of passage, MYWO and PATH sought both to empower and to protect girls, combining the best of modern and traditional education about sexuality and celebrating young women's passage to adulthood—everything but the cut. Project planners assessed the traditional wisdom imparted during seclusion as well as girls' need for education about sexuality and reproductive health. Formative research was first conducted in Meru and Kisii to understand prevailing practices and the desire of these communities to retain their beneficial aspects. Project leaders looked more deeply at the customary rite of passage, reexamined findings from the baseline research, and reviewed the literature on FGM. In focus group discussions with mothers and girls, we found that the custom of rites of passage was disappearing in urban settings but remained normative in rural areas.

Traditionally, circumcision and the rite of passage marked young women's readiness for sexual activity and marriage. Although in these communities marriage is now generally delayed a few years while some girls continue schooling, the ceremony is still associated with sexual maturity. Hence, girls receive mixed messages about sexuality: one warning that they are expected to avoid pregnancy and remain in school; and the other, more ancestral axiom that "once you are circumcised, you are mature." Indeed, girls often engage in unprotected sexual activity, whether willingly or not, outside of marriage.

In Meru, girls undergo fairly elaborate rites of passage. After the cutting procedure and before the celebrations, the young age mates are kept in seclusion for a week and receive messages about respect for oneself, parents, grandparents, community members, and peers. Girls receive guidance about relationships with the opposite sex and how to avoid situations that may lead to sexual relations or incest. They learn that their behavior is being monitored from multiple directions: peers, parents, grandparents, and the community at large. Mothers look forward with anticipation to the rite of passage ceremony for their daughters because it places the mother at the center of attention and represents a culmination of her achievements, demonstrating her success in rearing her daughter well and preparing her for marriage, as well as her organizational skills and the wealth she displays as she hosts family, friends, and prospective in-laws in her home. For fathers, it is a time to show off their daughters and wealth and to negotiate with prospective in-laws for the bride price—the customary payment that compensates the girl's parents for the loss of her labor, companionship, and support in old age and seals the bond between the two families. For grandparents, it is a time to ponder how far their family has come, to hand down ancestral teachings, and to feel proud of the new generation following in their footsteps.

Attitudes toward circumcision and the coming-of-age ceremonies associated with it were already changing in the two communities. Some people suggested that the ceremonies had become prohibitively expensive and a source of tension between families trying to impress one another. Some families abandoned the ceremony and simply had the circumcision done on an individual basis in a hospital or by a health professional who came to their homes. Some parents opted for less severe forms of circumcision or even faked the practice. When asked, some community members recommended that circumcision should be allowed to die a natural death without continuing the celebrations. MYWO knew that there was significant support for initiation ceremonies, but had no strong mandate to establish variations of the existing rites. The project developed a three-pronged strategy, which could allow parents who had already stopped circumcising daughters to come out of the closet; provide a way out for families educated by the project who were undecided or afraid of community pressure; and establish a strong and visible noncircumcising community within the locality. To offset fears that the project was trying to impose a foreign strategy, the initiative was designed to emphasize the relevance of the new ritual to the community and to build on existing traditions. Staff gathered ideas from mothers, girls, community leaders, and fathers through individual and group meetings. We asked what information the girls needed, who should serve as seclusion sponsors and teachers, what kinds of gifts girls should receive, what type of celebration the community should have, and who should participate.

In Meru, the team reached out to women who had already stopped circumcising their daughters and wanted to declare their position publicly and to those who were knowledgeable about the harmful effects of the practice yet still hesitant to stop on their own. Three mothers, one of whom had volunteered with the project since its early days and all of whom had participated in peer educator training, came forward. These women recruited additional families, creating the first cohort of thirty circumcision-age daughters. To avoid family conflict during the recruitment process, one of the ground rules for participating in the program was that both parents must agree to the decision not to circumcise their daughter. Women who wanted to have their daughters initiated through the alternative rite had to convince their husbands to participate, publicly declaring that they have stopped circumcising their daughters. These women were staking out new roles for themselves as custodians of the culture.

With advice from community members, the team designed a program that included all aspects of the traditional coming of age ceremony—seclusion, information sharing, and celebration—except cutting the genitalia. The alternative rite of passage provided an opportunity for parents and girls who chose not to cut to maintain the positive cultural traditions associated with this transition. It included up to a week of life skills education, followed by a day of festivities to mark the transition publicly and to celebrate with family and friends.

The alternative ceremony was called Ntanira Na Mugambo, meaning "Circumcision with Words." In August 1996, in Gatunga village in Tharaka Nithi, thirty girls experienced Meru's first alternative ritual. The mothers decided to have their daughters go through a period of seclusion similar to that which followed circumcision: a week of intensive instruction, guidance, and counseling. Project staff from PATH and MYWO joined community members in conducting the instruction. The content included accurate information about male and female reproductive anatomy, menstruation, and conception, as well as the prevention of pregnancy, HIV/AIDS, and FGM. The instruction also covered sexuality, dating, the consequences of adolescent pregnancy, marriage, family relations, self-esteem, decision making, and the rights of girls to education and healthy practices. Each girl had a sponsor, typically an aunt or godmother, who had informal after-dinner talks with the girls, meeting in groups and on a one-on-one basis. These discussions focused on positive aspects of the culture, such as respect for elders and parents and on religious teachings. Girls and their sponsors wrote and rehearsed songs and skits criticizing FGM to be performed at the coming-of-age ceremony and celebration.

At the conclusion of the period of seclusion, the district chief welcomed more than 500 participants, who were dressed for the celebration, to his compound. After the girls received gifts such as dresses, hats, shoes, and cosmetics, they performed the songs, dramas, and poetry they had prepared. Amid much feasting and dancing, mothers and daughters, fathers, younger sisters, and members of the community celebrated "Circumcision with Words" and condemned cutting. Mothers also received *bugidia*, sugars or gifts, from community members and families whose circumcision ceremonies they had attended in the past. Some community members who came out of curiosity joined in expressing support for the occasion. Finally, the girls were given certificates of "community wisdom" reinforcing messages of respect and ways of avoiding unwanted sexual relations and were declared mature, marriageable, and acceptable to society.

Widening Community Support for Alternative Rites of Passage

Advocates and activists were aware that, given the strong social pressure to maintain the traditional practice, uncircumcised girls desperately need to find at least one other uncircumcised girl and noncircumcising family in the community to overcome isolation and stigma. Families who participated in the first alternative ceremony, along with their community supporters, became the nucleus of a support group. Members agreed to work together to ensure that well-wishing community and extended family members did not overturn the families' decisions, to continue to advocate against FGM, and to recruit additional families for the next round of alternative ceremonies. Since local people participated in the conceptualization, development, and implementation of the project, they have a strong sense of ownership. Fathers and brothers have publicly supported the new tradition. Some boys have expressed their support for the program and promised to protect girls threatened with circumcision. The ARP program has been endorsed by religious leaders, who felt that the approach was consistent with their religious convictions.

The alternative program did meet with opposition. Some skeptics in the community expected the new tradition to fade quickly. Other groups supported the continuation of FGM and/or were opposed to sexuality education. Rumors spread about the program, including that it promotes sexual activity among adolescent girls, forces girls to drink blood under oath, involves injecting contraceptives into the girls' clitorises, and is sponsored by foreigners who do not care about the interests of the community. A vigorous campaign was launched to dispel these rumors and explain to the community what actually happened during the seclusion. The girls themselves became important public voices, as graduates of the program testified about what they had learned. On one occasion the Meru association, Ntanira Na Mugambo, invited six circumcised girls and one mother to observe the alternative seclusion process, so they could report back to the community. The girls and the mother not only reassured the community about the instruction being offered but asked Ntanira Na Mugambo to extend the seclusion training program to circumcised girls and called upon the community to enroll their circumcised daughters. Converting those who had practiced female circumcision into advocates of the instruction provided by the alternative program was a significant step toward public acceptance. Realizing that Kenyans, not foreigners, were behind the program made it easier for people finally to be convinced to support it.

Following the first Meru ceremony, MYWO began to receive inquiries from individuals and groups wanting to participate in a similar program. In contrast to earlier predictions that the alternative ritual would disappear, 200 families from eleven locations in Meru had participated within the first year. The alternative rites of passage program expanded to other districts and subdistricts. Each district has tailored the rite of passage to its distinct culture.

In Kisii, which has the highest FGM prevalence rate among the four districts, girls may be cut as young as six, and more than half had been cut by the age of ten. When the procedure is performed by health care providers, which occurs more often in Kisii than elsewhere, it takes place individually rather than in groups. Although a rite of passage did accompany the practice in Kisii, the alternative coming-of-age ceremony, with its instruction about sexuality and reproduction, was not as culturally appropriate as for girls who had reached adolescence. Project staff encouraged the Kisii community to explore more appropriate alternative approaches to initiation. Two types of ceremonies have been implemented: one following the Meru style, with formal training and coming-of-age ceremonies for large groups of 50 to 90 older girls; and home-based ceremonies for one or two families. In the small-scale rituals, the girls were secluded in relatives' homes while the family's home was decorated with flowers and banana tree leaves and food was prepared for the guests. The beautifully dressed and decorated girls were symbolically carried back to their mothers and accepted into the home by their fathers or other male family members. Everybody feasted and danced, and both the mother and girls received gifts of *bugidia* sugars.

The close association of FGM with girls' overall social status is central to the approach in Narok district. The Maasai of this region do not traditionally conduct ceremonies for girls, but circumcise daughters at around age fourteen. The project staff had been organizing seminars for girls during the school holidays to delay circumcision, early marriage, and withdrawal from school. After the Meru and Kisii experiences, the team adopted the Meru educational curriculum for girls followed by feasting and celebrations attended by community members and government leaders. Because of the low levels of education in Narok, education of the girl child is one of the key project messages in this district.

In Samburu district, a culturally conservative area that has been plagued by drought and security problems, the first ARP was held in December 2000 with 50 girls. The project has continued to provide institutional support to help girls avoid circumcision and delay marriage while continuing their education. Some schools have persisted in keeping girls at school over the holidays as a delaying tactic. In other cases, girls have run away from home to escape circumcision and early marriage; MYWO volunteers and the project pooled resources to enroll these girls in boarding schools and worked toward family reconciliation. The girls who participated in the ARP reported that the training helped raise their self-esteem and confidence to resist community pressure.

In several districts where people were initially more resistant to change, the demand for ARP now exceeds the ability of the project to respond with technical and financial support. For example, in December 2001, a record number of nearly 1,000 girls and their families in Gucha participated in ARP initiations that included a five- to seven-day seclusion period culminating in a ceremony. PATH and MYWO trained members of the Seventh Day Adventist Church, the Federation of Women's Groups, and other organizations to cosponsor some of these rites.

In all the participating districts, initiates continue to form support groups, consolidating their new role as public stakeholders in community culture. In Meru, the site of the original alternative ceremony, one of the first activities of the support group took place during the marriage of one of the girls. The initiates and their families flocked to the church to demonstrate that "uncircumcised girls are marriageable." The original group of Meru trainers, who formed the NGO Ntanira Na Mugambo, sponsors an initiates' support group oriented not only toward ending FGM but also toward obtaining girls' rights. They see their role as protecting, defending, and supporting all the community's girls, whether or not they are threatened with circumcision.

Changing Knowledge, Attitudes, and Practices

In 1999, after six years of work in these four districts, PATH commissioned an evaluation of the MYWO/PATH Female Genital Mutilation Eradication project to assess progress toward achieving its objectives. The methodology was designed to facilitate comparisons with the data collected in the 1992–1993 baseline survey, so questionnaires were administered at the household level to a random sample of 1,218 women between the ages of fourteen and sixty. Unlike the baseline, the end-line survey also included a representative sample of 1,220 men ages fourteen to sixty-five. In addition, 180 male and female youth in project-area schools, 19 service providers, 51 peer educators, and a purposely selected sample of 126 uncut girls were interviewed. Focus group discussions were held with a total of 267 respondents, including men, women, boys, cut and uncut girls, and health providers (Olenja 2000).

The findings of this survey are certainly encouraging. The proportion of women under age 20 who had undergone FGM declined from 78 percent in 1992–1993 to 56 percent in 1999, which represents a significant change. The proportion of all fourteen-year-olds who had already been cut declined from over half at baseline to less than a third six years later. There is no evidence of an increase in the average age of the cut, suggesting that the procedure is not merely being delayed. All indicators suggest that the decline in the prevalence of FGM will be maintained. Although no single intervention can claim sole responsibility for the dramatic social change that is now taking place in these districts in Kenya, it is clear that the collaborative work by PATH and MYWO has helped to bring about this change.

Since the prevalence and practice of FGM varies widely across ethno-cultural groups, we compared FGM prevalence rates in the project districts with the prevalence rates found among the same groups in a national survey. The significant differences between rates of FGM in a given group in the project districts and outside them show that the anti-FGM campaign in those districts has had a measurable positive effect among ethnocultural groups where the practice was nearly universal at baseline. In 1998, the Kenya DHS showed that nationally FGM prevalence rates remained high among the Kisii (97 percent) and the Maasai (89 percent). In the project districts in which these ethnic groups predominate, girls were less likely to be cut than their counterparts in other parts of the country. The realization that female genital cutting is not a universal norm and that other communities do not practice it helps people to acknowledge that cultural myths have built up around it. More importantly, learning that some families within their own cultural group have halted the practice can reinforce the decision to stop.

The 1999 survey revealed that the project had been effective in reaching women with its health and human rights messages about FGM and had influenced women to change their attitudes toward the practice. At least 65 percent had heard these messages during the six years of the project, 40 percent directly from MYWO staff. Twenty-seven percent of these women said that as a result of these messages they decided not to circumcise their daughters, and another 14 percent encouraged family members not to circumcise.

The project aimed to change social norms about FGM by facilitating a reassessment of beliefs and values that would ultimately lead to changes in attitudes and practices, so the surveys assessed these matters carefully. In 1992–1993, at baseline, the most common reason given to oppose FGM was that it was prohibited by religion; about one fourth of respondents said that FGM was against human rights. The project messages centered on FGM as a violation of human and women's rights and as a threat to the health of women and girls. By 1999, 68 percent of all women surveyed were able to recall a specific gender, human rights, or sexuality message promoted by the project, and the majority of those cited MYWO as the source of the message. An even larger proportion of women (72 percent) recalled hearing a health-related message, and these messages were often cited as crucial in making the decision not to circumcise. Those opposed to FGM were more likely to cite the practice as a violation of the human rights of women and girls than they were to say that it was prohibited by religion. Although control of women's sexuality was not commonly understood as the rationale for FGM, 18 percent of the respondents recalled this project message. Interestingly, the most commonly recalled message was that FGM reduces a woman's ability to enjoy sex.

Breaking the silence that had surrounded the subject in the past, the knowledge about female genital mutilation communicated in workshops and other venues led quite directly to changes in attitudes. The female anatomical model was especially effective as a teaching tool. Men were powerfully affected by being told and shown what happens during female circumcision. Prior to seeing the anatomical model, men said they had no idea what actually happens during female circumcision, particularly the extent of the cut. If they had thought about the procedure at all, they were under the misimpression that women underwent a minor procedure similar to the circumcision of their own foreskin. Many men incorrectly believed that FGM was beneficial to fertility and childbearing. By viewing the model, they were able to understand the potential health problems that are posed by the practice of FGM. Respondents emphasized the need to reach men, because they played important roles in making decisions about the procedure.

A majority of respondents thought that changes in attitudes and practices were occurring in their communities as a result of these efforts and that the practice was slowly dying. In 1999, 47 percent of the women interviewed expressed support for the continuation of FGM, a significant decline from the 63 percent who supported it in 1992–1993. Men, women, youth, peer educators, service providers, and uncircumcised girls all gave similar answers as to why FGM is still performed. FGM is viewed as a traditional practice that increases a girl's prospects for marriage, preserves virginity, prevents immorality, promotes cleanliness, and provides more pleasure to the husband. Interestingly, in the qualitative evaluation, respondents noted that FGM prepares and fortifies a girl for the pain and hardship that she will experience in life, especially during childbirth. Male and female respondents had similar views, except that women were much more likely than men to cite passage to adulthood as a reason to continue this tradition.

The forms of FGM that are practiced in the project districts have changed over time from more to less severe procedures, attesting to the influence of the anti-FGM project even on those who continue the custom. Historically, excision has been the predominant procedure in Kenya. In the project districts, infibulation was practiced to a significant extent only in Samburu. Comparison of the baseline with the end-point survey shows a shift to less severe practices. In Samburu, nearly 20 percent of women were subject to infibulation in 1992–1993, but this had declined to less than 1 percent by 1999. The qualitative survey also showed significant changes in attitudes and practices over the course of three generations. Each female respondent was asked about the type of procedure that she, her mother, and her daughter(s) had undergone. Nearly 58 percent of daughters, as compared to 38 percent of respondents and 22 percent of respondent's mothers, had undergone the less severe procedure commonly called sunna. Parents and traditional circumcisers who wanted to continue the practice but had been made aware of its health complications through the project proposed to reduce the risks of harm by advocating a milder form of the procedure rather than giving up the practice altogether.

One particularly problematic change over time that is visible in the data is a trend toward the medicalization and commercialization of FGM. A preference for performing FGM in a hospital or health facility is emerging in the districts of Kisii and Gucha. These districts had the highest proportion of health facility procedures in 1992–1993, and this preference became much more pronounced by 1999. These are also the districts where the procedure is being performed at younger ages. The conjunction of these two facts indicates that parents are increasingly becoming aware of the health dangers of the traditional procedure—in large part through anti-FGM efforts—and seek to have it performed under more hygienic conditions well before the girl herself might raise objections. In order to stem this trend, advocates' emphasis on the health consequences of FGM must be complemented by effective outreach to health care practitioners. Parents who seek out health professionals to perform FGM in aseptic conditions, with local anesthesia and antibiotics, also believe—in most cases correctly—that health professionals do less severe forms of the procedure, favoring clitoridectomy over excision. Health care workers who are asked by parents to perform the operation under safe conditions might rationalize that by doing so they are reducing the risk of harm.

Female circumcisers have traditionally been paid in cash or commodities, including foodstuffs such as meat, sugar, grains, drink, and snuff, as well as ornaments. The availability of a variety of foods during the harvest months of August and December makes these good times for FGM ceremonies. Because of increasing poverty in the country, traditional circumcisers view FGM as a key income-generating activity. One circumciser in Samburu affirmed in an interview that her family depended solely on the income she generated from the practice and explained that she was not willing to stop without obtaining an alternative source of income. We were surprised to discover in 1999 that nearly all traditional circumcisers in Kisii and a large number of those in Samburu had stopped performing the procedure. While a few had stopped as a result of the FGM eradication program, many were driven out of business by competition from health professionals.

Prior to the Presidential Decree issued in December 2001, many public and private health providers in Kisii and Samburu offered circumcision services. Focus group discussions revealed that nurses, junior staff, and private practitioners advertised their services, assuring the community that the procedure will be done in a "professional and hygienic manner." On average, the fee charged by health professionals is about Ksh. 600 per operation, but ranges as high as Ksh. 2000 (approximately US$ 8–26). Traditional circumcisers generally charge much less, about Ksh. 100 per girl (US$ 1.20). Female circumcision has become a source of supplementary income to augment health care providers' meager salaries, making it less likely that health workers will voluntarily give up the practice.

Prospects for the Eradication of FGM

Changing public attitudes toward FGM rested largely on increased awareness of its health risks and complications, although promoting the recognition that removal of healthy genital tissue is a violation of the human rights of girls was a central message of the PATH/MYWO project. When the project began, few women mentioned health reasons as a cause to oppose FGM, whereas in 1999, women were much more likely to cite such complications.

About 23 percent of women opposed circumcising their daughters in part because of health complications they themselves had experienced and now realized were a result of FGM. Male respondents were also aware of health issues associated with FGM. Of the 43 percent who knew of health problems that may result from circumcision, 62 percent mentioned infection, 43 percent mentioned difficult childbirth, and 23 percent cited difficulty enjoying sex. There was negligible difference between the male and female respondents in their ordering of reasons to oppose FGM.

The attitude of unmarried young men toward female circumcision is an important gauge of social change, since cultural perspectives on the relative merits of circumcised and uncircumcised young women as potential marital partners have been an important component of this practice's foundation. Whereas in 1992–1993, a majority of male youths strongly advocated the continuation of the practice and indicated that they would not marry uncircumcised girls, by 1999 the majority (55 percent) of unmarried men ages 18 and over said they would be willing to marry an uncircumcised woman. The main reason given (74 percent) was that they had learned that uncircumcised females could still give birth. This indicates that accurate information is finally beginning to counteract inaccurate beliefs. Whereas in the past boys were told that uncircumcised females were infertile, they now were aware that uncircumcised women actually had fewer complications during labor and delivery. Unmarried young men gave a variety of positive reasons for marrying an uncircumcised woman: 46 percent cited having fewer complications during delivery, and 45 percent said that uncircumcised girls might be better sexual partners.

Among the 45 percent of unmarried young men who said they would not marry an uncircumcised girl, the great majority explained that "it is against my culture." Some believed that uncircumcised females are unclean and tend to become promiscuous. The discussions we held with male youth elucidate the shift in attitudes. In 1992–1993, the men who said they would not marry uncircumcised girls offered a variety of reasons, including the belief that uncircumcised partners tend to seek divorce more easily since they are more independent. These concerns that uncircumcised girls are promiscuous and make disturbingly independent wives suggests that the control of female sexuality remains the fundamental rationale underlying the practice of FGM, and their declining salience in young men's thinking implies that support for this rationale may finally be eroding. It is important to note that the primary reasons young men gave for why they would marry an uncircumcised girl are the antitheses of reasons usually given for being unwilling to marry one: that is, uncircumcised women make better sexual partners as opposed to being more promiscuous; labor and delivery is easier for them rather than harder. The basic values—sexual fidelity and enjoyment, marital fertility and easier childbirth—are the same, but their presumed relationship to FGM has been changed. In this respect, at least, it may be possible to eradicate FGM by appealing to the same cultural values that currently support it.

This implication may be the attitudinal counterpart of what the project discovered through the ARP: preparing maturing girls for adult life through an intergenerational ritual that incorporates accurate and empowering information about sex and reproduction can be recognized as a traditional practice even if it does not involve cutting girls' genitals. Some fundamental values of these societies can be mobilized in support of change, once people understand that what they have been doing does not really accomplish their most deeply cherished goals. But in other respects, fundamental shifts of power are involved. Women themselves are acting to claim knowledge about and power over their own bodily health.

In order to work effectively to eradicate FGM, we must understand who participates in the decision about circumcision and how the respective roles of daughters, parents, grandparents, and other elders, as well as prospective husbands and their parents, are changing over time. In 1999, we attempted to clarify who makes the decision and to determine whether the locus of decision making shifted over the course of the project by asking who in the family had decided about a daughters' circumcision and who generally made such decisions. Mothers, fathers, and daughters did not entirely agree on how the decision was reached. The majority of women (69 percent) said that parents make the decision jointly, while some (23 percent) said that mothers could make this decision on their own. Men were less certain about how the decision was made: a slight plurality (38 percent) said it was a joint decision between husband and wife, some (22 percent) said they made the decision themselves, and 36 percent said they didn't know how the decision was made. Interestingly, as many men as women said that they could make this decision themselves, but fewer men than women said it was made jointly. This finding underlines the importance of raising men's as well as women's awareness of FGM and of involving men in anti-FGM activities.

The individual girl who will or will not undergo FGM has increasingly gained a role in decision making, particularly in those areas where intensive project activities and ARP ceremonies and support systems have built confidence among girls and parents who wish to abstain from the procedure. Of the uncircumcised young women whom we purposively selected to interview,

45 percent said their own decision not to be circumcised was paramount, and 51 percent said that parents were the key decision makers. Parental support for the girl's individual decision against FGM was probably critical in most cases. Among those who opposed the decision not to circumcise, the grandmother was often cited. Opposition from grandmothers and other relatives was overcome by strategies that included keeping the potential initiate temporarily away from home during the cutting season. Often a MYWO-trained peer educator came to the rescue by explaining the disadvantages of FGM to those who posed opposition. Armed with anti-FGM information and with the support of a network of girls and families who shared their opposition to FGM, parents and girls were able to defend their decision and resist the pressures of those who still insisted on the practice.

Parents' stated intentions about whether or not they would circumcise their daughters in the future changed dramatically over the duration of the project. In 1999, of men who had daughters of circumcision age, 43 percent said they planned to circumcise their daughters and 18 percent said they had not yet decided. Among women, 29 percent who had uncircumcised daughters said they planned to circumcise them. This figure represents a substantial drop from 1992–1993, when nearly 66 percent of women said they would circumcise their daughters when they reached the appropriate age. Those with little formal education remain the most committed to the practice; 75 percent of men and women with no schooling indicated that they intend to circumcise their daughters. Men and women practicing traditional indigenous religions were much more inclined to circumcise than those belonging to other religious denominations. Religion, general awareness of human rights issues, and the declining cultural significance of the practice were cited as being important in the decision not to practice FGM. Men who did not plan to circumcise any (or any more) daughters were more likely to cite violation of human and women's rights (46 percent) than any other reason to oppose FGM. The project appears to be responsible for raising awareness of women's rights and human rights in these communities.

Among unmarried young men, 60 percent indicated that they would not circumcise their future daughters, revealing a marked shift in attitudes. These findings suggest that unmarried youth were exposed to FGM eradication messages and that advocacy and education in the community has begun to affect social norms. Since marriageabllity has been cited as the key factor in maintaining FGM, the abandonment of the practice also has been seen to rest on the abandonment by both sexes of the belief that FGM is a prerequisite to marriage (Mackie 2000). The positive attitudes of young men toward uncut girls have great potential to bring about change in the practice of FGM by alleviating young women's fears that without the cut they might be undesirable marriage partners. Once FGC is no longer viewed as a prerequisite to marriage by potential husbands, substantial proportions of parents and girls will be more likely to forego the practice.

Despite this progress, many factors mitigate against the elimination of FGM. Myths and misperceptions still surround the practice and remain especially entrenched in remote areas. The older generation remains resistant to eradication efforts. In one district, although people had been sensitized by the MYWO project, people were afraid to speak out against FGM for fear of being "cursed." In some areas, FGM has increasingly gone underground, as community members perform the procedure clandestinely and require the circumciser to maintain confidentiality. In other places, the practice is shifting to medical professionals and hospital or clinic settings. From the perspective of parents, using health facilities and health care providers to perform FGM is an understandable response to concern about the health risks of FGM. Although some view this as a step in the transition to eliminating the practice (Shell-Duncan 2001), medicalization is unlawful in Kenya and it poses a serious challenge to anti-FGM efforts. Health care providers experience a conflict of values when approached by parents who are determined to cut their daughters with or without the benefit of pain medication, antibiotics, and sanitary equipment. Financial gain is also an incentive for some medical personnel to perform the procedure, creating a conflict of interest. Enlisting the support of health providers in efforts to eliminate the practice will be effective not only because it closes off one seemingly safer form of FGM but also because it undermines the legitimacy of the entire procedure.

Conclusion

MYWO deliberately focused its grassroots efforts to combat FGM on rural communities where the practice remained much more prevalent and culturally entrenched than in urban areas, where it was fast disappearing. Promoting women's health and well-being and bringing the message of women's rights and human rights to the people who live there was regarded as an urgent task of national development and a major effort to redress inequalities experienced by Kenyan women. Questioning and transforming the social norms and customary practices of these communities required a multipronged approach, using activists, peer educators, teachers, parents, religious leaders, the media, and women's groups to raise awareness and mobilize for change. The combination of intensive community sensitization about FGM and the alternative rite of passage program has fueled attitudinal and behavioral changes in the project districts in Kenya. Working together, these newly mobilized social actors have developed effective strategies to promote the demise of a harmful cultural practice (see also Mohamud, Ringheim, Bloodworth, and Gryboski 2002).

Alternative rites of passage ceremonies promote group cohesion and allow those parents and girls who have decided to forgo FGM an opportunity to share and celebrate this decision openly with other like-minded families. The decision to abandon FGM is generally arrived at after girls and their families have been exposed to program messages through peer educators, teachers, religious leaders, and others trained by the project. Although ARPs were not instituted in all the districts with the same intensity, the program proved especially valuable where community pressure to conform to traditional practices remains strong and where those who did not circumcise felt ostracized. Many parents had hesitated to stop the practice because they feared the social stigma for themselves and its potential impact on their daughter's marriage prospects. Through 2002, in addition to the nearly 7,000 girls in the four project districts who had participated in an ARP, the alternative coming-of-age ritual was spreading to new communities.

Although the ARP program is predicated on the assumption that parents and girls who participate have already made the decision not to circumcise, an evaluation of the program by the Population Council noted that for some "the ARP may offer the impetus to take the final step of actually stopping the practice." Making the ARP available to those who would most benefit from participation is an important strategy for the future. Participation in an ARP is not expected to convert girls and families to a decision that they have not already made, however. An ARP may well strengthen the resolve of those whose decision is somewhat tenuous, but "the sensitization activities that have preceded the Alternative Rite are critical for creating the conditions in which the rite itself can be introduced" (Chege, Askew, and Liku 2001). There is a legitimate concern that groups wishing to emulate and expand upon the success of the PATH/MYWO project may adopt only the ARP without investing in the longer term efforts to foster sustainable social change. Although some girls and families did not feel the need for the social support offered by the ARP or were not facing ostracism or criticism for their actions, the demand for ARP has continued to grow and presently has outstripped the capacity of the project to organize and support the seclusion period, instruction, and initiation ceremonies.

Once a critical mass of people abandons the practice of FGM, the custom has the potential to die quickly (Mackie 2000). The significant reduction in prevalence of FGM among younger adolescents in the project areas is a hopeful sign that this process is occurring. Sustaining the momentum of anti-FGM efforts until that critical mass has been reached will require intensifying the work in the more remote parts of the current districts and broadening coverage to other districts—a process MYWO has already undertaken. Only then will this social transition in the making be complete.

Chapter 5
A Community of Women Empowered:
The Story of Deir El Barsha

Amal Abdel Hadi

> *Women might endure exploitation within the confines of their*
> *traditional community and shun commitments that would provoke*
> *opprobrium, but not when they have an active sense of their existential*
> *dilemmas and alternative possibilities.*
> —L. Amede Obiora, 1997

The community of Deir El Barsha, a Christian village in Egypt, discontinued the practice of female circumcision in 1992 without the intervention of policymakers, politicians, or medical experts. Village leaders and religious clerics, spurred by local women's groups, made an agreement with midwives, traditional birth attendants, and hygienic barbers to declare their commitment to abstain from the practice and to advise other people to abandon it. In this document, Deir El Barsha's leaders and traditional circumcisers announced:

Having elucidated the harmful and pernicious effects of female circumcision, all the undersigned decided to refrain from performing this practice, and to strive to enlighten people of the village to follow suit. All individuals present here asserted that whoever engages in this practice from this day onwards would be questioned before God, the village committee and state law. This is an attestation to this effect.

Signed by Priest Safwat Ghabriel; co-signed by
Saida Abdel Sayed and Louisa Labib

This declaration was the culmination of nearly a decade of many-sided efforts focusing on female circumcision among the inhabitants of Deir El Barsha.

The discontinuation of female circumcision in this community resulted most immediately from the increasing recognition that the practice violates women's rights to health and well-being. Seminars were organized where specialist physicians spoke about the health problems that result from the procedure, and priests from various churches explained that the circumcision ritual is not a Christian tradition. Women contributed to the eradication of the practice as they paid home visits and discussed female circumcision and its implications for women's lives in great detail. The most important reason for the shift away from the practice of female circumcision, however, was not the campaign targeted specifically at this problem but a more fundamental change in gender relations in local society. For many years the village has been a site of consistent development efforts that promoted women's participation and reconfigured gender roles in a noticeable way. Women's empowerment enabled them to articulate their critique of female circumcision and to persuade village leaders to use their influence to abolish the practice. This attitudinal shift has been expressed in action, as is evident in the rising numbers of uncircumcised girls in Deir El Barsha compared to the near universality of female circumcision in neighboring villages and the Egyptian countryside. More than ten years after this public declaration was made, we have strong reasons to believe that this attitude will persist and the practice will disappear.

These exemplary developments in Deir El Barsha demonstrate the possibility that communities can address the problem of female circumcision themselves. Indeed, the case of this village suggests that local efforts are very effective in stopping the practice, provided that they arise from more fundamental shifts in values and power relations that promote respect for women and increase women's autonomy. To illuminate the significance of the Deir El Barsha experience, I begin with an overview of female circumcision in the Egyptian context. I then present the findings of the Deir El Barsha study, which was conducted under the auspices of the Cairo Institute for Human Rights Studies (CIHRS). This village's remarkable success in eradicating FC/FGM was first brought to the attention of the Egyptian Task Force Against Female Circumcision in 1995, when Samira Louqa from the Coptic Evangelical Organization for Social Services, an NGO active in Christian rural communities, surprised everyone by announcing that Deir El Barsha had stopped practicing female circumcision after signing a declaration three years previously. The medical and social science researchers involved in CIHRS and the task force were convinced that this achievement was worthy of careful documentation and analysis. The study had two major objectives: to ascertain whether female circumcision had actually been halted in Deir El

Barsha and whether this change was sustainable; and to identify the factors that enabled people there to stop the practice. Both quantitative and qualitative methods were employed in this study; given my medical expertise and concern for women's health, I participated in the collection and analysis of the data. The guiding theoretical position of my analysis, and the central argument I present here, is that development efforts in the village, combined with male labor migration to urban centers in Egypt and to oil-rich Arab countries, created an environment that enabled women to achieve greater autonomy in their household decision making and thus to abandon the practice of female circumcision. I conclude by drawing important lessons from the experiences of Deir El Barsha and exploring their significance for the abolition of the practice elsewhere in Egypt and beyond.

Female Circumcision/Female Genital Mutilation in Egypt

The ancient practice of female circumcision remains widespread in contemporary Egypt. It is not clear when the practice was first introduced, but it certainly predates both Islam and Christianity (see Aldeeb, this volume). Some modern historical works suggest that this is a Pharaonic ritual, a claim that remains unproven because ancient Egyptian drawings illustrate only male circumcision. Female circumcision is a traditional or customary practice rather than a religious obligation; both Muslims and Christians in rural Egypt practice it, while their coreligionists in other regions do not. Even in some exclusively Christian communities, the available evidence suggests, all women were circumcised (Assad 1980).

The most prevalent form of female circumcision in Egypt is the partial or total removal of the clitoris and the labia minora. Infibulation, which entails excision of the clitoris and the labia minora, the partial removal of the labia majora, and suturing the remaining labia majora to leave only a small opening for urination and menstruation, is limited to the southernmost areas of the Nile Valley, Aswan and Nubia (see El Guindi, this volume). Young girls are usually circumcised between seven and twelve years of age. The 1995 Demographic and Health Survey (DHS), the first national study to survey a representative sample of nearly 15,000 Egyptian women, indicated that 97 percent of ever-married women ages fifteen–forty-nine have been circumcised.

The reasons for the prevalence of female circumcision in Egypt have been documented in the national Demographic and Health Surveys and analyzed by numerous ethnographic studies. They include upholding tradition, preserving female virginity and chastity, enhancing male sexual pleasure, gaining social acceptance, and following the teachings of religion. Primary among the justifications underpinning the practice is curbing female sexuality. In this respect, the rationale in Egypt bears a strong resemblance to the reasons advanced in the Somali and Nubian contexts as explained by Abdalla and El Guindi (in this volume). In previously published work, I have demonstrated the linkage between concepts of sexuality and the performance of this ritual, and I explore this matter later in this chapter.

The 1995 DHS revealed that some 82 percent of adult women in Egypt support female circumcision and intend to circumcise their daughters. This figure was an embarrassment to the Egyptian government, which had claimed since the 1950s that the practice was declining and that only half of the women in the country were circumcised (Tadros 2000; Abdel Hadi 2000). Previous efforts to eliminate female circumcision had obviously failed, despite the concurrent increases in the level of education and urbanization in Egypt. Female circumcision was not eliminated or markedly diminished, even in particular localities, until the 1990s, when women themselves began to mobilize their entire communities to address the cultural and social values upholding the practice.

The terms used to refer to female circumcision have changed as public debate over this practice has intensified in Egypt. The term female genital mutilation was adopted during the early 1990s by physicians and proponents of women's rights who advocated that the practice be discontinued as harmful to health and a violation of women's bodily integrity. Those who sought to justify continuing the practice responded by adopting terms that endowed it with religious sanctity and positive moral value. One such term is *tahara*, which means ritual purification in Egyptian colloquial Arabic. The classical Arabic term *khitan al inath* signifies the female equivalent of male circumcision, which is required by religious laws and teachings. The more specific Arabic term *khifad* has been propagated by those who support female circumcision as an Islamic practice parallel but not identical to male circumcision. *Khifad* literally means lowering or decreasing the height of the clitoris. This notion is based on a hadith, or teaching, in which the Prophet Muhammad advised a circumciser to lower the clitoris but not to cut so much. The authority for this hadith is regarded as weak, so the force of this teaching is questionable. Speaking of female circumcision as *khifad* while reserving *khitan* for male circumcision suggests that the female procedure is less severe because less genital tissue is removed, while asserting that the practice is based on Islamic teaching. This term has increasingly been used in the media and by the Egyptian population during recent public discussions of the practice. The term *sunna* circumcision, especially when used as a synonym for infibulation, has equally deliberate religious resonances. Proponents of female circumcision resist the term female genital mutilation for political reasons, criticizing it as an alien, Western way of speaking and thinking that condemns a deeply rooted Egyptian cultural tradition and criminalizes communities that practice it. The terms they employ cast religious sanctity on the circumcision ritual and depoliticize the debate by distancing it from discourses on women's rights as human rights that have gained significant support among grassroots organizations and women's groups in Egypt.

Throughout this chapter, I use the coupled terms female circumcision/female genital mutilation (FC/FGM). As a physician, I am deeply convinced that the practice is a mutilation of the genital organs. Medically, it interferes with the natural functioning of a healthy organ. Under the Egyptian legal code, any act that leads to total or complete loss of function of a bodily organ is a crime. Yet it is very difficult to use the term female genital mutilation in everyday interactions. For example, you cannot ask a mother or father, "Why did you mutilate your daughter?" You cannot ask a community member, "Why do you think people here mutilate their daughters?" Implying such deliberate ill-will on the part of parents, circumcisers, and respected leaders is offensive enough to end the conversation, short-circuiting any chance of persuading people to reconsider the practice and embrace positive change. As numerous interactions we have had in the field demonstrated, the terms we use have direct bearing on the acceptability and success of our advocacy efforts. The term female circumcision is more helpful at the outset of such discussions because, although it has the shortcoming of conveying a similarity with male circumcision, it is devoid of moral or religious connotations, particularly those associated with purification. The neutrality of the term makes it especially useful when the issue has become such a battlefield for conflicting factions. As our educational and advocacy efforts proceed, people come to recognize that what they had thought of as a religious ritual done for the moral benefit of their daughters inflicts pain and lasting harm; then they are ready to condemn the practice as female genital mutilation.

The history of the movement against FC/FGM in Egypt demonstrates that this concern did not arise recently and originate from the outside, as some defenders of the practice argue. They maintain that the issue was superimposed on Egyptian society because of Western propaganda and pressures brought to bear by Western women's organizations. However, these assertions are groundless. Numerous Egyptian groups, including religious leaders, physicians, social scientists, and national nongovernmental organizations, have all focused their energies on eradicating FC/FGM and preventing its harmful effects on women's health.

In 1959 the Egyptian Minster of Health banned the performance of FC/FGM in public health facilities and took steps to prevent nonmedical personnel from performing the procedure. Considerable time and effort has been required to develop a consensus on this issue in the medical community. Some physicians maintain that it is necessary to perform FC/FGM "according to the needs of their patients." They suggest that, since parents who are determined to have their daughters circumcised will seek nonmedical practitioners if they refuse, less harm will result to girls if they agree to perform a less severe form of the procedure under hygienic conditions. However, medicalizing the practice not only perpetuates it but also lends it new legitimacy, when it is entirely without medical benefit. In 1997, the Egyptian Association for Obstetricians and Gynecologists took a definitive public position declaring that there are no scientific grounds for FC/FGM. This decision provided opponents of the practice with important tools for advocacy.

An important step forward came with the creation of the Egyptian task force to combat female genital mutilation in 1994. Activists and researchers joined together in preparation for the International Conference on Population and Development (ICPD), and after the conference many feminist and human rights groups joined the task force. Some had already initiated legal proceedings against government officials and religious leaders for promoting FC/FGM, and their active participation in the task force's deliberations was crucial to framing the issue in terms of human rights as well as medical wrongs. The task force condemned the practice as a gender-based violation of women's rights and took a solid stand against FC/FGM regardless of where it is performed or who performs it. Taking this position was not easy, given the cultural importance and prevalence of the practice. The task force members conducted significant internal debates, as some members advocated a "milder" form of FC/FGM and its performance in public hospitals as a necessary step on the road to ending it. Finally the task force decided on the slogan "No to any type of FC/FGM" (Tadros 2000; CEDPA 1999; El Katsha et al. 1997). This stance shifted the approach from medicalization to fighting FC/FGM within a human rights framework. Dealing with the practice as a violation of women's rights pulled the carpet from under groups advocating harm reduction approaches.

The public silence surrounding FC/FGM was broken during the early 1990s. All sections of society were involved, and heated public debates were conducted in the press and other mass media. The task force's preparation for ICPD raised the question of women's reproductive and sexual rights, and during the conference the airing of the famous CNN film showing the circumcision of a young Egyptian girl had tremendous impact. The movement to combat FC/FGM provoked intense political controversy. Opponents and proponents exchanged arguments and presented cases to the Egyptian courts in an unprecedented manner. Advocates of abolishing FC/FGM took both the Minister of Health, Ali Abd El Fatah, and the Sheikh Al Azhar, the late Gad Al Haq, to court on charges of abusing their authority to the detriment of Egyptian women. Ali Abd El Fatah, who had supported the continuation of the practice, was succeeded as Minister of Health by Ismail Salam, who prohibited doctors from performing FC/FGM in public hospitals or private clinics. Proponents of FC/FGM then took Minister of Health Salam to court on the grounds that he interfered with the freedom of the medical profession. The controversy was settled by a historic court decision in 1996, which supported the health minister's decree and declared that FC/FGM is not an Islamic practice. Since the Constitution of Egypt states that Shari'a, Islamic law, is the main source of legislation, the status of female circumcision within Islam was relevant to the court's ruling. Although the Islamic religious institutions in Egypt are not unified in their position, the Al Azhar Mosque in Cairo played a central role in shaping opinion on this matter. This thousand-year-old mosque has long been respected for religious scholarship, and from the nineteenth century on it was a center of national resistance against colonialism, so the opinions of its spiritual leader are seen as having a bearing on what is authentically Egyptian as well as what is authoritatively Islamic. The current head of Al Azhar, Sheikh Mohamed Tantawy, reversed the position articulated by the previous Sheikh and publicly declared that female circumcision has nothing to do with Islam. He not only contradicted the argument made by some physicians that they were compelled to perform female circumcision for religious reasons but also issued a fatwa, a legal religious opinion, in support of the health minister's decree prohibiting doctors from practicing FC/FGM. (See the reproductive health manual published by the anti-FGM task force: Abdel-Salam and Helmy 1998).

Deir El Barsha and the Coptic Evangelical Organization for Social Services

The Cairo Institute for Human Rights Studies, in collaboration with the research committee of the task force on FGM, decided to embark on an extensive investigation of the factors influencing the abandonment of female circumcision by the Deir El Barsha community. In order to elucidate the distinctiveness of this experience, some comparisons were made with its neighboring village, El Barsha. Unlike Deir El Barsha, which is entirely Christian, El Barsha includes both Muslim and Christian residents. El Barsha and Deir El Barsha have such strong neighborly relations that they are often referred to as the "twin sisters." Deir El Barsha is also more closely connected with the nearby Muslim villages than with its Christian neighbor, Abou Hanas.

Deir El Barsha is situated between El Barsha and Nazlat El Barsha. The three villages are treated as one administrative unit for the distribution of social services, water, electricity, roads, schools, and health care. The train journey to Deir El Barsha from the city of Mallawi, the major city in the El Menia governorate of Upper Egypt more that 400 kilometers south of Cairo, takes three and a half hours. Timeworn cars and pickup trucks transport people between the station and the ferry, an old, kerosene-operated boat that runs from sunrise to sunset. In the countryside, where villages are small and isolated, outsiders are easily spotted. When we started our research, timid questions mingled with welcoming comments, but before long drivers came forward and asked: "Going to Deir El Barsha, right?"

Deir El Barsha has nearly 2,500 households distributed in four geographic regions. The inhabitants are connected by myriad ties of kinship and long association, as well as through formal social institutions. The village has one primary school with nine classes and 1,100 pupils, a water station that serves four neighboring villages, weak electricity networks, and a health care unit that only provides first aid. In its relative poverty, reliance on agriculture, and customary ways of life, Deir El Barsha is rather similar to other villages in Upper Egypt; Christians and Muslims differ only in their religious beliefs. However, Deir El Barsha's close association with the history of the Egyptian Coptic Church distinguishes it from other rural communities.

The village of Deir El Barsha is deeply rooted in Coptic tradition. (The term Coptic comes from the Greek term for Egyptians and applies to all Christians; the Egyptian church has been unified since the fifth century.) The Ansana region where Deir El Barsha is located was important during the early Coptic epoch, around the fourth century c.e. Its name is derived from a Greek word meaning "the place of the president," which refers to a convent that Coptic bishops established nearby during the fifth century. Deir El Barsha encompasses several ancient Egyptian Coptic sites, including cemeteries and temples. In 1972 two cemeteries were found intact in the village center, along with jewelry and archeological treasures that were transferred to the Egyptian Museum of Cairo. The five Christian churches in Deir El Barsha— established by the Orthodox, the Evangelists, and the Belamis Brothers— coexist with a strong spirit of tolerance.

Deir El Barsha is also distinctive because it has been the site of long-standing and diverse development programs introduced by the Coptic Evangelical Organization for Social Services (CEOSS), an Egyptian grassroots organization. CEOSS plays a momentous role in the fight against FC/FGM, both directly through its activities addressing public health and indirectly through its commitment to advancing women's participation in community development programs. Established by Priest Samuel Habib in the late 1950s and recognized by the Ministry of Social Affairs since September 1960, the organization works predominantly in social services, including the promotion of development projects in rural communities irrespective of religious affiliation. Initially CEOSS gave considerable attention to literacy programs. The scope of its social services soon expanded to incorporate activities oriented toward health and farming, as well as education. During the late 1980s, the organization embarked on close partnerships with communities in Cairo, Menia, Giza, Beni Sweif, and Assuit, including both major cities and rural villages. It sought to broaden participation in its programs, allowed women full access to its activities, and began to address gender directly as well.

CEOSS deals with local communities upon their own request and follows an integrated, participatory approach to development. The organization's relationship with the community goes through three stages. (1) Participation: A CEOSS team settles in the local community and assumes a leading role in various programs that bolster communal development and participation. (2) Follow-up: Then the leadership of development projects is handed over to community residents. The staff begins to minimize its role, limiting its activities to advice, supervision, and follow-up. The primary concern during this stage is to implement local leadership. (3) Self-reliance: Finally, the local leadership supervises and operates development programs and establishes its own independent agencies, which usually take the form of community development associations that operate as mediators between the CEOSS and the local community.

Deir El Barsha was among the first Upper Egyptian villages where Priest Samuel Habib operated in the 1950s, even before the establishment of CEOSS. In the early 1980s, the NGO's new emphasis on the promotion of educational programs aimed at the elimination of traditional social practices harmful to the health and well-being of women and children—including but not restricted to FC/FGM—was implemented there. This program was situated within an integrated approach to development in which the involvement and empowerment of the community was a primary concern. This participatory perspective facilitated the incorporation of local views into development programs, which was especially important when long-established cultural practices were called into question.

Many village elders received training for eradicating illiteracy and discouraging harmful social practices that were prevalent in the village; such as early marriage, public defloration at wedding nights, and barren women seeking fertility by making *talaa*, cemetery visits, and *adid*, eulogizing and mourning the deceased. At the same time, since 1982 the CEOSS helped Deir El Barsha establish a potable water network, sewage systems, vocational training for youth, revolving loans for small enterprises, family planning, mother and child health services, literacy classes, and reproductive health education for young women. The promotion of development projects was probably the most significant factor influencing cultural transformation in the village. These projects included income-generating activities, such as loans, training, and capacity building; health literacy courses on nutrition, disease prevention, hygiene, family planning, and reproductive health; agricultural and environmental projects, including animal husbandry, poultry, tree planting, and protection of the environment; and educational programs for the whole community, with a specific focus on women and girls.

Most Egyptian villages have committees that function like local governments for community decision making. Usually composed of village leaders, representatives of prominent families, religious leaders, doctors, school headmasters, teachers, and other notable residents, they vary in structure and effectiveness. These committees seldom include women, and most villages lack any forum for women to express their own concerns. CEOSS has addressed this problem by creating independent women's committees in the villages with whom it works. This fact underscores the importance of the CEOSS approach to grassroots participation and gender representation. The inclusion of women in development programs has contributed significantly to the success of efforts to eradicate FC/FGM. The underlying structures of gender inequality were challenged and reformed by establishing frameworks that enabled women to play an active role as influential leaders in their community.

In Deir El Barsha, CEOSS helped establish a women's committee with twelve members who represented the various Coptic denominations found in the village and were known for their activism, boldness, spirit of initiative, and trustworthiness. CEOSS was keen to include married women, who have more freedom of movement and enjoy community acceptance. Married women are particularly important to the discussion of sexuality and reproduction since single women, even if they are professionally trained, cannot bring up such subjects comfortably. CEOSS provided committee members with opportunities to develop their skills and add to their knowledge through seminars and workshops. The women's committee divided the work, and each member shouldered the responsibility for a specific section of the village. She recorded the names of women in her section and followed up with monthly home visits. The work was done in two shifts a day, since women's housework begins early in the day and ends shortly before their husbands return.

Home visiting proved a very effective means of promoting health education in general and of combating FC/FGM in particular. If families had girls at the customary age of circumcision and one of the parents insisted on circumcision, the women's committee turned to the village leaders to dissuade him or her. Over the years, this approach gained the women's committee genuine credibility and a reputation for competence. The committee played, and is still playing, a crucial role in the work against circumcision within the village. Alongside sustained educational programs through meetings and seminars, the women's committee maintained follow-up through home visits.

From the early 1980s, the women's committees supervised various projects involving women, such as classes in literacy, family planning, and household economy, and worked to raise people's consciousness about social practices harmful to women and children, especially early marriage, public defloration, and incorrect beliefs about infertility. In cooperation with CEOSS, the committees were able to stop these practices in the villages relatively quickly. Then, in the early 1990s, the focus shifted to the elimination of female circumcision as part of a comprehensive program on knowledge of the body and reproductive health. In Deir El Barsha, the reduction in the prevalence of FC indicates that women have indeed become more self-reliant and capable of making their own choices and have gained greater control over the resources needed to implement these choices.

Factors Influencing the Decline of FC/FGM in Deir El Barsha

Researchers affiliated with the Cairo Institute for Human Rights Studies (CIHRS) undertook a large-scale study of the factors influencing the decline of FC/FGM in Deir El Barsha, focusing on the relationship between development and cultural change. The research committee of the task force to combat FC/FGM sought to go beyond the descriptive level to explore the attitudes and behaviors of the various players involved. (See also Abdel Hadi and Abd-El Salam 1998.) CIHRS designed the study, with advice from experts in the field, and recruited and trained researchers to carry out in-depth interviews in Deir El Barsha. CEOSS provided moral support by introducing the team to key community leaders, including the village committee, religious clerics, and members of the women's committee. Gaining community acceptance and trust was essential to enable us to understand cultural practices in Deir El Barsha, as well as the social relationships among various groups that shaped local society. Communal leaders, particularly members of the women's committee, advised us on the design of our study and explained the history of the village's involvement in CEOSS-supported development projects. We then interviewed women and men in the community, collecting demographic information, asking about their participation in development activities, and inquiring into their attitudes toward and practice of FC/FGM. For comparative purposes, we also studied the neighboring village of El Barsha, which has both Christian and Muslim residents. This approach addressed a central question: what are the characteristics of Deir El Barsha that helped its members to abstain from female circumcision, as compared to El Barsha? The analysis concluded that those characteristics are: (1) development efforts in Deir El Barsha throughout its recent history, particularly during the 1980s and 1990s; (2) the effects of temporary male migration for work elsewhere on gender relations in the local community; and (3) the influence of religious leaders in enlightening inhabitants about female circumcision. These factors varied in their relative importance, but their interaction produced a radical departure from attitudes that previously governed male-female relations in the village. After explaining the basic demographic characteristics of Deir El Barsha, I analyze each of these factors in turn.

In Deir El Barsha, the research team interviewed 497 respondents, 399 females and 98 males, drawn from a random sample of households based on the recent census. Most were native to the village, although a few (9 percent) came from other villages. This pattern conforms to prevalent patterns in the

Egyptian countryside, where marriage is mostly endogamous—spouses from the same community are preferred to those from elsewhere—and residence is patrilocal—the woman moves to her husband's house after marriage. Since men who migrate for work have greater opportunities to find marriage partners in other places, more women than men are newcomers to the village. Almost all of the adults we interviewed were married. The majority of women were aged 20–49, while the majority of men were aged 30–49. This difference reflects the fact that women almost always marry before they are twenty, while most men marry between the ages of 20 and 29. In Egypt, girls marry at a younger age in order to protect themselves, while men marry later, after they get settled in a job and have performed military service.

Given the development programs' prominent focus on literacy and the importance of education in local efforts to combat FC/FGM, the survey assessed literacy carefully. Three-quarters of the women were illiterate, compared to just under half of the men. Those illiteracy rates are higher than those given in the 1997 World Bank reports for Egypt as a whole and reflect the general lack of educational opportunities in rural areas. Because the village has no secondary schools, students who wish to continue their education must travel daily to Mallawi city or settle down there. This imposes a great financial burden on most families, and living alone in the city poses a particular problem for girls. Only 10 percent of the men and 5 percent of the women had intermediate school certificates, and only four of the men we interviewed had obtained a university education. Still, 23 percent of all respondents could both read and write, a figure that registers the benefits of the village's adult literacy programs.

The income-earning activities in which Deir El Barsha residents engage include both formal employment and production for use and sale. The primary economic activities in the two villages revolve around agriculture and fishing, as well as handicrafts. Two-thirds of the female respondents in Deir El Barsha did not work for money. But 34 percent of them mentioned that they perform paid work, which is higher than the 28 percent given in the World Bank report on female employment in Egypt. Most of the work activities that women in Deir El Barsha mentioned, such as producing food items for sale and making baskets and scuttles, are not usually listed in official statistics on labor force participation but are regarded as part of women's household duties. Nor does the "labor" category on the official statistics include agricultural activities such as plowing, except when women themselves declared that they worked. Our survey documented all of women's and men's income-generating activities, no matter how they were recompensed.

This study provided persuasive evidence that development played an essential role in the community's ability to stop FC/FGM. Approaching FC/FGM from a development perspective meant that it was seen as part of a wider campaign for empowering the community and enhancing the possibilities of upward social mobility. In turn, community engagement enabled many people to build their own capacity for fighting harmful social practices. Because of the participatory approach to development activity in Deir El Barsha, the issue was discussed in detail with all members of the family, including youth, wives, husbands, and grandparents. The level of participation in local development activities was significantly higher in Deir El Barsha than in El Barsha, and women were more likely to participate in such programs than were men, especially in positions of leadership. The level of participation rose not only over time but across the generations.

Participation in development activities had a significant effect on attitudes and practices of FC/FGM. The study found a positive correlation between respondents' involvement in development activities and their tendency not to circumcise girls. The proportion of noncircumcised girls among daughters of respondents of both sexes who were involved in development projects (42 percent for mothers and 60 percent for fathers) was twice as high as that among the daughters of those who did not participate (28 percent for both mothers and fathers). A similar correlation was found regarding the circumcision of respondents' sisters. The positive correlation between participation in development projects and the tendency not to circumcise girls was higher among the younger generations, suggesting that the expansion of programs focused on literacy, health, and empowerment has accelerating effects on FC/FGM.

The practice of FC/FGM in Deir El Barsha has actually declined substantially, and this trend can be expected to continue in the future. More than 95 percent of the female respondents and the wives of male respondents had been circumcised. This rate corresponds closely with the national average reported by the Demographic and Health Survey, although it is lower than the rate for rural Egypt as a whole.

In order to analyze the practice of female circumcision among the younger generations growing up in Deir El Barsha, we ascertained the proportion of respondents with daughters below, at, or above the ages when circumcision is typically performed. We found that the typical age for female circumcision in the village is between seven and thirteen, so daughters of respondents were classified into three categories: those over thirteen, those aged seven–thirteen who were at the usual age for circumcision, and those under seven. Respondents who did not have daughters and those whose daughters were all less than thirteen were eliminated from this analysis, since it was not possible to ascertain their actual practice relative to FC. We classified the rest into two major groups. (1) Respondents with noncircumcised daughters. This group included those with one or more uncircumcised girls who had reached the typical age for circumcision, even if they had older daughters who had previously been circumcised, because the presence of even one uncircumcised daughter reflects a shift in the parents' behavior. (2) Respondents with circumcised daughters, even if they also had daughters at or under the typical age for circumcision. Although these respondents might assert that they would not circumcise their younger daughters, that had not been proven by their actual behavior. We then compared the group of parents who had stopped circumcising daughters with the group of parents who had not demonstrably stopped the practice.

When we examined the prevalence of FC among the daughters of respondents, we found that exactly one-third (33 percent) of respondents had circumcised daughters, while almost one-fifth (19 percent) did not circumcise girls, a proportion that is considerably higher than that among their mothers. When we exclude all those who do not have daughters past the typical age for circumcision (unmarried respondents, those who have not yet had any children, those who only have sons, and those whose daughters are under or have just reached the typical age for circumcision), 63 percent have circumcised daughters and 37 percent have noncircumcised daughters. The gap between this prevalence rate and that among adult women is highly significant, indicating a process of change over time. This rate for daughters is substantially lower than the actual and expected FC prevalence rates given in the 1995 Demographic and Health Survey for Upper Egypt: 53 percent had at least one circumcised daughter, and 44 percent intended to circumcise their daughters in the future. In Deir El Barsha, a large proportion of those who had daughters at or under circumcision age claimed they would not circumcise their girls.

Contrast this experience with El Barsha, where FC/FGM is still alive and well. We surveyed one hundred families in the neighboring village, choosing Muslim and Christian families according to the relative numbers of each. The group of 122 respondents from El Barsha included 113 females and 9 males. As in Deir El Barsha, most were born in the village; almost all were married; the majority of women were ages 20–49; and, since men tend to marry later than women, more of the men were 30–49. Illiteracy rates for male and female respondents were close to those in Deir El Barsha, but fewer residents in El Barsha could both read and write. A significant difference between the two villages was the lower rate of participation in income-earning activity among women in El Barsha. Fully 73 percent of female respondents did not perform paid labor, a rate almost identical to that given by the World Bank report. In El Barsha, as in Deir El Barsha, more than half of the women who did earn income produced foodstuffs and handicrafts for sale. Men in El Barsha were engaged primarily in agriculture.

The major difference between the two neighboring villages is that a significantly larger proportion of the residents of Deir El Barsha had participated in development projects. In El Barsha, less than 5 percent of female and male respondents had taken part in any development-related activities, while in Deir El Barsha 21 percent of the female and 17 percent of the male respondents had done so. All of those who participated in El Barsha were Christians, and most had been involved in literacy classes conducted by the church. The development activities in Deir El Barsha were qualitatively different from projects in El Barsha; not only did they address broader concerns, but they involved more women and gave local leaders a larger role in project management.

In Deir El Barsha, patterns of labor migration have facilitated the efforts of community members to combat FC/FGM. The connections between male labor migration and the decline of female circumcision within the village are both direct and indirect. Over three-quarters of the men (78 percent) had left the village in search of employment; the majority (58 percent) had worked in foreign countries, although they did not remain outside of Egypt for very long periods of a time. The rest made migrated within Egypt to find employment. In this village, there was a strong positive correlation between the migration of fathers for work abroad and their tendency not to circumcise their daughters. Nearly half (44 percent) of the daughters of respondents who migrated to work outside Egypt were not circumcised, compared to one-sixth (16 percent) of the daughters of those who did not travel at all.

Migration affected both men and women in dramatic ways. In-depth interviews indicated that male migration abroad had a great influence on the status of women in the village. Financial remittances from their husbands allowed women to establish independent households away from the authority of their in-laws, allowing women to prove themselves by assuming leadership of the domestic unit. Many women shouldered double responsibilities: their normal household duties, the upbringing of children, and management of the household economy. Unless women had sons who could work in the field, they took responsibility for performing agricultural work, such as plowing, seeding, harvesting, and selling crops. Women left alone in the village found many ways to contribute to the family's income.

Women living away from the extended family generally managed the money their husbands sent them very wisely. As one man maintained in an interview, "many men came back to find they owned red-brick houses and land." Women made sure that these houses also had electricity and potable water, using men's remittances to raise the family's standard of living. The perception that many men had of their wives changed, and so did their perception of women in general. They came to trust the abilities of women to handle money and deal with difficult situations. This attitude has extended to trusting women's capability to preserve the family's honor even if they are not circumcised.

Their husbands' absence gave women the opportunity to make decisions about educating their children and finding marriage partners for them. The migrant father is consulted and is supposed to have the "final" say in the decision, but his opinion is built on his wife's assessment of the situation and the options she has presented. Some respondents indicated that the father's absence gave young girls greater freedom to develop their personalities and to make independent decisions concerning their lives, particularly regarding marriage. Even though the daughter's new-found independence is often mitigated by the father's homecoming, her personality has already gone significant change. Now, unlike in the past, some girls even turn down suitors.

A comparison of Deir El Barsha with the neighboring village, El Barsha, reveals a striking difference in the rate of male labor migration that corresponds with the significant difference in the prevalence of female circumcision. In Deir El Barsha, nearly every household had at least one male who migrated abroad to earn money to improve the family's economic situation. In El Barsha, on the other hand, only two-fifths of the women respondents reported that their husbands had traveled outside of the village to work, and very few of them remained away for long periods of time.

Unlike the men and women in El Barsha, who both tended to favor female circumcision, those in Deir El Barsha maintained that in Arab countries female circumcision is not practiced. This idea, which was based on their experience of living in other Arab societies, played an important role in bolstering the belief that the practice is unnecessary.

The absence of men permitted women in Deir El Barsha to expand their activities beyond the roles that had previously been assigned to them. This transformation was crucial in enabling women to take a critical view of cultural traditions and to abandon those practices that are detrimental to them. The in-depth interviews showed that migration affected women's image of themselves as capable beings and men's perception of women's capabilities. Involvement in development activities created an enabling atmosphere for women. It helped them get out of the home and interact with others. They gained new skills and expertise, as well as management experience. Through their income-generating projects, they contributed to their family's income. Women were also exposed to urban influences through the workshops they attended in the city.

The clergy played a crucial role in influencing the decline of the practice of FC/FGM in Deir El Barsha. Qualitative analysis of questionnaires and in-depth interviews indicated that a large number of respondents of both sexes received their information about the practice through churches and that all churches asserted that FC/FGM is not a Christian ritual. This teaching divested the practice of religious sanctity and encouraged inhabitants to relinquish it. The commitment of religious leaders not to circumcise their daughters and their public proclamation of this abstention created an atmosphere in which ordinary people felt empowered to follow suit. The clergy signed the village anti-FC document, and the religious formula that "whoever practices it from today onwards would be questioned before God" endowed the agreement with religious sanctity and infused it with positive cultural implications. The moral weight of religious leaders reinforced the commitment of midwives and hygienic barbers not to practice circumcision and not to yield to any pressures exerted on them to do so. As a midwife put it, "every time someone in the village asks me to circumcise his daughter, I say if Father Daniel accepts, I am ready to do it. I know quite well Father would not accept." When people attempted to obtain Father Daniel's consent, he would tell them, "If you find that I circumcised my daughters, then do the same thing with yours." The clergy have become a model for the rest of the village to follow. When Father Daniel proclaimed that he was refraining from circumcising his daughters, others within the communal leadership and among the village's inhabitants were encouraged to abandon the practice.

The rich qualitative evidence gathered in interviews and focus group discussions at Deir El Barsha illuminates the connection between the control of female sexuality and the practice of FC/FGM. The moral dimensions of this matter were the topic of considerable debate among women themselves. When a team of researchers inquired about the factors influencing the practice, women offered varied opinions about the effects of the procedure on female sexuality and its personal and social consequences. It was clear that the ritual had been regarded as an important part of preparing young women for marriage, intended to guarantee their virginity and purity. But the procedure had longer-lasting effects on women's sexuality as well as their physical and reproductive health. After one woman asserted that FGM made women frigid, diminishing their enjoyment of sexual relations in marriage, another responded that "It would be better to cut off part of the body that could put her at the sexual mercy of her husband, than to be needy and vulnerable." In a society where it is considered shameful for a married woman to initiate a sexual encounter, the restraint on women's sexual impulses that results from female circumcision might be regarded as a benefit. Women whose husbands were away for long periods were, like unmarried women, regarded as more likely to maintain their sexual honor if they had been circumcised. In our interviews, we frequently encountered a pattern in which women attempt to convert a form of bodily harm and emotional violence into a form of empowerment; for example, some women accepted public defloration in exchange for freedom of movement (Seif El Dawla, Abdel Hadi, and Abdel Wahab 1998). These attitudes, which register the power of patriarchy, were called into question and transformed in Deir El Barsha as the practice of FC/FGM was abolished.

To sum up, the prevalence of female circumcision is decreasing in Deir El Barsha because the cultural constructions of gender relations and the status of women are changing through education and literacy programs, women's participation in the market, and religious dialogue.

Conclusion

The decline in the practice of FC/FGM in Deir El Barsha is likely to continue. When we inquired whether this new attitude would persist in the village, the overwhelming majority of female and male respondents (70 percent) answered in the affirmative. Only 17 percent thought the practice would reemerge, and 12 percent said they could not predict whether the practice would reemerge or not. The substantial change in the attitudes of the inhabitants of Deir El Barsha toward female circumcision was manifested in their actual behavior; the prevalence of female circumcision had declined over time, and the rate of decline was accelerating.

In 2002, when we went back to Deir El Barsha to celebrate the tenth anniversary of the declaration against female circumcision, young girls at the age of circumcision presented a short drama titled "Girls' Dreams" showing

how circumcision violates their hopes of leading healthy lives. In several pre-
sentations, the women's committee addressed a large audience from their village and neighboring villages, in addition to the governor and visitors from
Cairo, about their experience in challenging this long-standing tradition.
The prominent role they played in the Deir El Barsha campaign demonstrates why earlier efforts that excluded women had failed to combat the
practice, as most of the advocacy ignored the matter of gender relations in
local communities. This failure, along with increasing medicalization, was an
inevitable result of the tendency of most previous anti-FC/FGM efforts to
restrict their attention to the health framework. What was most innovative
in the case of Deir El Barsha was the emphasis put on developing the capabilities of local communities by bolstering the role of women as leaders in
their own right. The CEOSS focused on empowering the local community
by creating and developing local tools, expertise, and experience, establishing
the necessary conditions for the continuation and expansion of self-generated
local development action through a comprehensive understanding that encompasses all aspects of life in the local community with a variety of inhabitants. This approach entailed a systematic coordination of activities, including
provision of services, education and socialization, and the promotion of
technical and administrative skills, and took into consideration gender-
related aspects of development.

    The position of women in rural communities can be transformed, and
in order to end FC/FGM it must be transformed. Women must no longer be
captives to their roles as housewives and reproductive machines and subjected to the hegemony of customs and traditions that are detrimental to
them. FC/FGM is a social practice that aims to control women's sexuality
and subjugate them. Their bodies are surgically altered to keep them in line
with patriarchal norms and ideologies. Unless FC/FGM is addressed from a
gender and human rights perspective, we will be missing the point. What is
unique about the Deir El Barsha model is that it addresses the FC/FGM
problem in an integrated and a comprehensive manner. The struggle against
FC/FGM is seen as part of a wider approach to development that addresses
all aspects and sectors of the community with emphasis on women's empowerment. The members of the Deir El Barsha community signed their
document in 1991, before the ICPD and other UN conferences on the problem of female circumcision. This act demonstrated that long-standing cultural structures could be challenged if the political will is present, and that
empowering women within local communities and respecting their own
wisdom and experience is the most effective way to combat FC/FGM. Equally

significant is fact that the whole community was involved in the fight against the practice. This community-wide approach proved to be as important in Deir El Barsha as it has been where Public Declarations and Alternative Rites of Passage programs have been adopted (see El Guindi; Mohamud, Sampson, and Ringheim; and Diop and Askew; all in this volume). Individuals are empowered by their communities in ending a rite that has impinged on women's health for centuries. The case of Deir El Barsha illuminates the basic forces that enable committed grassroots organizations and communities to put human rights into practice.

Chapter 6
Strategies for Encouraging the Abandonment of Female Genital Cutting: Experiences from Senegal, Burkina Faso, and Mali

Nafissatou J. Diop and Ian Askew

The understanding, cooperation, determination, and know-how of the principal participants in circumcision are imperative for a workable solution. Programs tempered with an interest in, and respect for, grassroots initiatives and local knowledge of needs which are designed, delivered, and managed by the community women have a better prospects of sustainability.

—L. Amede Obiora, 1997

What we call Female Genital Cutting (FGC) is prevalent in much of West Africa, and grassroots activists, nongovernmental organizations (NGOs), and national committees are working together to end it. This essay evaluates strategies employed to encourage the abandonment of FGC in three adjacent nation-states: Mali, Burkina Faso, and Senegal. The proportions of the population practicing FGC vary both between countries and within them. FGC is almost universal (92 percent) in Mali (CPS/MS, DNSI, and Macro International 2002), and it is widespread (72 percent) in much of Burkina Faso (INSD and Macro International 2000). In Senegal, where the national prevalence rate is estimated to be 20 percent (Mottin-Sylla 1990), the practice is restricted to some ethnic groups (Fulani, Mandingo, and Soninké, among others), and among them the prevalence rate is high (80–90 percent).

The rationales given for this practice in West Africa and the underlying social and cultural reasons for its continuation are similar to those found in other places where FGC is prevalent. Studies conducted in Burkina Faso (Ouédraogo et al. 1996; Dera et al. 1997), Mali (Diallo 1997), and Senegal (Ndiaye et al. 1993; Bop 1999), using both qualitative and quantitative research methods, describe how the practice is carried out—by whom, where, and at what ages—and record the many and varied reasons used to justify FGC: preserving cultural identity; defining females' gender identity; maintaining personal hygiene (the clitoris is seen as a source of germs and possible infection during childbirth); reducing sexual desire, thereby controlling female sexuality; and complying with religious teachings.

A variety of interventions to encourage individuals, families, and communities to abandon the practice have been undertaken in these countries since the early 1990s (see Diallo 1997 for a review of approaches taken in Mali). NGOs have led the way, but governmental bodies have actively advocated against the practice: in Burkina Faso, the Comité National de Lutte Contre la Pratique de l'Excision (CNLPE, the National Committee for the Struggle Against Excision); in Mali, the Programme National de Lutte contre l'Excision (PNLE, the National Program for the Struggle Against Excision). Religious groups have also been supportive. For example, in Mali, the Catholic Church is credited with initiating the first campaign against FGC (Diallo 1997). In all three countries, Islamic academic teachers are denouncing perceptions that the Qur'an sanctions FGC. However, as they are not recognized as national Islamic leaders, their voices are not reaching the wider population, unlike the prominent role that Islamic leaders have played in the Sudanese context described by Ahmed (in this volume).

Although there is great variety in the approaches taken, the major strategies for encouraging abandonment of FGC in these countries can be broadly categorized as follows:

- Undertaking awareness-raising campaigns among the general population that highlight the health problems associated with the practice and advocate its abandonment because it is harmful to women and children and contravenes their basic human rights.
- Implementing community-level behavior change strategies that educate key actors in the community, build the capacity of women to participate actively in decisions affecting their lives, and create supportive mechanisms for widespread abandonment of the practice.
- Persuading traditional practitioners to stop the practice and supporting them to become educators and advocates against FGC.

- Educating health care providers working in formal medical settings to act as change agents among their clients and communities, as well as to convince their colleagues who are currently carrying out the procedure to stop doing so.
- Introducing legislation to prohibit and criminalize the practice.

While these strategies are not mutually exclusive, they represent distinct approaches to the problem and its solution.

For the most part, these interventions have been implemented with little attempt to document how they work, or to evaluate their influence on knowledge, beliefs, attitudes, and behavior. As a consequence, there is little empirical evidence regarding their relative effectiveness. Unfortunately, this limitation characterizes almost all interventions aimed at encouraging the abandonment of FGC. During the past decade, however, the important contributions made by systematic evaluation have begun to be appreciated. As Izett and Toubia aptly stated: "Monitoring and evaluation of programs are among the most important items on the FC/FGM agenda. Although there is a history of over 20 years of progress to persuade communities to stop the practice, few of them have been assessed to date. Before further investment is made in expanding existing approaches or experimenting with new ones, it is crucial to determine whether activities are achieving their objectives and whether there are measurable outcomes in terms of changing attitudes or a reduction in circumcision" (1999). Since 1995, the Population Council[1] has undertaken a series of studies in Burkina Faso, Mali, Senegal, and other countries where the practice is prevalent to test and evaluate several of these strategies using experimental designs. Other studies have analyzed the sociocultural context in which FGC is practiced and the interventions operate, and participatory learning approaches have been used in various communities to identify strategies that would be acceptable and effective (LSC 1998; Tapsoba et al. 1998).

This essay briefly describes three strategies that have been tested and systematically evaluated in Mali, Burkina Faso, and Senegal and then discusses the key findings of those studies. The research conducted by the Population Council is based on a methodology that social scientists in the field call operations research. The distinctive characteristic of this experimental approach is that evaluation is not entirely separate from the design of the intervention; implementation of the intervention being tested can, to some degree, be controlled or influenced by those undertaking the study (for a description of this approach, see Fisher et al. 2002). Evaluation is formative as well as summative, and the activities involved in carrying out the intervention are the major source of data about their influence on participants. Equally important, attitudes and actions are linked systematically in the applied research design. Not only does this approach decrease the costs and burdens of formal evaluation, but it allows for more systematic analysis of various factors that contribute to or inhibit the success of different strategies and specific features of intervention programs. With a problem like FGC, where the strategies being employed are based on a wide range of assumptions about the conditions that support continuation of the practice and what interventions are effective in creating change are so little known, such an approach is especially valuable. The essay concludes with a discussion of the lessons learned and recommendations for directions that efforts to change behavior in this region should take.

Community-Wide Awareness Campaigns

The strategy that has been most commonly used to address FGC is mass or community-level campaigns to educate people about the health risks associated with it, usually within the context of portraying FGC as a traditional practice that is harmful to women and children and contravenes their fundamental human rights to bodily integrity. This approach can certainly be successful in raising awareness; the large-scale campaigns conducted by the CNLPE in Burkina Faso (CNLPE 1997) have been cited as a good example (WHO 1999). Improving knowledge about the health risks that may be associated with the practice is a necessary but insufficient step toward changing behavior (WHO 1999). Many women who undergo genital cutting, especially the less severe types, do not suffer any obvious health consequences, and this perception weakens the argument's persuasive power (Obermeyer 1999). Equally serious, knowledge of the health risks is pushing many people who strongly want to sustain the practice to seek medical assistance in performing the cutting rather than abandon it. Medicalization is an unintended consequence of strategies focused narrowly on women's health (Shell-Duncan 2001).

Effective strategies designed to change practices that, like FGC, are based on and enforced by social conventions, rather than merely individual preferences, require strategies that address the social dimensions of the practice and provide support for those who act for change. An educational component is necessary to generate initial awareness and promote consideration of the disadvantages of continuing FGC. Translating this knowledge into be-havior requires a sequence of components to follow this first stage, which are usually implemented community-wide, to build the commitment of the majority of families to decide not to allow their daughters to be cut, to implement that decision despite opposition from others, and then to ensure that they sustain this change over time (Izett and Toubia 1999, Mackie 2000).

First we consider evaluations of two strategies that focus on changing the behavior of individuals who play key roles in the practice of FGC: traditional practitioners who carry out the genital cutting; and health care providers who work in medical settings and may perform the procedure themselves or support others who do. Second, we present the findings from an evaluation of one of the best-known examples of a community-wide be-havior change strategy, the Village Empowerment Program developed by the Senegalese NGO, Tostan.

Traditional Practitioners

The vast majority of girls in Mali, Burkina Faso, and Senegal who undergo FGC are cut by traditional practitioners, usually called excisors: 91 percent in Mali, 97 percent in Burkina Faso, and 93 percent in Senegal. Excisors usually carry out the cutting with crude implements and in unhygienic conditions, so the health risks of the procedure are easily highlighted during educational campaigns. Traditional practitioners are obvious targets for efforts to en-courage abandonment of the practice, but only if it can be assumed that a strategy to decrease the supply of those doing the cutting will also reduce de-mand for the service.

In Mali, several NGOs have developed and implemented strategies that seek to persuade traditional practitioners to stop agreeing to cut girls. The Centre National de la Recherche Scientifique et Technologique (CNRST, the National Center for Scientific and Technological Research) and the Population Council undertook an evaluation of the programs of the three main organiza-tions using this strategy: the Association Malienne de Suivi et d'Orientation des Pratiques Traditionelles (AMSOPT, the Malian Association for Monitor-ing Traditional Practices), the Association pour le Progrès et la Défense des Droits des Femmes (APDF, the Association for the Progress and Defense of Women's Rights), and the Association de Soutien au Développement des Ac-tivités de Population (ASDAP, the Association for the Development of Popu-lation Activities).

In brief, the strategies followed by the three NGOs comprised the same two initial phases:

- Identifying traditional practitioners and educating them on the physiology of female genitalia, the harmful consequences of FGC, and their role in perpetuating it.
- Raising awareness of the harmful consequences of FGC in communities.

Because excisors gain social status from performing the procedure and may be dependent on the remuneration they receive from it, two of the NGOs developed alternative income-generating activities for practitioners, and one of them also provided excisors with financial assistance. Similar to the Sudan National Committee on the Eradication of Traditional Practices Harmful to Women and Children, one NGO educated practitioners to become change agents within their communities.

To evaluate this strategy, data were collected through interviewing the heads of the three NGOs, 10 field staff members, and 41 practitioners. In addition, 45 focus group discussions were conducted with 380 community members in six of the districts where the NGOs operate. The study sought to understand the content and means of communicating messages to the practitioners, determine community attitudes following implementation, and assess the efficacy of these strategies (Population Council and CNRST 1998).

Health Care Providers

In several countries, many families now seek the services of medical professionals in an attempt to avoid the dangers of unskilled practitioners performing FGC in unsanitary conditions (for Guinea, see Yoder et al. 1999; for Egypt, see El-Gibaly et al. 2002; for Nigeria, see Mandara 2000; for Kenya, see Shell-Duncan et al. 2000, Njue and Askew 2004, and Jaldesa et al. 2005). Health care workers find themselves under pressure from individuals and families to carry out FGC. While those who support the practice may willingly accede to the request, even those who do not may find the financial incentive hard to resist. Medicalizing the procedure constitutes a violation of a girl's right to bodily integrity and does not address the long-term sexual, reproductive, and mental health complications that may result from FGC. Virtually all international organizations are unequivocal in their opposition to medical providers engaging in the practice, and several are working to engage health care providers actively to oppose FGC within their clinics and communities (WHO 2001). Most importantly, this trend toward medicalization is contrary to the WHO statement that "female genital mutilation in any form should not be practiced by health professionals in any setting" (WHO 2001). Numerous other organizations have made explicit statements against medicalization, including the International Federation of Gynecology and Obstetrics, the Inter-African Committee, and the U.S. Agency for International Development (USAID). They unequivocally declare that no health professional should practice FGC in any setting—including nurses and midwives as well as physicians, and clinics as well as hospitals (WHO 1997). However, the issue remains contentious and complex (Shell-Duncan 2001; Shell-Duncan et al. 2000).

Health care providers interact regularly with people from diverse backgrounds and have the opportunity to discuss the health implications of FGC with their clients, as well as to identify and deal with medical problems arising from circumcision. They constitute an underutilized and potentially important resource in educational campaigns against FGC. In 1998, ASDAP, the Malian Ministry of Health's Department for Community Health, and the Population Council developed and pilot-tested an intervention that consisted of two main activities:

- Training clinic staff in identifying the types of FGC and related health complications and in communicating messages against FGC to their clients.
- Introducing FGC topics within group health talks at the clinics and during individual consultations with clients whenever feasible.

During three days of training, providers were given information on the prevalence of FGC, reasons for the practice, female anatomy, types of cutting, complications that result from the procedure, and how complications can be managed. Participants spent an entire day learning how to do counseling and give health talks, using role-playing and a flipchart developed specifically for this purpose.

The intervention was evaluated in terms of the extent to which these activities improved providers' understanding of FGC-related health problems, increased the proportion of them identifying and managing such complications, and reduced the likelihood of their agreeing to cut girls. The study also measured whether clients were more likely to hear messages against FGC after the training. The interventions were implemented by training a team of master trainers (eight doctors and two midwives) and developing a special set of educational materials. In turn, the master trainers trained 59 staff in eight clinics. These providers were then compared over time with 49 providers drawn from six similar clinics. Both sets of clinics were located in the capital city of Bamako and in the rural region of Ségou. The knowledge, attitudes, and actions of practitioners were measured immediately before the training and three months afterwards through interviews with providers and observations of group health talks in the clinics. Interviews were held with 1,633 clients to assess their exposure to FGC messages during their consultation (Diop et al. 1998).

Village Empowerment

The Village Empowerment Program (VEP), also known as the Tostan program after the international NGO based in Senegal that developed it,[2] evolved out of a functional literacy program for women that seeks not only to equip women with knowledge and skills for personal development but also to empower them to participate more actively in community development, a field traditionally reserved for men. This program was developed with the philosophy that literacy skills alone are not sufficient to prepare learners for active participation in the social, political, economic, and cultural decisions related to the development of their community and ultimately their country (Tostan 1999). Tostan promotes an integrated approach to learning, offering a comprehensive curriculum in national languages not only for reading, writing, and mathematics, but also for improving life skills and the socioeconomic conditions of participants. The use of innovative pedagogical techniques inspired by African traditions and local knowledge has contributed to making the sessions relevant, lively, and participatory.

The program consists of two interrelated components: a basic education program to raise women's functional literacy, and through this to advance their understanding of reproductive health and basic human rights; and an awareness-raising and social mobilization process to educate local leaders and the whole community about the harmful consequences of FGC and encourage them to make a public declaration in favor of its abandonment. Classes of approximately 30 women per village study four modules— on human rights, hygiene, problem solving, and women's health—over a period of seven to eight months. Recently, in response to their requests, Tostan has added classes for men, held separately but at the same time. Social mobilization activities are undertaken within each village, and then several villages are gathered together in order to debate issues concerning FGC, early marriage, and the use of family planning. Village committees play a key role in organizing these meetings, and women involved in the literacy program and their facilitators are bringing the issues to the debates.

The Population Council evaluated the effectiveness of the VEP in two different but comparable situations: in the Kolda region of southern Senegal, where Tostan has expanded its existing program into 90 villages; and in the Bazega province of central Burkina Faso, where Tostan has mentored a national community development NGO called Mwangaza to implement the VEP in 23 villages. Both studies were financially supported by the German organization Gesellschaft für Technische Zusammenarbeit (GTZ) and the United States Agency for International Development (USAID).

To test the effect of the basic education program and the social mobilization process on community members' attitudes toward FGC and on their willingness to hold a public meeting to declare community-wide abandonment of the practice, which is used as the ultimate indicator of social change, both studies compared these indicators before and after introducing the intervention, and compared the study villages with similar villages where the intervention was not introduced. During surveys carried out immediately before and 12 months after the interventions were introduced, all women who participated in the programs were interviewed (approximately 600 women in Senegal and 580 women in Burkina Faso). In addition, the majority of their husbands or partners and a sample of women living in the same villages who did not participate in the education program were interviewed to gain an understanding of the degree to which the intervention had diffused beyond those directly participating in the program.

Key Findings from the Evaluation Studies

Traditional practitioners continue to perform FGC despite making statements that they had abandoned the practice.

Attempts to convince traditional practitioners to give up the practice were not successful. FGC was still being performed in all but one of the six sites visited for the evaluation, and in that site it had not been performed for the past two years only because it was not the customary time for circumcision. Most people did not know of any excisors who had stopped working, as they

were still responding to requests from families. Out of 41 excisors interviewed, 29 declared that although they had been sensitized by the NGO, they
were still performing the procedure when requested and were not convinced
that what they were doing is wrong. Others explained that they had given up
the practice but took it up again because the NGO did not provide them
with the alternative sources of income they had been promised. The five
practitioners who had genuinely discontinued FGC actually did so for reasons unrelated to the intervention: they retired because of advanced age or
poor eyesight and were replaced by their daughters. Most practitioners remained unconvinced that FGC is harmful to women, and community members had no difficulty finding a replacement for any excisor who gave up the
practice, either through another traditional practitioner or a health provider
(Population Council and CNRST 1998).

*Most health providers are opposed to FGC and are willing to play an active
role in discouraging the practice. But many remain supportive, and several
continue to perform the procedure in medical facilities.*

Interventions targeted at health care professionals who work in medical settings have been more successful in influencing their knowledge and attitudes
than in changing behavior. After training, the majority of health providers
(62 percent) supported efforts to encourage the abandonment of FGC in
principle. The beliefs that uncut girls are immoral, that men prefer cut girls,
and that FGC guarantees virginity until marriage decreased slightly among
providers as a result of training. Nevertheless, 28 percent of them said that
they were not really against the practice, and another 10 percent indicated
support for its medicalization. While no training intervention is likely to influence the beliefs and attitudes of all health providers, this intervention did
succeed in changing the opinions of 47 percent of the providers. A significant
number (13 percent) recognized that FGC is being practiced at their facility,
although understandably, very few (2 percent) admitted performing the procedure themselves.

The gap between what providers know is happening and what they admit to doing is as telling as the apparent medicalization of this harmful practice is alarming. Unless providers who actively oppose the practice persuade
their colleagues to refuse to perform it, little headway will be made toward its
abandonment. As a direct consequence of this research finding, the Malian
Ministry of Health immediately issued a policy directive to all its providers
explicitly banning the practice by MOH employees and in MOH premises.

The Ministry of Women's Affairs also circulated a decree to all its central and local service providers that they should be aware of the MOH policy and do their best to promote and reinforce it.

Although providers' knowledge of FGC increased as a result of training, they remained uncomfortable discussing FGC with their clients.

The dramatic gains in health providers' factual knowledge of the various types of FGC did not translate into their taking actions to discourage it among their clients. The proportion of providers who believed that FGC poses no significant risk to women's health did not decrease much as a result of training, suggesting that medical information did not erase their support for the practice. Those professionals who were opposed to FGC and well aware of its health risks found few opportunities to talk with their patients about it. Most providers indicated that, because of the large number of clients during the morning clinic sessions, they felt too rushed to be able to spend time discussing FGC with their patients. Indeed, during exit interviews only 0.5 percent of women said that they had been counseled about FGC.

More than one third of providers interviewed had referred a client for further treatment of complications resulting from FGC. Although health professionals are better able to recognize those complications, providers acknowledged that they have limited competence in treating them and would appreciate further training. Since completion of this study, USAID has supported a training program in Mali to strengthen providers' skills in managing FGC-related complications and in educating their clients on the benefits of abandoning the practice. This program, implemented by IntraHealth's PRIME II Project, resulted in an increase in knowledge of FGC, with nearly three quarters of providers passing the test on counseling skills, up from 12 percent at the baseline (Newman and Nelson 2003).

The Village Empowerment Program improved knowledge and attitudes concerning reproductive health, human rights, and gender relations.

Women who participated in the basic education program in Senegal showed tremendous improvements in their awareness of reproductive health, human rights, and gender relations and substantial shifts in their attitudes toward FGC. The data demonstrate that women living in these villages who did not directly participate in the education program also gained greater awareness of these issues. Similar increases were found among men living in these villages, suggesting that the education program can also influence others, perhaps through discussions between participants and nonparticipants which are actively encouraged by Tostan as part of the implementation process.

The Village Empowerment Program decreased the practice of FGC.

Participation in the Village Empowerment Program had significant positive effects in reducing the practice of FGC. For example, the prevalence of FGC reported among daughters under 11 years of age decreased significantly among women who participated in the program (from 54 to 40 percent). Rates of FGC also declined among the daughters of women in these villages who did not participate directly in the program. The girls who were cut, however, were now being cut at younger ages than before, suggesting that those who chose to continue the practice were taking steps to ensure that the girls would definitely be cut before they could oppose the decision. This finding, although not the main effect of the intervention, is a matter of some concern.

Social mobilization has been successful in leading to public declarations against FGC, as well as supporting other improvements in the position of women in civil society.

In both Senegal and Burkina Faso, social mobilization strategies have been used to build on this increased awareness in the villages by seeking to shift group attitudes in order to change behavior. Following these group discussions within the 90 villages in Senegal, these and over 200 other communities were brought together and publicly declared, during a specially organized event in the town of Karcia, that they would no longer practice FGC on their daughters. The additional villages participated because reconsideration of the value of FGC had diffused widely through participants' networking with their friends and relatives in other villages where the VEP program had not been introduced. Also, each intervention village conducted social mobilization activities in two other villages of their choice.

In addition to building a community-wide consensus to declare an end to FGC, the social mobilization strategy facilitated several other initiatives that have improved the position of women and girls in civil society. In Burkina Faso, the 23 project villages led movements to enroll girls in school, to register children so that they can get identity cards, and to organize campaigns for massive voter registration. For example, in one village 43 couples decided to get married legally; in another 10 villages it was decided that all families should receive an official family record book; and in all 23 villages environmental hygiene and health activities to improve living conditions were undertaken (Diop et al. 2003).

Lessons Learned

Understanding the ways in which a community consensus in favor of FGC is sustained and can be overturned in practice enables grassroots activists, NGOs, international agencies, and all those concerned with ending this violation of women's rights to bodily integrity to identify appropriate and effective strategies for social change. Without systematic research, the cause-and-effect relationships between intervention activities and desired outcomes are seldom clear (Izett and Toubia 1999). Integrating evaluation studies into the design of interventions need not be complex or burdensome (see Population Council 2002 for a discussion of the key issues to be considered with this type of research). This approach does, however, require a commitment to two principles: that an intervention's effectiveness cannot be assumed simply because it is feasible and acceptable to the community; and that its effectiveness cannot be measured or demonstrated without a quasi-experimental study design. Pilot-testing strategies for encouraging the abandonment of FGC and evaluating their effectiveness can be a crucial step in developing a successful program of action that can then be implemented on a larger scale. The empirical information collected and insights generated through carefully documenting the process of implementing a strategy and systematically measuring its effectiveness provides those responsible for developing, implementing, and funding anti-FGC programs with concrete evidence of what works, what does not, and why. These research studies offer many lessons for decision makers at various levels to consider when developing strategies appropriate for their particular context.

The strategy of encouraging traditional practitioners to stop performing FGC and to become change agents is not effective because so few give up the practice permanently. The excisor is a community member, and her stopping the practice depends on the level of awareness within the community that FGC contravenes basic rights and can be harmful. As long as there is still community-level support for the practice, parents will continue to seek someone to do the cutting, so it is much easier for an excisor to continue her practice than to stop. The low social status and relative poverty of traditional practitioners make the recognition they gain and the livelihood they earn through performing the procedure valuable personal assets. Since it is in their interest to continue the practice, they are in no position to influence the community to abandon FGC. Programs intended to furnish them with alternative sources of income have not been successful, as any alternative would also have to provide them with a level of social recognition similar to that enjoyed as a practitioner.

In these West African societies, the power to influence community-wide behavior is vested in the chiefs and elders, so anti-FGC strategies must address community support for the practice by persuading these groups to advocate against it, rather than trying to cut off the supply of practitioners with the expectation that this will also curtail demand. The results of this evaluation are similar to what has been observed in northeastern Africa, which led the WHO to recommend that "while excisors should be included in programming, finding alternative income for excisors should not be the major strategy for change" (WHO 1999).

The strategy of working with health care providers had two components: training them in basic skills to manage FGC-related medical complications; and educating them to become active advocates against the practice during consultations with their clients. There was a clear need to train health staff to recognize medical problems induced by FGC and to provide the specific care needed. Health professionals' lack of knowledge reflected the general lack of public awareness of the linkages between women's reproductive health and the practice of FGC. Even relatively simple training significantly improved health care providers' levels of knowledge about FGC and its complications. Consequently, it was recommended that such training be incorporated into preservice medical training. It was not possible to document whether the training improved management of complications, but the proportion of providers identifying complications and referring patients for treatment increased. The research suggests that such training is essential in countries where gynecological and obstetrical complications due to FGC are widespread.

The strategy of using health care providers is compromised, however, by the fact that many of them support the practice, and in some cases actually cut girls themselves. For providers to be able to encourage change among their clients and the broader community, they themselves must first go through a process of attitudinal and behavioral change. Any strategy focused on using health professionals to convince communities to abandon FGC that does not begin with real changes in their own attitudes and actions will not achieve its objectives. Even those health care providers who are well informed about the negative medical consequences of FGC do not necessarily pass on that information to their clients. Given their status in the community and influence over their patients, heath providers are an important potential resource in campaigns to abandon FGC, but a concerted and well-planned effort is needed to ensure that they become effective change agents. Training for health care professionals must be supported and extended by broader efforts at the community level.

The use of community-based strategies like the Village Education Program (VEP) show real promise, as their multifaceted approach addresses knowledge, attitudes, actions, and communal support in an integrated manner. A comprehensive education program that includes human rights, reproductive health, and gender relations and is coupled with strategies that give women more confidence and empower them to participate in community-level discussions and activities concerning their bodily health and their position in society is more likely to lead to changes in social behavior. The participatory methods used in the basic education program create an opportunity for self-determination; women themselves decide which actions they and the wider community should take. Because education on human rights and gender relations was included along with information about FGC, women understand that this practice is not merely an individual concern or a health-related problem but must be viewed as an integral component of their rights, their roles in society, and community development.

The VEP strategy builds on the fact that in these village-based societies, as is the case across rural Africa, a public declaration is more powerful than individual expressions of opinion about a socially approved practice. According to the sociological principles on which the VEP is based (Mackie 2000), these declarations are the most important factors facilitating abandonment of the practice. Put briefly, the normal lack of public discussion or debate about the practice of FGC makes it difficult for individual families to judge the opinions and expectations of others within their community, so they remain uncertain and anxious about others' attitudes when their own attitudes have shifted. Until the subject is brought into the open, people will not risk damaging their reputation by ceasing to practice FGC. Mackie argues that the most important reference group against which people judge their decision is not the community as a whole but the social grouping within which the family marries, since FGC is seen as a prerequisite for making a socially acceptable match. Thus, if there is a critical mass of families within a community, or within a group of intermarrying families, who have individually come to the decision that they would like to abandon FGC, then holding a public declaration against the practice by their representatives enables each of them to know that a critical mass of significant others holds the same view. What may have been perceived as a minority view is now known to be a majority view and becomes the new social convention for that group.

Two key unknowns play important roles in promoting or inhibiting this process of change. First, how can individuals and families become sufficiently concerned about the harms entailed in FGC that they seriously contemplate changing their behavior? Is educating a group of 30 women in a village through a functional literacy program enough, at least when undertaken together with social mobilization activities organized by an NGO? Secondly, how can an NGO actively support and organize a public declaration so that it represents a sincere and widespread pledge that the majority of the community will change its actions? The public declaration in Karcia, Senegal, included many more villages than had participated in the VEP. Can villages that did not participate in the VEP be expected to be at the same stage in the behavior change process as villages that participated directly in the program? In order to understand the diffusion process, we must know more about the ways in which the other villages became involved in the public declaration activity. Evidence (Diop et al. 2004) suggests that this involvement was strongly based on familial and friendship ties among the leaders of different villages—that is, on the dynamics of intermarriage within the geographic area. More research is needed on the information diffusion process that takes place among village leaders and on the role of these leaders within their villages as communicators of ideas for change.

Conclusion

Since community-based programs to encourage the abandonment of FGC are relatively new and deal with a sensitive and deeply embedded cultural practice, it is crucial that the strategies they employ are based on a comprehensive understanding of the values, beliefs, practices, and rules of social interaction that prevail at the community level. The lack of a theoretical and empirically tested sociological model informing the strategies targeting traditional practitioners and health care professionals may well explain their relative ineffectiveness. Those who perform FGM and provide health care are not easily persuaded to become advocates of change, and the health care practitioners who oppose FGM evidently do not exercise the kind of influence that these programs assume. In order to be effective, strategies should be designed to generate social change rather than merely influence individuals, and they must offer social support for families to carry their new ideas through action. FGC is usually undertaken to prepare daughters for marriage in compliance with what is perceived to be a social convention in the communities within which marriages take place. The VEP approach seeks to initiate and support a community-wide behavior change process. Its demonstrated effectiveness appears to support the theory that changing social behavior requires building a community-wide agreement that such a practice is not desirable and then publicizing and demonstrating widespread agreement with this change through a pledge ceremony. The way forward lies in implementing interventions that are based on a thorough understanding of the communities involved and on facilitating grassroots involvement in the process of social change.

Chapter 7

The Sudanese National Committee on the Eradication of Harmful Traditional Practices and the Campaign Against Female Genital Mutilation

Hamid El Bashir

"Al sayga Wasila"—No matter how slowly, a caravan that walks steadily ultimately reaches its faraway destination.
—Proverb from Western Sudan

The Sudanese feminist movement has not launched an explicit campaign against female genital mutilation. Until the 1970s, the movement was overwhelmingly concerned with the achievement of basic economic and political rights. During the 1980s, however, the feminist movement turned to combating cultural prejudices and practices harmful to women, including female genital mutilation (FGM).

The first campaign against female circumcision in the Sudan occurred during the late eighteenth century under the Sinnar Sultanate, well before the formal incorporation of Sudan into the Ottoman Empire in 1821. That movement was believed to be initiated and supported by the holy religious Sheikh, Hassan Wad Hossona, in central Sudan. Detailed documentation of its progress and achievements has not been found. It vanished with the death of its leader, without visible or lasting effects on the people.

The next initiative came from the British colonial authorities. In 1946 the British administration in the Sudan officially passed a law banning circumcision. In 1945 a traditional birth attendant in Rufaa, a town on the eastern bank of the Blue Nile in central Sudan along the Khartoum-Wad Medani Road, was sentenced to six months imprisonment in Hasaheisa town, the district capital, for circumcising a girl. A campaign against the circumciser's imprisonment was launched by a graduate engineer from Gordon Memorial College, which later became the University of Khartoum, and a Sufi Sheikh known as Mahmoud Mohammed Taha. The campaign against the law was nationalistic, denying the right of the colonial rulers to intervene in Sudanese cultural practices. The movement gradually developed into a popular uprising in that locality known as "the Circumcision Revolution."

Ironically, both the first campaign against circumcision and the first campaign to defend it were based on religious grounds. The contradictory use of religious discourse in relation to FGM stems from the obscure and controversial nature of the issue within Islam. But the nationalist dimension of the 1945 circumcision revolution deeply influenced subsequent developments, affecting the strategic and programmatic approaches taken by activists in national and international nongovernmental organizations and the relevant government departments in the country, such as the ministries of Health and Social Welfare. Since 1945, the law prohibiting female circumcision has never been implemented, and criminalization of FGM has never been discussed by those campaigning against the practice in the Sudan.

In 1946, after encountering concerted resistance, the British administration decided to give up enforcing the law and focus on other measures against female circumcision. The administration asked the two major Islamic religious leaders in the Sudan, Imam Abdel Rahman Al-Mahdi of the Ansar sect and Sayed Ali Al-Merghani of the Khatmiya sect, to approach their respective clients and followers (*murides*) and advocate the eradication of FGM. The two leaders made strong anti-circumcision statements to their followers, but had no success.

Although the origin and history of female circumcision in the Sudan remain controversial, the practice is deeply embedded in the dominant patriarchal cultural framework of Sudanese society. FGM arises from and reinforces the subordinate status that women occupy (see, for example, Hayes 1975). The modern campaign against FGM originated from within the Sudanese feminist movement and became an integral part of its objectives and strategic agenda. Like other traditional practices that are harmful to the health of women, FGM centers on women's reproductive capacities, beauty, and sexuality.

A process of fundamental social and cultural transformation has been in motion throughout Sudan during the last century. Sudan became a modern nation-state, with supporting institutions and organized efforts at economic development. Mass communications and transportation networks have increased geographical mobility and urban growth. Ethnic groups that formerly had marked cultural differences have become more integrated. As education has expanded, women's education has made gradual progress, particularly in central Sudan. The division of labor changed as educated women entered the civil service on equal footing with men. Education has had revolutionary implications. The traditional family structure has been transformed by all these socioeconomic shifts, as well as by particular factors affecting women directly. The influence of male and female elders has declined. As their vested interests have been jeopardized, many elders opposed sociocultural change. But the socializing role of the family has also diminished in the face of such new state-sponsored institutions as schools, the mass media, and civic organizations. The economic transformation stimulated by the monetization of indigenous economies, the hegemony assumed by market relations and forces, and the process of globalization have all had deep and far-reaching implications for the Sudanese social fabric. The acceleration of social change has contributed to women's emancipation and empowerment.

In the late 1970s, a national nongovernmental women's organization, the Babiker Badri Scientific Association for Women's Studies (BBSAWS), based at Ahfad University for Women, was formed with a central focus on the health and well-being of women and children. BBSAWS was the first civil society institution and organized women's group ever to launch a campaign against female genital mutilation, which it conducted in urban areas. Later the campaign was integrated into the extracurricular activities of students at Ahfad University for Women. This initiative arose from the pioneering and committed feminist inclinations of the Babiker Badri family in modern Sudan. Ahfad University, the first institution in the country to offer women a higher education, was established by the Babiker Badri family and became a major feminist training institution. Ahfad was very much disliked by the far right-wing, military and Islamicist regime that has ruled the country since 1989.

In 1982, a National Committee for the Eradication of Female Circumcision (NCEFC) was formed through a decree by the Ministry of Social Welfare in Sudan. But, given the absence of any institutional and organizational structure to launch an anti-circumcision campaign, both the decree and the formation of the NCEFC remained a matter of the state's will and commitment rather than of practical action until 1984. In 1985, a subcommittee from the NCEFC was formed in order to coordinate with the Inter-African Committee (IAC) on Traditional Practices Affecting the Health of

Women and Children. During the IAC conference held in Addis Ababa, Ethiopia, in 1987, a resolution was passed to establish the Sudan National Committee on the Eradication of Harmful Traditional Practices Affecting the Health of Women and Children (SNCTP). In 1988, the SNCTP became a full-fledged national nongovernmental organization and a branch of IAC. In June 1989, SNCTP was dissolved by the new military regime along with all the other NGOs in the country, but in March 1990 it was allowed to pursue its anti-circumcision campaign. Since then, SNCTP has assumed the leading role in the national campaign against FGM.

Traditional Practices Harmful to Women

The Faculty of Medicine at the University of Khartoum carried out the first nationwide sample survey on the magnitude and prevalence of female circumcision in 1977. In 1989, the National Population Committee of the Ministry of Health and Department of Statistics conducted a nationwide Demographic and Health Survey (DHS). The procedures employed were categorized in three types. Pharaonic circumcision, defined medically as infibulation, involves the most severe surgical alteration of the genitals: the clitoris, labia minora, and labia majora are removed and the vulva is stitched closed, leaving only a small opening for urination and menstruation. The intermediate type, which resulted from the incorporation of midwives into the modern health system, is a modification of the Pharaonic procedure in which the clitoris and labia minora are totally or partially removed and the labia majora are partially removed and stitched together over the vaginal opening. While this procedure is generally less severe than infibulation, it varies widely between different groups and regions in the Sudan. In fact, this intermediate category is often blurry, and some groups see only two types of female circumcision. What is called sunna is a less severe procedure, known medically as clitoridectomy, in which the hood and part or all of the clitoris are removed.

The overall prevalence of FGM in the Sudan was high: 92 percent in 1997 and 89.2 percent in 1989. Pharaonic circumcision was the most prevalent type; around 80 percent of women surveyed had undergone infibulation. But between 1977 and 1989 there was a marked shift from the intermediate types of FGM to sunna, a less severe form. Although the data are imperfect, it is clear that, even prior to the commencement of SNCTP and its campaign, there were two positive trends of change in relation to FGM: a very slow quantitative decline in its prevalence, as a much faster qualitative shift in the type of FGM practiced.

SNCTP and the Campaign Against FGM

In its campaign, SNCTP identified major beliefs and prevalent practices that directly affect the health of women and children. Because under this banner there are too many harmful traditional practices to campaign against all at once, SNCTP and IAC identified four practices as the most harmful and urgent to eradicate: female genital mutilation; nutritional taboos; early marriage; and unspaced pregnancies. Among these practices, FGM is believed to be the most harmful, and therefore worthy of the biggest share in SNCTP efforts.

SNCTP has taken several steps toward changing popular opinion and educating the public in its campaign to eradicate female genital mutilation. By implementing programs in several different social and political sectors at once, SNCTP has been able to affect public perceptions of the practice. The organization has used four main implementation strategies: a mass media campaign; a training and information campaign; training of trainers; and lobbying and advocacy at the governmental and organizational level. The organization's linkages with other institutions and ad hoc activities incorporate several programs and agendas.

The efforts of SNCTP, along with BBSAWS and NCEHTP, in coordination with many other autonomous organizations and individuals, have led to a gradual and slow, yet demonstrable, shift in public attitudes toward FGM. The very fact that the issue of female genital mutilation is now publicly discussed in the media and among women, men, and young people of both sexes is in itself a major indicator of change. Discussion of the issue used to be taboo; at best, it was regarded as "a women's private issue and cannot be discussed by men," as a woman interviewed in central Sudan commented.

Health messages related to the complications of FGM have predominated in SNCTP's campaigns against the practice. These messages have been especially effective in urban areas, where the general public is becoming more health aware. The expansion of health institutions and personnel in rural areas has also played an important part. Maternal mortality and morbidity are declining throughout the country. However, the predominance of the health component has led to the medicalization of the issue. Two dangers are associated with the medicalization of FGM. First, opponents can easily challenge the medical arguments about the complications of FGM. In many instances women say that "our grandmothers were circumcised and they gave birth to our mothers who gave birth to us. We are also circumcised. This has been going on for generations now. We are not seeing any of these problems you are now talking about. We are married, enjoying our sexual life, and have children who will also be circumcised." The second danger is that many medical personnel will be involved in the practice under the justification of using a medically safe method of circumcision. This trend is now occurring in the Sudan, as well as in Egypt.

Promoting discussion of the health consequences of FGM is a powerful means of mobilizing people against it. Presenting such information in technical terms is less effective for the masses of the people than telling personal stories. SNCTP has facilitated the sharing of personal experiences and the discussion of health problems at the local level and published such testimony in its educational materials. One especially powerful story epitomized many family tragedies.

My name is Sua'ad Omer El-Hag Ahmed, from the Maqharba tribe. My husband's name is Haj Mohamed Meskin Ali Al-Sayed from the Ja'afra tribe (originally from Upper Egypt). I'm 55 years old and my husband is 80 years old. He has been blind for three years now. I suffer from diabetes and hypertension. I got married when I was less than 15 years. Our parents believed early marriage is good for girls because it protects them and their honor, which can be destroyed through fornication. I don't have sons; I have only three daughters: Fatima, 21 years old; Adla, who was married at the age of 13 and died last year at the age of 15; and Intisar, the youngest, who is now 13 years old.

Let me tell you the story of my deceased daughter Adla. She was circumcised, Pharaonic type, when she was six years old. Pharaonic circumcision is the only type we know, and frankly speaking we think sunna circumcision is no circumcision. All these new versions are not good; circumcision is circumcision, and it has to be good and well tied. Let me go back to the story of my deceased daughter Adla. Since she reached the puberty age, she continuously had problems during the menstruation period. Two years later, we took her to a doctor in Sinnar City who told us that was due to the very tight nature of the Pharaonic circumcision she had. At the age of 14 years Adla got married to a blacksmith in Omdurman. Her problems and complications continued and even worsened after the initiation of marriage. Her husband and I took her to a doctor called Ali in Omdurman Military Hospital who gave her some medicine. A few months later, Adla became pregnant, and when about to deliver, her husband brought her to Sinnar to have her first baby with us. She gave birth to a girl and four days later Adla died of tetanus infection, according to the doctor. Adla (may Allah bless her) used to support us through her husband who was kind to us. After she died her husband got married to a Danaqla woman in Umbada, Omdurman. He is no longer supporting us or his young daughter. I sometimes beg in Sennar market but without much gain. My husband is now begging in the marketplace as well. People of the Zakat Department used to support, us, but they stopped for almost one year now.

Last year one of my nephews from Rabak asked for the hand of my daughter Intisar who is 13 years old. We all accepted and felt happy because we are unable to support ourselves and her. We are also happy because she can support us through her husband. A few months later, two ladies and a male doctor came to us in the quarter and had a discussion with all the people about the negative consequences and complications of FGM for girls, particularly when they grow older. It was during the discussion with this group that we realized that Adla had died due to complications of FGM and early marriage and delivery. Immediately her sister Intisar, who had already been betrothed to her cousin, refused to get married because she is only 13 years old and she feared the fate of her sister Adla. My brothers and relatives are very angry at us because we failed to force her into marriage, and as a result they stopped all assistance to us. My husband is insisting that Intisar should marry her cousin as soon as possible. We put pressure on her but she is adamantly refusing the marriage. Hiyam, the little daughter of Adla who is now under my custody, will never ever be circumcised or married at a younger age. (see also El Bashir n.d.: 11)

This story shows that when parents and girls realize the harm done by FGM, they may decide to forgo the procedure, but they have difficulty doing so in the face of pressure from relatives and potential marriage partners.

Educational programs targeting traditional birth attendants (TBAs) and midwives, who perform many circumcisions, have had limited effectiveness in bringing about broad changes in practice. Focusing specifically upon those who provide this service does not do much to restrict the demand for it, and few practitioners who depend on the income from performing the procedure forgo it voluntarily. However, when coupled with broader efforts to educate the public, some gains may be made. The training programs offered by SNCTP have been more effective with health care paraprofessionals and health educators, who occupy positions of some influence within their agencies and communities. The reflections of Sa'adia Addaw Mohamed Nour, a nutritionist and health trainer in Sennar in central Sudan, show the far-reaching effects that training programs may have when the health care workers who participate continue as SNCTP volunteers and organize grassroots activities in their communities. Nour concludes by describing the stubborn obstacles campaigns to end the practice encounter.

I was born and bred in Karima Al-Bahar village in the eastern bank of the Blue Nile facing Sennar town in 1969. I have worked as nutritionist since 1992 with Sinnar Province based in Sennar town. I also work as a volunteer with SNCTP in Sinnar since I got my first training course in Sennar in December 1993. I attended a second advanced training course entitled Training of Trainers (TOT) in Wad Medanin in December 1993, which also included training on FGM. I'm single and currently living with my family, which is composed of my mother, brother, widowed sister, and her little daughter.

The training courses conducted by SNCTP . . . were turning points in both my conscience and my public activities. I found my true self in the campaign against FGM launched by SNCTP. I felt the campaign deep inside myself. Originally, apart from being a nutritionist, I'm an activist; I'm the Deputy President of the Women's Union in Sinnar province and the Finance Secretary of the Youth Association in our village.

The first thing I did with my friend Mona, who is also a nutritionist, was to inject all that we had learned in the SNCTP training into our regular nutrition program in the province. We usually have four training courses in nutrition every year for trainees from different departments.

The second thing I did was form a social and religious benevolent society in our village called "Peace be upon the Prophet" (Al-Sala a'ala-Al-Nabi). Its objective was to support one another in funerals and marriage ceremonies. I gradually injected messages against some harmful traditional practices and female circumcision into its agenda. Of course, we began by campaigning against extravagance in ceremonies and gradually moved into practices such as early marriage and female genital mutilation. Our preaching found good acceptance by the members and the village community at large. The training workshop influenced me very much, to the extent that I formed my own NGO.

As regards our collaboration with other grassroots NGOs in the pursuit of our objectives, we either receive an invitation from them or we send a request to them. In either case, we always find warm acceptance of the idea. In case we find some opposition to our ideas, we repeat our session with them. We always invite a religious leader to accompany us. He has been very convincing. Of course, he did not receive any formal training; but we trained him (because we received TOT).

The *daya* (midwife) in rural Sinnar attended the training course in Sennar with us. Because they taught us that circumcision is dangerous, she became more conscious. Every time somebody approaches her for circumcision she tells them they have to get permission from me. I usually try to convince them. If they refuse, I then tell the midwife to circumcise the girl sunna type—that is, only to cut the tiny upper part of the clitoris. I usually keep an eye on and closely monitor the circumcised girl and her family, because sometimes the mother changes her mind and recircumcises her daughter into the Pharaonic or intermediate type. After four months of close coordination with and supervision over her work, the midwife felt uncomfortable about this relationship. She sued me before the village Sheikh and the popular committee. Her main point was, why do I interfere in her work and attend every circumcision operation she performs? The Sheikh and the committee members supported me. Then gradually she changed and now she is practicing a mild sunna type of circumcision. She did not stop it completely because the people do not want to stop it completely but are willing to make a qualitative shift. If I insist on them stopping it completely, they will just reject my campaign and me altogether.

I think that here in the village the situation is very much different from Khartoum or Wad Madani or the other big towns where there are many educated people who are willing to accept the complete abandonment of FGM. Here in the rural areas such an objective is impossible to achieve.

After we got the training in both Sinnar and Wad Medani, my friend Mona and I started to approach some of the officials to facilitate our campaign in villages and town quarters. We were expecting them to solve our logistical problems since we don't have any funds. They were not cooperative. The only cooperative person was the head of the nutrition department in Sennar. He was always giving us a ride. Some of our friends and relatives are also very cooperative. They were offering their cars free of charge to take us to remote villages.

In July 1994, Ahfad University for Women through the Ministry of Planning and Investment organized a workshop entitled "Gender Incorporation in Development Planning." In that workshop, we decided to criticize the formal state's apparatuses and the top officials for their attitude of apathy toward our activities. Accordingly we composed a short play and played it in front of the audience. The Deputy Commissioner was present. . . . After that critical play, the officials changed their attitude towards us. The Provincial Executive Officer has directed his staff to support us and facilitate our campaign. The commissioner himself showed interest.

We have various strategies for distributing campaign messages. Apart from the formal lectures, we usually conduct group discussions on various occasions, such as marriage and funeral ceremonies and tea and coffee gatherings within the village or neighboring villages. For example, during the last nine months, we participated in five public events in Sennar. I personally participated in group discussions at twenty funeral ceremonies, eighteen marriage ceremonies, and four circumcision ceremonies (see also El Bashir n.d.: 22)

Although SNCTP does not compromise its stand against FGM, the campaign against the practice must be tailored to local circumstances and enlist community leaders.

As social and attitudinal change is often spearheaded by elites, the changing beliefs and practices of Sudan's modern, educated, prosperous elite in relation to FGM may well be influential. Among well-educated groups in major urban centers, as one person who was interviewed reported, "the practice of FGM is viewed by many as a symptom of backwardness [and] anti-modernity, and shameful." Some people now perform it only in secret and without ceremonies. In addition to the overall trend toward the sunna type, which is less harmful than infibulation, a new version called "funny" or "false" circumcision is being practiced. Called *lazga* (literally, plaster band circumcision), it involves only the placement of a plaster band around the labia majora as a symbol for the operation, intended to deceive the girl's relatives and perhaps the girl herself into thinking that an operation has taken place. In other cases, the midwife simply pricks the clitoris. These strategies of deception are adopted when the parents oppose

FGM but seek to avoid incurring the opposition of their relatives and others who insist on the practice.

The influence of SNCTP on the programs of government institutions, government-organized NGOs (colloquially known as GONGOs), grassroots NGOs, and international NGOs in the campaign against FGM has produced a promising proliferating and multiplier effect. The movement against FGM is now sustainable: spontaneous, continuous, and self-generating.

A variety of examples attest to the liveliness of this campaign at the grassroots level, even though SNCTP seldom has an ongoing presence in local communities after conducting training sessions. A monitoring system for the practice of FGM has emerged among activists and NGOs in some of the villages and towns where SNCTP or its offshoots have conducted sensitization exercises. Local groups or individuals approach SNCTP branch offices and activists to report cases of FGM in their communities. In some villages, volunteers have forced midwives and traditional birth attendants to practice only sunna circumcision under their direct supervision; care is taken to ensure that these girls will not be recircumcised into a Pharaonic type few days later. In many cases, the local community has prevented the midwife from practicing infibulation or group circumcision. Some communities, inspired by SNCTP volunteers, have formed their own grassroots organizations to eradicate FGM and enlisted the aid of local government. In Kosti province in central Sudan, top health and administrative officials had asked the local police to detain some traditional birth attendants and midwives for violating this new community norm. Attitudes have changed dramatically. In some villages in northern Sudan, where people threw stones at SNCTP campaigners and activists and called them "immoral" because they were talking publicly about FGM, three years later, they filed requests for SNCTP to open branch offices. The demand for sensitization workshops and publications from SNCTP often exceeds the supply. The considerable recognition that SNCTP has received from the ministries of health and social planning and from administrators at the state and provincial levels is also encouraging.

Indications of Change in Attitudes and Practices

Although systematic evaluation of programs and assessment of progress has not been done since the SNCTP began its intensive campaign, indicators of change in the prevalence of and attitudes toward female genital mutilation are visible in central Sudan. The decline in the general prevalence of female circumcision and the shift from infibulation toward sunna circumcision that is visible in some groups is counteracted, to some extent, by the recent adoption of the practice of FGM by some ethnic groups, especially those from the southern Sudan, Nubia, and West Africa, who have moved from areas where FGM is uncommon to areas where the practice is more prevalent. The adoption of FGM in any form by women who convert to Islam or marry Muslim men is particularly alarming.

The trends in the major cities, among younger women, and among the educated middle classes are quite encouraging. In a study conducted in 1992 among female pupils aged ten–fifteen years in the Khartoum International School, an exclusive primary school that serves the elite, 78 percent of pupils reported that they were not circumcised; since most had passed the customary age for circumcision, they would likely remain uncut. Although none of their mothers was illiterate, the mothers of the uncircumcised girls had significantly higher educational levels than those of the circumcised girls. Among the 22 percent of girls who were circumcised, 86 percent had the sunna type of procedure. These data indicate a strong correlation between the education of mothers and the decision to refrain from the circumcision of daughters.

Empirical clinical investigation was conducted on the actual type of circumcision found among 210 women at the delivery rooms in Khartoum, Khartoum North, and Umdurman maternity hospitals, and the data were analyzed by the socioeconomic status of the neighborhood. The survey revealed that the sunna type of circumcision is dominant in the areas with higher socioeconomic status, while the Pharaonic type is dominant in the lower-class and rural areas.

The education of parents is the most influential factor in the abandonment of FGM among young girls in Sudan. The decline in circumcision among young girls is evident in studies done at primary and secondary schools in Khartoum, Wad Medani, Sinnar, Kosti, and Atbara. A significant proportion of girls had passed the customary age of circumcision without being circumcised: the average was about 36 percent. The uncircumcised girls whose parents were illiterate came from ethnic groups that have traditionally not practiced female circumcision. But the main correlation was with parents' education, especially the mothers' educational level. Among those whose parents had acquired a university education, the percentage of uncut girls was much higher: over half with university-educated fathers and two-thirds of those with university-educated mothers were uncircumcised.

The practice of FGM in the Sudan is basically a function of women's subordinate position in society. The campaign against FGM should address the practice from this structural angle and link it to the empowerment of women, particularly through the education of young girls. Interestingly, parents from all educational levels attributed their decision to refrain from circumcising their daughters to the conviction that FGM is both harmful and non-Islamic. The influence of the mass media in raising the awareness of those parents is evident.

When high school girls aged fourteen–nineteen were asked about their intentions for the future, 83 percent said they did not want to marry early and 77 percent said they intended not to circumcise their future daughters. These girls are likely to get married within the next seven years, so they represent the society's future mothers. Compared to their own mothers, these girls have much greater access to information. In a question posed to high school girls in the states of Khartoum, River Nile, Gezira, and White Nile about the sources of their knowledge of the campaign against FGM, they responded that written materials (posters, pamphlets, and newsletters) and the media (particularly TV and radio) were the most important sources. Lectures and group discussions represent a less important source of information. The growing awareness among girls and young women in Sudanese schools portends well for the future.

Opposition to the Campaign Against FGM Within the Medical Establishment

Despite the gradual quantitative and qualitative changes in the practice of FGM in the Sudan over the past two decades, the campaign to eradicate it has encountered real difficulties. Analyzing these limitations and constraints offers valuable lessons for designing more effective campaigns in the future.

First, the medical profession in general and obstetricians and gynaecologists in particular include proponents as well as opponents of FGM. The central argument of the opponents of FGM in Sudan is that it is harmful and entails a risk of medical complications when girls grow into womanhood, including urinary and menstrual problems, difficulty in sexual intercourse, and complications in childbirth. Psychological trauma is often associated with the practice as well. These arguments represented the medical point of view that was central to the SNCTP campaign, along with the violation of the girl child's basic human rights to development, protection, growth, self-esteem, and self-realization.

The proponents of FGM from within the medical establishment make two main points. First, they assert that the theory that medical risks and complications arise from the procedure is unfounded in scientific evidence and without validity. They argue that, because there is no single, controlled study comparing circumcised and uncircumcised women, the proponents' argument is an activist campaigner's proposition rather than a scientific statement. Through their domination of the media and their ability to set new values and standards of modernity and gender sensitivity associated with opposition to FGM, this wing of physicians maintains, opponents of the practice were able to influence the objectivity of the medical profession.

Second, some prominent obstetricians, practitioners of other medical specialties, and university professors have spoken repeatedly and publicly about medical advantages purportedly associated with the practice of FGM. For example, they suggest that uncircumcised women are more liable to develop certain types of vaginal cancer than circumcised women. Unfortunately, at the height of the anti-circumcision campaign in 1995, this point of view found its way into the public media, along with a supporting religious statement. The same view had been expressed at the Cairo Conference on Population and Development. Although held by only a few medical professionals, this view is likely to influence medical students and younger medical professionals. These proponents of FGM represent a counter-campaign and pose a major threat to efforts to eradicate FGM. Furthermore, these views are often expressed within the broader framework of "authenticity" and the discourse of getting "back to the origins" that is articulated by the Sudanese Islamicist state.

Many front-line health workers express ambivalence toward the eradication of FGM. Some say that they are opposed to the practice in principle, but continue to perform it because it is a major source of income and, they suggest, they can ensure that the procedure entails less risk for the girl. As one trained nurse who has a lucrative practice in midwifery and circumcision repeatedly told me, "If I refused to do it some other untrained people will do it the worse way." However, this woman does all types of circumcision upon request. Such health professionals set a bad example for paramedical health visitors, midwives, and traditional birth attendants.

FGM is never taught in any of the medical or paramedical training institutions in the country. As a traditional practice, it is supposed to be practiced by only traditional practitioners, mainly traditional birth attendants. However, most of the paramedical staff, especially female nurses, midwives, and health visitors, are deeply involved in the practice. At least 90 percent of

circumcisions in urban areas are performed by "modern" paramedical workers. This represents a major source of frustration emanating from the medical establishment. Optimistic guesstimates suggest that only about 6 percent
of health care professionals and paraprofessionals who participated in training sessions have actually stopped the practice. Of course, economic factors,
especially the need for supplementary income since health care workers'
salaries are so low, and social factors such as community pressure support
the continuation of the practice. Yet the involvement of the paramedical staff
in the practice is implicitly supported and perpetuated by the legal apathy
and relaxation in the enforcement of the existing medical and legal rules regarding the practice of FGM.

In its campaign against FGM, SNCTP has to adopt a holistic and multidi-
mensional perspective, ranging from inventing alternative income-generating
activities for midwives and traditional birth attendants to the use of legal
mechanism to enforcement of the existing laws. SNTCP has sought the incorporation of instruction about FGM in the curricula of the national medical and paramedical training institutions.

The Ambiguous Stance of Islam Toward FGM

The position of Islam relative to female circumcision remains ambiguous
and controversial. Many Muslim leaders consider FGM a *makrama*, that is, a
teaching of lesser importance, rather than treating the practice as strictly
prohibited or anti-Islamic. This lack of clarity allows many interpretations to
be offered and permits a variety of opinions regarding the practice. The ambivalence among clerics is not solely responsible for the current confusion,
however. The high illiteracy rate among the population and the dominance
of popular versions of Islam mean that widely accepted views, rather than
clerical scholarship, shape public attitudes. Many traditional cultural practices have found expression and legitimization through relating them to Islam. It does not help that the Arabic word for circumcision, *tahara*, refers
both literally and metaphorically to purity and purification.

Modern Islamic scholars have been influenced by these overwhelming
popular misconceptions and constrained by the lack of innovative interpretations of the historical texts of Islamic jurisprudence in the light of the
progress of human achievements in all walks of life and in harmony with the
rhythm of time and history. Under such societal, structural, and intellectual constraints, the existence of a single hadith (a saying of the Prophet

Muhammad) supporting a limited form of FGM has caused a great deal of controversy. The renowned hadith of one of the prophet's female companions, Umn Atiya, reads "Akhfidhi wa La tanhiki" and literally means "Don't cut deep; cut at the surface of it." This teaching, which lends Islamic legitimacy to the practice, has never been strongly counteracted by modern Islamic scholars. Most scholarly statements about FGM say merely that it is a teaching of the third order—that is, the practice is Islamic, but not as binding an obligation for believers as first- and second-order Sunna. However, the three orders of Sunna lie along a continuum and, by implication, the most pious people observe the third-order commands. This notion creates a loophole for the religious campaign against FGM. Very few of the religious master trainers and activists within the SNCTP campaign say that the practice is *haram*, strictly prohibited by religion.

When this religious obscurantism is linked to the medical and professional stance of proponents of FGM, it may form a deadly alliance. SNCTP must work at the highest levels among those who crystallize religious opinions in order to arrive at a *fatwa* announcing a unanimous judgment against FGM. Since the stand of Islamic leaders remains ambiguous, trained paramedical people and other activists can avoid taking a strong stand against the practice. Instead, they pragmatically accept and sometimes even recommend *sunna* circumcision compared to the more harmful versions, such as infibulation.

Still, progress in this regard is possible. Religious leaders have been deeply influenced by sensitization workshops. Some wept while watching a documentary film showing the cruelty and horror of the practice. They might well weep for their own past neglect of the harms done by female genital mutilation, which contradict the fundamental message of Islam to respect and honor human life.

Eloquent testimony on this matter comes from the Imam of a mosque in Kosti town in central Sudan. Daw El beit El-Bashir is the Imam of Al-Hila Al-Gadida North (nicknamed *qhoba*). He also works as a freelance clerk, writing court applications for illiterate people in the town. His family consists of his elderly parents, his sister, his forty-year-old wife, and their seven children—four sons and three daughters—ranging in age from seventeen to one year old, all but the youngest of whom attend school. The Imam explained his views of the status of female circumcision within Islam.

In 1994 I was selected through the Religious Affairs Department in Kosti Province to participate in a training workshop on female circumcision organized by SNCTP. After the training workshop I was fully convinced of the health hazards and negative consequences associated with FGM and its irrelevance to Islam. I told my wife not to circumcise my daughter Amal who was then 9 years old and was due for circumcision. My wife refused, and was even surprised that such remarks came from me because I never objected about any of the older girls. Moreover, it is not part of our tradition or of any people we know not to circumcise girls. Circumcision of girls is taken for granted as something Islamic and appreciated by the culture. I told her I could not do something non-Islamic and harmful to my daughter. When my wife insisted, I told her that if she did so she had to leave the house, which effectively means she is divorced. Then she complied with my point, although without being convinced. Gradually I reflected to her what we learned in the workshop, and now she is convinced.

The Islamic principle is very clear: "No harm should be exerted on an individual from a presumably Islamic practice." The minute that harm is detected, then the practice is prohibited. This principle applies to more than female circumcision. For example, a specialized physician can tell a patient not to eat something because it harms you. According to the main principle of Islamic jurisprudence of "No harm," this food is *harem* (prohibited) for that individual. Islam respects science and scientists. We have seen material evidence through documentary films that FGM causes major health problems for the young girls and married women. Moreover, the Qur'an prohibits any changes in the natural state of the human body, especially if that is for beauty or sexual satisfaction as in the case of FGM.

During this month, I made two public speeches in the mosque about this issue. Women come to my house every other night to attend a Qur'anic teaching session and they regularly ask me about this issue. Many of them have been convinced. I think we are going slowly but steadily. . . . Women should be our target group; and a group of experts and religious leaders should organize special tours in every town to target women in particular. SNCTP should train the tribal leaders and native administration people in the countryside because of their role in effecting mass mobilization for the eradication of this practice.

One final word: I feel morally committed to the eradication of this practice. I'm ready at any time to stop anything and join any campaign for this humanitarian objective. (see also El Bashir n.d.: 21)

Committed clerics like this Imam, who teaches that there is an Islamic basis for the elimination of FGM, must play a central role in any effective campaign.

The Contradictory Positions of Traditional Birth Attendants and Health Educators

Although programs to train traditional birth attendants (TBAs) and midwives to abandon and oppose the practice of FGM have not been very effective, some practitioners have been influenced by formal midwifery training and by Islamic teaching to give it up and to advocate that others refrain from FGM as well. The shift in the practice of a traditional birth attendant who received formal training as a midwife that included direct instruction against FGM is documented in the narrative of Salima Khamis Karrar. Her account also analyzes the reasons for the persistence of this practice among displaced women and traditional birth attendants.

Salima Khamis Karrar is an energetic, forty-year-old women who lives in Dar Es-Salam, Omdurman. Because of the difficult events she has been through in her life, Salima looks much older than her age. The mother of six children, she lost her husband ten years ago and remarried two years later, in 1986. Since the devastating drought and famine of 1985, she has lived in a displaced camp in Omdurman. Her family includes Hawa'a Ali, a daughter who married at the age of thirteen and is currently living in Gezira, and Rabha, fourteen, Dar Al-Salam, thirteen, Maymouna, twelve, and Salman, nine, all of whom live at home and attend school. Haja Salima (her official title after she performed the *haj*, the pilgrimage to Mecca, in 1985) recalls her past with mixed feelings of nostalgia and remorse.

We had seen better days when we were stable in our *dar* (homeland) in El-Duweim as nomads. We had abundant milk, meat, honey, and sorghum we got through barter and the exchange of milk with the settled communities next to us. We never experienced hardship; everything was abundant, even the clean desert air and the green banks of the White Nile River. Our movement was as strict and systematic as a watch; we went into the plains of Kurdufan, and those of the Upper Nile and Gezira. Now everything is lost and we finally found ourselves in this barren land as beggars in the equally barren city of Khartoum. We lost everything because of the drought of 1985 and we are now displaced at the outskirts of Omdurman.

Although we were happy as nomads, we very ignorant of basic health and hygienic measures. Now we learned a lot by being in the city. You know sometimes being in a city has its advantages. Education and health services were completely absent among the nomadic communities; now we have these services available for us and for children here.

As you can see, the spacing period between all my children is just one year. We didn't know that could have any health effects or consequences for women. We thought the woman who delivers many children is both lucky (*bakheita*) and fertile— a good woman with a soft belly, as we believe in our own culture. In fact we never even thought that a woman could control when to become pregnant or give birth. We never heard of such things like contraceptives. We only heard of these things after we migrated to Khartoum as displaced and after I had been trained as a midwife in Omdurman to serve our displaced community.

I remember when I was pregnant with my last baby, Salman, I had a difficult time. The delivery was difficult delivery as well. Immediately after childbirth, I requested the doctor to "tie up the vein" (lit. to tie up the womb).

My mother, Mastoura Abdella Ali, was a trained midwife. When I was nine years old, I used to accompany my mother to both circumcision and delivery operations. I used to assist her; sometimes carrying a small lamp (*masraja*) for her and sometimes inserting the thread on the needle (for stitching women after deliveries) because she was growing old and she could not see well.

When I was 13 years old my elder sister Rabha was pregnant. She was in the last days just before giving birth to the baby. My mother was very anxious about her because she was very young, about 14 years old, and that was her first delivery. Such young girls are usually tied very tightly and are expected to have some difficulties during childbirth. One morning my mother went to the market to do some errands and requested us to keep an eye on my sister Rabha. While we were eating our breakfast, Rabha told me that she felt like going to the bathroom. She went and came back without doing any thing. She went inside the small hut and laid down quietly. I came in and started investigating her. I noticed that the baby was coming out. I immediately took the midwifery case of my mother, opened it, and started to recall the steps my mother used to do: Firstly, I inserted my finger in her *naffs* (lit. soul—vagina) and made a first cut upward. The baby didn't come out. Then I made another cut on her thigh near the vagina; the baby came out. My sisters came in and they were happy that I did it.

From that day I became a traditional birth attendant. I was also practicing Pharaonic circumcision. In the 1970s I started to use anesthesia for the circumcision by injecting the clitoris, and then eradicate the clitoris and cut the two labia from the deep bottom in one shot. Then I would make the stitching of the two sides of the labia to each other, leaving a very small opening that only allows the penetration of a matchstick. For us nomads, if the opening of the vagina is much wider than that, then that is bad circumcision, and we believe it is good neither for the husband nor for the wife.

I recall two important incidents that happened to me in the mid-1980s. First, when I went to Mecca to perform the *haj*, a religious leader (who was not Sudanese) gave us a lecture about female circumcision stressing that it is *haram*, prohibited, according to Islam. I really felt bad because I had been practicing it for more than 30 years. I prayed to Allah and asked him for forgiveness in that Holy Land. All sins are deleted during *haj*, especially if you are serious and genuine about your repentance.

The second incident occurred when I first came to Omdurman as displaced in 1985. Some of my relatives warned me that female circumcision in Khartoum is illegal and punishable by law. They told me to be careful in case I start practicing it. Although I brought new equipment for delivery and circumcision from Saudi Arabia, I decided to stop immediately. All the new equipment (the knife and scissors) I brought with me from Mecca I kept for delivery operations only. I attended a crash course on delivery for three months in El-Duweim town in 1984. Immediately after that came the drought and the famine and I accompanied my people who migrated to Omdurman. In Omdurman, they again selected me for the course on "modernization of the traditional birth attendant (TBA). I learned a lot from that training course: safe maternity, hygiene, and many things. I also learned a lot about the health hazards of FGM; I have been increasingly convinced. Unfortunately, some of our colleagues are still practicing it. A trained TBA from the Nuba Mountains is still practicing it. She gets £s 2000–3000 per girl (the equivalent of US$ 2–5). She is actually making a good living out of it. (see also El Bashir n.d.: 19)

This traditional birth attendant's account shows why efforts to convince trained health professionals and paraprofessionals not to practice FGM are seldom effective.

This problematic situation is also analyzed by a heath visitor in central Sudan. Although Amna Abd Allan Idirs no longer practices FGM, she is well aware that the practice continues among her peers.

My name is Amna Abd Allah Idirs; I was born and raised in Wad Medani town. I completed my middle school education and joined the nursing profession in 1964 when there was a general strike in the health services in the country. My father was very old and sick and he couldn't support us. I decided to work in order to support my younger brothers and sisters in order to continue their education. Thanks to Allah they are all educated now. I worked as a nurse for twelve years and then I was selected for health visitor's course. In 1977 I became Assistant Health Visitor and in 1980 I was promoted to Health Visitor.

In 1980 I started to practice female circumcision in the city for the first time. I was only circumcising girls of the upper class who can afford the high fee for the operation charged by a Health Visitor. In 1981 I joined the Blue Nile Health project. At that time I never got any formal or informal training about FGM; I just saw some of my colleagues were practicing it. One of the strong reasons to do it is, of course, the economic gain. In 1981, I circumcised a girl from a rich family who paid me about LS 20 in cash and about the same amount in kind (soap, perfume, sugar, etc.). At that time, my salary was about LS 79 per month; that means income accrued from the circumcision of one girl from a rich family amounted to about one-quarter of my monthly income. It was, frankly, quite appealing to circumcise girls. Poor families pay half of that paid by the rich, and they often go to midwives or TBAs rather than to expensive health visitors. During that time, I used to circumcise two or three girls per month; that means I used to get between half and three-quarters of my monthly income from circumcision. The business is seasonal, especially in urban areas, because people prefer to circumcise their girls during school holidays, particularly during the dry season.

During the period 1983–1989 when I was working in a small urban center about 40 kilometers to the west of Wad Medani, the price of circumcision dramatically increased from LS 50 to LS 100 and even to LS 1000. In 1989 my monthly salary was about LS 1300; that means, if I circumcised two or three girls per month, it doubled or tripled my monthly salary.

About 80 percent of my circumcisions used to be Pharaonic, since only a few educated people, and especially few men, request the sunna type. I remember a high school teacher who asked me to circumcise his two daughters and insisted on the sunna type. When he left, his wife asked me to do it the Pharaonic way, as "the Sunna, she believes, is no circumcision." I refused because was afraid that the father might check on his daughters and that might cause me some troubles. A year later, the woman had recircumcised her daughters in the Pharaonic type without the knowledge of their absent father.

Another incident I remember was that of a young girl in Wad Madani who was really frightened about the operation. We tried to convince her that the operation is simple, as it will just be Sunna. When I started to cut and, of course, it was painful, the girl screamed "No. No. I swear to Allah that is a real Pharaonic one."

Since I got training by SNCTP I completely stopped FGM and, in fact, I regretted that past experience very much. So far, during the past two years, I have trained more than 150 paramedical workers about female circumcision. (see also El Bashir n.d.: 33)

The Adoption of FGM by New Groups

In Sudan, the practice of FGM has been largely correlated with Islamic and Arabic affiliations. However, there is mounting evidence that as some non-Arabic and non-Islamic groups are incorporated into the majority's culture, through both assimilation and acculturation, they have embarked upon the practice of FGM. (This trend occurs elsewhere as well; for a case study in Chad, see Leonard 2000.) Both Christians and practitioners of indigenous religions within the Sudan, and Muslims of West African origin who did not practice FGM in their own country, have increasingly become involved. The evident preference of infibulation in some groups is particularly alarming.

The processes of cultural assimilation that lead to the adoption of female circumcision among migrant groups are visible among West African communities. Mayerno is one of the most famous and biggest West African settlements in central Sudan. The town is located in the eastern side of the Blue Nile at about 15 kilometers to the south of Sennar. It has a total population of about 20,000, mostly Fulani and members of other West African ethnic groups. Their history of migration into Sudan dates back to the late nineteenth century as supporters of the Mahdist movement, as agricultural laborers after the establishment of the giant Gezira scheme, and occasionally as pilgrims on their way to or from Mecca, the holy Muslim city in Saudi Arabia. In spite of the observed process of their acculturation and adoption of many aspects of the Sudanese-Arabic culture, Mayerno's population still preserves considerable Hausa-Fulani cultural practices, which distinguish them from the rest of the population in the region.

Khadiga Sajou, a forty-year-old woman, belongs to the third generation of West African migrants from Hausa land in north Nigeria. She started her paramedical career as a midwife in 1977, and in 1983 she became an Assistant Health Visitor. She worked in Mayerno and Sheikh Talha village on the eastern bank of the Blue Nile River in central Sudan. Through her work in health care, as well as through the active role she played in the social and political life of the village, Khadiga Sajo advocated the elimination of FGM. She discussed what was going on in relation to FGM in her own community.

In our indigenous traditional cultures, both Hausa and Fulani, women do not practice circumcision, and it is not part of the men's sexual taste either. We simply don't know it, and because we are Muslims that is another testimony for its not being Islamic. Fulani migrants into Sudan were able to maintain this tradition for just so long. During the last 30 years or so, a drive toward female circumcision has been in motion, especially for the Pharaonic type. (see also El Bashir n.d.: 30)

The figures Khadiga Sajou provided demonstrate this trend. In Mayerno, none of the women over the age of thirty-five years are circumcised. But the prevalence of circumcision is rising steadily among younger women. One-sixth of women aged twenty-five to thirty-five are circumcised, one-fourth of those aged eighteen to twenty-four are circumcised, three-quarters of those aged sixteen and seventeen are circumcised, and all of the girls between seven and fifteen are circumcised.

Khadiga Sajou explained:

That means circumcision has been very popular during the last 8 years or so in our community. Ironically, this is the time when the campaign against it was started in central Sudan by SNCTP. When I talk to women in the village health centre or in any ceremony in the community about the health hazards and future complications of FGM, they usually respond to me by saying: "how come female circumcision has only become bad when we started to circumcise our daughters?" Not only that: in Mayerno village, even grown-up girls at the age of 18–25 years come to me in my house and ask for private circumcision operations. Some of those grown-up girls are students in high schools and universities. It is also very common for grown-up girls to come and ask secretly for circumcision operations when they are betrothed and about to get married. In our village the performance of the operation has become part of the preparation for marriage. For the other non-Fulani communities that is not the case, because the girls are usually circumcised at the age of 6–8 years. Moreover, some women in our village ask me to circumcise them immediately after delivery. This is not recircumcision (*a'adal*) because they were not originally circumcised. For our women this is a new circumcision. Recircumcision (*a'adal*) is also common after the delivery. We practice it the same way other women practice in the neighboring communities. If a woman is not recircumcised after delivery other women will ridicule her. Not being tight is a symbol of slackness, and that means the woman is not meticulous and not taking care of herself, which could lead to the loss of her husband to another woman. The recircumcised woman is usually very proud of herself. Even her sisters, mother, aunts and close relatives feel proud of her.

The circumcision of adult women has caused many problems in our village. Let me tell you two stories that took place in the village in that connection.

Three years ago a man in the fourth quarter took a second wife. His first wife was very unhappy. Deep inside, she thought it may be because she is not sexually satisfying him. Maybe the man wanted a young woman with a tight vagina. Since she was uncircumcised, she immediately went to a midwife in the village and got circumcised into the Pharaonic type. When her husband came to her [when it was her turn] he realized the change [i.e., that she got circumcised]. He immediately divorced her because he believes that this practice is *haram*, prohibited according to Islam. Now she is living with her five children; of course, she cannot rectify the situation.

The second story is of a 22-year-old girl. She was engaged. The groom's family brought the gifts and did the betrothal. While the girl was kept on the house [in a period of confinement] waiting for the imminent occasion, she secretly went to a midwife in the Nile quarter and got circumcised. Immediately after marriage the groom brought the bride back from the honeymoon and divorced her in front of her family. He told them there must be something wrong with your daughter that caused her to get circumcised at this age and immediately before marriage. He suspected that the girl might have not been virgin. I personally think the girl might have been virgin; but it is almost a fashion among our girls here to get circumcised before marriage since they are not originally circumcised.

Unfortunately, we are going in the opposite direction. At the time when all the peoples in the nearby towns and villages have started to talk about health hazards and complications of the practice, we just got into it. (see also El Bashir n.d.: 30)

The same trend has been observed among the Nubian and southern Sudanese groups who have migrated to urban areas in central Sudan.

The testimony of a southern Sudanese midwife who lives and works in the Goz Al Salaam camp near Kosti town for southerners who have been displaced by the ongoing civil war is equally revealing. Members of her family, like other displaced southerners living in central Sudan, have been drawn into this practice despite her instruction about its complications.

In 1978 I was selected to join the midwifery school in Melekal. The midwives who came to train us from Khartoum told me that I have to get circumcised since I myself will be a midwife in the future. I was about to accept, but due to the unexpected sickness of my mother I quit the training program to sit next to my ailing mother. Now, 17 years later, I joined the midwifery school in Kosti in order to graduate after one year of training and be a certified midwife to serve the community of the displaced southerners in Goz Al Salam Displaced camp.

I was really surprised when they taught us this time in the midwifery school that female circumcision is bad and we shouldn't practice it. I told them it is Islamic; they said no, that is not true, that is only a wrong popular belief.

In my family we are very much mixed: My sister Nabita is a Muslim through marriage, I'm a Christian by birth, and my daughter Sua'ad is also a Muslim. Nabita became Muslim when she got married to a Muslim soldier in Malakal in the late 1960s. He became part of our family and he told my sister that they should circumcise me. My sister liked the idea and called the midwife, but I ran away and hid with my aunt for few days. When I came home they were laughing at me and accused me of being a coward for not daring to have a small operation like circumcision. So I never got circumcised until I grew up and got married to a Shilluk man and had my daughter Sua'ad.

Sua'ad became a Muslim through her uncle [my brother-in-law] Mubarak, who was a primary school teacher. She was living with him when she was young. He circumcised her with his daughters in 1980, and from that time she automatically became Muslim. Three years ago Suaa'd got married to a Christian man from the Shiluk tribe, but she is still Muslim. Now Sua'ad is living with us in Goz Al Salam displaced camp. (see also El Bashir n.d.: 26)

It seems reductionist to assume that the processes that lead to the adoption of FGM are related solely to Arabization and/or Islamization. Rather, it is safer to say that the adoption of FGM is a manifestation of acculturation assumed by the majoritarian culture of northern Sudan. How ironic that, just as the movement against FGM is making its way into the majority public, minorities are adopting the practice in their attempts to assimilate.

Men's Sexual Preferences and Power Relations in the Perpetuation of FGM

My field research indicates that FGM is more than just a cultural practice; it has far-reaching connotations and is associated with deep-seated dynamics at the personal, familial, and societal levels. In the Sudan, men's sexual culture favors a tightly circumcised rather than a loose vagina. Testimony collected in the field from married and unmarried women and midwives documents this preference. Women often express their fears of divorce and psychological or moral punishment from the husband if they are not circumcised or recircumcised immediately after childbirth (a practice known as *a'adal*). Some cases of divorce have occurred, even during the honeymoon period when husbands discovered that their wives were not circumcised. Many women who do not come from minority subcultures have been recently been initiated into the practice, especially after marriage or delivery.

A nurse related several stories of such women, including the daughter of a gynaecologist in central Sudan who chose to be circumcised after marrying at the age of twenty-five. Men's preference for tightly circumcised women would frustrate our efforts if circumcision just before or immediately after marriage were to become a trend.

For circumcised women, recircumcision is usually associated with valuable gifts from the husband of cloth, money, gold, and the like. The wife who is repeatedly recircumcised after childbirth in order to keep herself tight hopes that the practice provides a measure of security against her husband's taking another wife, which she fears would result in her being neglected and abandoned. Men's preferences and their ability to act on them have a strong influence on women's practice of FGM for themselves and their daughters.

Yet the matter is even more complicated, as considerable evidence indicates that female circumcision is often used by women to manipulate power relations within the household, which are generally characterized by a serious imbalance in favor of men. Within patriarchal cultures, women often resist domination by means of subterfuges which they carry out within their gender-specific domain. In the Sudan, although this matter is rarely stated explicitly, it is evident implicitly and circumstantially within the women's subculture that women intend to have a "tight circumcision" in order to make penetration difficult, both during the early period of marriage and after delivery. This situation has cultural and psychological implications that may be favorable to the woman. The husband who fails to effect a quick penetration "comes under the mercy of the wife," since his failure to penetrate implies his "sexual weakness." "The woman can almost blackmail the man for that." It is likely that he provides presents and gifts and sometimes grants a "delegation of powers" within the household with the hope that she will maintain "the fatal secret of his sexual failure to effect penetration." Although the prevalence of such a dynamic cannot readily be assessed, it seems to exist in some instances.

These explanations regarding the sexual preferences of men and the subversive strategies adopted by women stem from the deeply rooted dynamics of power within the culturally defined context of the household. These dynamics of male sexual tastes and women's attempts to manipulate the household power structure both arise from the imbalanced relationship of patriarchal domination, making patriarchy—whether imposed or subverted—a fundamental contributor to the perpetuation of FGM in the Sudanese society. Thus both the genesis and the perpetuation of FGM are related to the society's culture and structures of power. For this reason, the eradication of such harmful practices should be viewed through a holistic perspective, as part of an overall cultural transformation in society.

Relationships with Governmental and Nongovernmental Organizations

In its multilevel campaign to eradicate FGM in the Sudan, SNCTP has established links of cooperation and coordination with a variety of organizations and institutions. These relationships extend from the national level to local groups and international organizations. SNCTP has established working relationships with such international organizations as OXFAM USA, OXFAM UK, Radda Barnen, and Community Aid Abroad. These international organizations provide financial support to SNCTP, while multilateral agencies such as UNICEF provide expertise as well as funding. Within the Sudan, SNCTP has especially strong relationships with such organizations as the Da'awa Islamic Organization, the Babiker Badri Scientific Association for Women's Studies (BBSAWS), the Abu Gadoum Social Center for Women in Khartoum North, and the African Charitable Organization for Mother and Child Care.

SNCTP has been especially effective in its high-level work with government policymakers. Through lobbying and advocacy, SNCTP persuaded the government to adopt the strategic objective of eradicating harmful traditional practices within the National Ten-Year Plan of Action (Al Istratigia). The eradication of harmful traditional practices has become part and parcel of the work plans of the Ministry of Health and the Ministry of Social Planning. SNCTP benefits from the human resources, infrastructures, and logistical support of these two giant institutions. Many professionals have described the "revolutionizing effect" of SNCTP's injection of its programs into their institutions.

The national influence exercised by SNCTP has been facilitated by its close working relationship with international and multilateral organizations such as UNICEF. UNICEF sponsored Sudan's National Steering Committee for the Eradication of Harmful Traditional Practices and helps to fund and coordinate research studies as a basis for planning more effective campaigns. SNCTP's influence and inspiration on the national level is widely recognized, but because of what some call "professional tribalism," competition, or a "desire for empire building," SNCTP has been criticized by both UNICEF and NCEHTP "for not being cooperative and coordinating to the extent the country is partitioned in areas of jurisdiction among the two, SNCTP and NCEHTP, which itself a legal offshoot of SNCTP and its efforts." A recent arrangement specifies distinct geographical jurisdictions for SNCTP and the NCEHTP within the Ministry of Health; SNCTP is to campaign within Khartoum and the Central and River Nile states, while the NCEHTP is to campaign in Eastern, Western, Northern, and Southern Sudan. Within less than two years NCEHTP succeeded in sensitizing and training most of the midwives in Kordofan and Darfur states.

The Ministry of Health administers health and health education programs, the national AIDS program, and a special program on the modernization of traditional birth attendants, while the Ministry of Social Planning conducts many development-oriented activities. The aim in these relationships is to inject the eradication of harmful traditional practices into these institutions' agendas through training and influence on the planning process. The campaign utilizes all the institutional resources and logistical capacities of the Ministries of Health all over the country. At the state level, programs are run by senior medical staff who formulate policy and make decisions.

Through its leading position within the governing board of the Sudanese Council of Voluntary Agencies, SNCTP is in a position to influence policy formulation at this high level. The eradication of harmful traditional practices has been incorporated into the strategic objectives of these voluntary organizations, both national and international.

The campaign has indirectly influenced academic research in the field of FGM. One professor of Community Medicine reported to me that the SNCTP campaign has influenced scientific work to the extent that scholars cannot publish any research findings or take any professional stand against the strong and widely supported discourse of SNCTP. "Of course," he explained, "we do hold different views from that of the campaign, but we cannot utter them in public. They look odd and disgraceful."

Another potentially revolutionizing effect of SNCTP has been its influence on the religious establishment. The organization has gradually influenced the formulation of a *fatwa* or authoritative Islamic religion opinion on the practice. By sponsoring influential religious leaders, such as Professor Abdella Al-Tayib, to take a clear stand against female circumcision, SNCTP and other institutions working in the field are seating a religious discourse.

SNCTP's involvement with government and other national institutions has been strikingly effective in some respects, yet has had limited results in others. Through participatory rapid assessment, these institutions—along with other organizations with whom SNCTP works—were given the chance to speak their minds with respect to their relationships with SNCTP, its impact on their programs and the larger community, the constraints and shortcomings of our cooperative efforts, and indicators of change. In addition to government ministries and agencies, participants included the Abu Gadoum Social Development Centre for Women, Community Development Administration, and National Population Committee. These discussions led to several important recommendations. While SNCTP has been effective in raising awareness of harmful traditional practices and injecting the issue into these institutions' strategic objectives and regular activities, not all these efforts were as effective as their planners had hoped. Some participants believe that the awareness-raising campaign conducted in the media and though sensitization activities have seriously shaken traditional beliefs. Others think that NGOs and social reformers and activists have been more deeply affected than the general population.

SNCTP was criticized particularly for not adopting a systematic, scientific approach to the eradication of harmful traditional practices. SNCTP has no baseline data and does not conduct formative or summative evaluation research. SNCTP is highly centralized, with little or no delegation of powers to the lower levels of the organization. Cooperation and coordination with state-level government institutions is rather weak. The number of trainers available at SNCTP is insufficient to allow it to respond to requests for sensitization programs without delay. The language used by SNCTP trainers and sensitizers in public lectures is often too technical for illiterate members of the audience. These critical observations are especially valuable because they originate from cooperating institutions in the social and medical field which are in almost daily contact with SNCTP. "Had it not been for these" problems, one colleague commented, "SNCTP programs would have been better and their impact would have been more noticeable." Feedback from colleagues in cooperating institutions is especially helpful in improving these programs' effectiveness.

One prominent NGO official commented that "SNCTP is maintaining stronger relationships with government institutions than with the grassroots . . . this makes SNCTP look more like a GONGO rather than an NGO." SNCTP needs to be more people-oriented and pay more attention to grassroots organization in pursuing its strategic objectives.

SNCTP cooperates actively with local NGOs campaigning against FGM, but most of these programs are carried out on ad hoc basis rather than being institutionalized. SNCTP offers training, distributes publications such as pamphlets and posters, and sometimes conducts sensitization activities in form of lectures and group discussions. Among the NGOs with which SNCTP works are the Sudanese Red Crescent (SRC), particularly its program for women; the Sudanese Family Planning Association (SFPA); the Women's Youth Association, a branch of the National Youth Association; and the Sudanese Women's Union. The chain and multiplier effects of SNCTP training of NGOs are quite noticeable. In the Sudanese Family Planning Association, for example, at least 3000 of its volunteers have got the message through internal training and sensitization. The message has been smoothly incorporated within their strategic objectives and work plans. SFPA has recently formed a National Network for Population and Development of which SNCTP is a member. They regularly campaign against harmful traditional practices using SNCTP materials in all their branch offices in most of the Sudanese cities. However, the cooperative relationship is limited by the fact that SNCTP branch offices often lack a sufficient supply of materials and do not accomplish smooth and systematic coordination.

Relationships with other NGOs in the field, such as SRC, the Women's Youth Association, and the Women's Union, are improvised rather than institutionalized. Some of these organizations are continuously requesting materials and lectures to be conducted by SNCTP resource persons. The SNCTP should seek to develop sufficient training capacity within these organizations to reduce their dependence. Some of these organizations, especially the Women's Union and the Women's Youth Association, are critical of the fact that "they have more of a personal rather than institutional relationship with SNCTP."

At the provincial level and in rural areas, various relationships exist between NGOs and SNCTP. SNCTP provides materials for exhibitions organized by regional and local organizations. For example, in less than a year, SNCTP branch office in Wad Medani had participated in more than 50 such exhibitions. SNCTP volunteers in Sinnar and Kosti have magnificent relationships with grassroots organizations. In Sinnar two active volunteers have conducted more than 60 sensitization activities in collaboration with the local NGOs. In Kosti, where an almost institutionalized relationship has been established with Working Women Union, two volunteers are conducting one or two activities per day in work places.

Thus, despite shortcomings which are normal in this stage of development, SNCTP's relationship with grassroots and government-organized NGOs is a positive one and shows great potential for the future sustainability of the campaign. All these organizations have described both direct and indirect effects of the relationship with SNCTP on their institutional orientations and programs. As part of its advocacy and lobbying effort, SNCTP as one of the most focused organizations in the Sudan, has succeeded in sensitizing these organizations and securing support for its campaigns. Programs promoting the eradication of FGM and other traditional practices harmful to women have been brought to the forefront of their funding priorities. Although this impact is indirect, it is clearly recognizable and socially powerful.

Chapter 8

The Babiker Badri Scientific Association for Women's Studies and the Eradication of Female Circumcision in the Sudan

Shahira Ahmed

Since efforts against female circumcision are proving futile, women themselves must now take the initiative. For it is they who suffer the effects in their daily lives and their social status as mothers and leaders in the community.

—Yusuf Badri, 1981

Throughout much of northern Sudanese history, female circumcision remained a taboo subject that was not addressed publicly. It was a ritual performed by women on women, and for a long time it was hard for local communities to fathom why certain groups campaigned to abolish it. This traditional rite, passed on with pride from generation to generation, uplifted the status of the circumcised girl to a respectable, marriageable woman, and the event was conducted with much fanfare and honor. The first serious waves of resistance began at the turn of the twentieth century when a few religious leaders and politicians, both Sudanese and British, began to speak out against infibulation, known locally as Pharaonic circumcision.[1] In 1946, the government finally passed legislation that outlawed infibulation and made performing it punishable by a fine and imprisonment. Unfortunately, opponents of the law attacked it, claiming it was only an effort by the colonialists to undermine Sudanese culture and traditions. Although the law increased awareness of the issue and has not been revoked by later governments, the practice did not diminish. The period following the Second World War brought a growing women's movement, development programs, and increased education, which renewed interest in the issue. The efforts and objectives of those working against female circumcision have been diverse, however, and ranged from supporting medicalization of the practice to abolishing all forms of it.

A survey conducted between 1996 and 2000 by the Sudan National Committee on the Eradication of Harmful Traditional Practices (SNCTP) and Save the Children Sweden estimated the prevalence of female circumcision at 87 percent among urban women and 91 percent among rural women in northern Sudan (U.S. Department of State 2001). In urban regions, and to a lesser degree in rural areas, women born after 1980 were likely to be subjected to one of the less severe forms of circumcision, rather than infibulation. (For more information about the practice in the Sudan and the work of the SNCTP, see El Bashir, in this volume.)

In the past several decades, many nongovernmental and governmental organizations, in addition to local, regional, and international institutions, have taken on the challenge of addressing female circumcision in all its complexity. Opponents argue that it inflicts unnecessary suffering on women of all ages. Anti-female circumcision campaigns are faced with a practice that remains deeply embedded in society's sense of tradition, honor code, and sexual identity. These efforts have been various, reflecting differing agendas, mission statements, and values. A wide range of activities have been conducted by various agencies and organizations. Major Sudanese groups involved include Physicians in Obstetrics and Gynecology; the Medical Association; the Higher Nursing College; the Sudan Family Planning Association; the government's Department of Social Welfare; the Maternal and Child Health Service of the Ministry of Health; the Sudanese Women's Union; and the National Committee for the Eradication of Female Circumcision, sponsored by the Ministry of Internal Affairs. The Babiker Badri Scientific Association for Women's Studies (BBSAWS), under the patronage of Ahfad University for Women, emerged as an eminent force in calling for an integrated, unified campaign to tackle female circumcision. This essay highlights the work of this group, translating some of the materials BBSAWS has produced and exploring the principles and strategies that shape its campaign against the practice.

We begin with a story from a booklet produced by BBSAWS and UNICEF as part of their joint campaign to eradicate female circumcision.

Bakheeta lives in a small village on the outskirts of Khartoum in the Sudan. She left school after completing grade six and stayed home to help her mother with the house chores. Several years later she married her first cousin Ibrahim and moved in with his family. She joined a class in the village that teaches women how to read and provides them with information on how to take care of their families and children. Bakheeta soon became pregnant and she carefully followed all the instructions she received in her class in order to have a strong and health baby. She made sure she ate vegetables and drank two glasses of milk a day. She also went to the clinic twice a month.

Bakheeta and Ibrahim were happily looking forward to the birth of the baby. The day came when Bakheeta told Ibrahim that she thought the baby was on its way. Ibrahim hurried to fetch the midwife, who agreed the baby was going to come soon. He jovially rushed to let their families and neighbors know and they quickly rushed to Bakheeta's side. Bakheeta's contractions grew, but she was showing signs of distress. Her mother began to worry and told the midwife that maybe it would be wise to take her to the clinic. The midwife brushed her worries off and told her it's normal for a new mother to take some time before she delivers. After a while Bakheeta's screams became anxious and agonized. The midwife finally told Ibrahim and her mother that they should get her to the hospital. At the hospital, the doctor rushed her into the operating room but she bled profusely. Finally the doctor came out and told them the sad news that Bakheeta had died. Her mother started to cry and blamed the doctor for killing her daughter. She wished that she had never taken Bakheeta to the hospital.

The doctor compassionately said to her, "But it was you who caused her death." This shocked Bakheeta's mother, who asked how that could be. Bakheeta had bled because she was circumcised, the doctor explained. He told the shocked and confused mother, "Hasn't God told us in the Qur'an that He created Man in an ideal state? So we should not then remove an organ that God has surely created for a purpose!"

"Son," the shocked mother said, "I have not heard of circumcision killing anyone before; everyone I know, including myself, is circumcised and we are doing fine."

"But it is a well-known fact that circumcision has many harmful physical, social, and psychological effects," the doctor replied. He went on to list and explain the harmful effects, until Bakheeta's mother was convinced that she should not let any of her grandchildren be circumcised. She asked the doctor how she could help wipe out the practice and bring awareness to the rest of the village. The doctor urged her to tell Bakheeta's story, exposing how circumcision cut her life short. (*The Story of Bakheeta*, BBSAWS 1997)

This fictionalized narrative draws on the experiences of the many circumcised women, their families, and health service providers in the Sudan. Although death is one of the most extreme consequences of female circumcision, this story eloquently describes a community and circumstances Sudanese people can relate to. The harmful ramifications of female circumcision are highlighted through the series of events and ensuing dialogue. The simplicity of the language makes the message clear and powerful.

This booklet is part of a comprehensive campaign led by the BBSAWS to abolish one of the most persistent afflictions of women in Sudanese society. This campaign to eradicate all forms of female circumcision began three

decades ago. BBSAWS has succeeded in putting together one of the first unified movements to break the silence on the harmful effects of female circumcision in the Sudan and the neighboring countries where the practice remains
prevalent. BBSAWS's pioneering initiative integrates the health, legal, psychosocial, and religious debates surrounding female circumcision.[2] By translating selected material from the organization's awareness booklets, interviews,
and workshop proceedings, I bring to light the strategies adopted by the organization as well as the obstacles it faces, stressing the complexity of tack-
ling a practice that is deeply embedded in the society's sense of cultural
tradition. The selections also provide a description of the reasons and justifications given in relation to female circumcision by local people with various
backgrounds and outlooks. I hope that, through profiling this organization,
the lessons learned and best practices used by BBSAWS will serve other
grassroots organizations working in female circumcision eradication campaigns and provide insight for international organizations on how best to
support local efforts.

The Vision of Babiker Badri

The Babiker Badri Scientific Association for Women's Studies was launched
in 1979. The Ahfad University for Women, the oldest and largest private university in the Sudan, houses the organization and supports its work. The
man for whom the group is named, Sheik Babiker Badri,[3] founded the first
elementary, intermediate, and secondary schools for young women in the
Sudan. Ahfad University publications succinctly tell the story of this pioneer.

Following the battle of Omdurman[4] in 1898, when the Anglo-Egyptian army deci-
sively defeated the Sudanese nationalist forces, a young Sudanese survivor of that
battle, Babiker Badri, journeyed up the Blue Nile and settled in the village of Rufu'a.
There he opened a secular school, as opposed to the traditional religious schools, for
boys. Babiker was a deeply religious man and widely respected for his knowledge of
the Qur'an, but he also had the radical idea that even girls should receive at least a
minimum education so they could provide more companionship to their husbands.
The fact that Babiker had thirteen daughters as well as some sons may have influenced his views. In 1904, he asked the British authorities for permission to open an elementary school for young women. Fearing a negative popular reaction because of
the radical nature of this request, the British Commission of Education for Sudan denied it. A similar request in 1906 was also denied. But Babiker was a determined man,
as the British were to learn. His request was finally granted by Sir James Currie,

Director of the Educational Department of the British administration of the Sudan at that time. In granting approval, Sir James noted that "I would myself prefer that the government should not undertake the task—girls' education—for some time, but I cannot see that any possible harm can come out of starting something here (at Rufu'a)." Finally, in 1907, Babiker began his secular school for girls in a mud hut with nine of his own daughters and eight of those of his neighbors. (Ahfad University 2002)

From this humble beginning, the Badri family has nurtured private education in Sudan for over three generations. Babiker's son, Yusuf, carried on his father's work, and in 1966 he established the Ahfad University for Women in Omdurman, which is across the White Nile from Khartoum. Beginning with only 23 students and a faculty of three, including Yusuf Badri, by the end of the twentieth century Ahfad University had an enrollment of over 4,600 students and 157 full-time and 34 part-time faculty members.

The Mission of BBSAWS

BBSAWS currently conducts its work under seven different program areas: Women and Development; Environment and Appropriate Technology; Women, Law, and Peace; Training and Advocacy; Family and the Child; Information and Research Office; and a Humanitarian Office (BBSAWS 2002). The organization's overall mission is to address issues affecting Sudanese women, encourage research on their social status, and seek ways of effectively applying research findings. It has successfully carried out various projects that include setting up training centers for women and kindergartens in rural areas and producing educational materials on issues involving legal rights, human rights, and conflict resolution. The association has also funded and produced films (*Our Village Calls Us* and *Dura Bride*) that have been well received at local and international forums.

Female circumcision represents one of the main concerns tackled by BBSAWS since its inception. One of the first accomplishments of the organization was the establishment of the Committee on the Eradication of Female Circumcision. This committee's plan of action was to conduct national and international workshops and conferences on female circumcision, run media campaigns advocating eradication of the practice, and produce awareness and advocacy material on the subject.

National and International Workshops

The 1979 WHO seminar on "Traditional Practices Affecting the Health of Women and Children," held in Khartoum, Sudan's capital city, put female circumcision on the global agenda and provided the impetus for the campaign in the Sudan.[5] In 1981, BBSAWS organized a national workshop titled "Female Circumcision Mutilates and Endangers Women—Combat It!" in Khartoum (BBSAWS 1981). The workshop sought to put forth strategies and recommendations based specifically on the Sudanese context with the ultimate goal of totally eradicating all forms of female circumcision in the country. To guarantee involvement of all segments of society, BBSAWS sent invitations to over 23 grassroots, governmental, academic, and community organizations and agencies and established an executive organizing committee comprised of 40 people representing these different institutions to coordinate the workshop. The outcome was a comprehensive, three-day agenda with broad participation from across Sudanese society. Experts from other countries were invited to contribute their insights on the challenges they faced and their successful practices that might be suitable to Sudan.

The workshop began with speeches from Asma Abdul Raheem El Dareer, one of the leading voices and researchers on female circumcision in the Sudan (see El Dareer 1983), and Khaled Hasan Abbas, the Minister of Health at the time. Participants then heard from obstetricians, gynecologists, psychiatrists, social scientists, and religious leaders, who offered a concise and thorough picture of what makes female circumcision a harmful tradition threatening girls and women in the places it is practiced. During the next two days, through a series of discussions and debates, participants presented their insights and recommendations. For the first time, Sudanese women and men heard one another describe the extent to which female circumcision had influenced their lives. The importance of research that identifies appropriate and effective methods sensitive to local attitudes was stressed. Participants discussed the importance of highlighting the physical and psychosocial dangers of female circumcision and of dispelling misconceptions about religious views on the practice. Participants arrived at a consensus that any campaign must promote the complete eradication of all forms of female circumcision, not just infibulation. As these translated excerpts from the workshop proceedings (BBSAWS 1981) indicate, women from different backgrounds and educational levels offered their personal insights on why reasons the practice continues to be prevalent and how it can be addressed.

Alawia Abdul Faraj (from southern Sudan): I am a mother of two uncircumcised girls. And this is not because I am from the South, but because I personally suffered from circumcision. My education helped me a lot. I followed the teachings of the Prophet Muhammad and my husband also supported me in this decision. The time has come for all of us to tackle this problem seriously, not only in Khartoum but in all parts of the country. People living far from the city may rush to circumcise their girls if they hear of this workshop. So awareness is more important than passing laws. I would also like to address a point made by one of the participants that there might be some benefits to circumcision. They say that circumcised girls or recircumcised women find more pleasure with their husbands and that the husbands have more pleasure too. The women that I know say it is the men who ask for this. And as all women know, if someone wants to marry an uncircumcised girl, they will say she is not a virgin. I want to be frank and tell you what I know. These days in the big cities like Khartoum and Madani, some girls have sex before getting married. Then they go get recircumcised a few days before their wedding day. The poor husband never finds out. So I say this should be a good reason to stop circumcision because it doesn't stop these girls from anything. It would be better to focus our attention on the moral upbringing of our girls instead. I start by telling my girls that their private parts are private and should not be touched but be saved for special times. Then we have to continue education in the schools and I don't think anyone will stray after this. In the South, the girls walk the cattle with the boys until the ages of 15 and 16 and never have sexual relations before getting married.

Nadia (medical student): As part of a study we conducted in school, we visited several rural areas and conducted interviews. It was striking that in every single village people were immediately untrusting and said, "You are from the medical school, which means the government sent you and is going to ban female circumcision." So they rush and circumcise the girls in fear of the impending law. We tried all the time to explain that we have no relation to the government and that we only wanted to get their points of view on the practice. So I think it is more productive to focus on awareness and not on passing laws.

Awatif Ahmed Othman (Dean of the College of Nursing): I am pleased that we are finally discussing this subject openly. I have three sisters and 20 years ago I had to convince my family that they should not circumcise them. My sister, now 30 years old, was unlucky. At the age of 16, she got engaged when I was out of the country. Her friends convinced her that her fiancé would leave if he found out that she was uncircumcised. Sadly, I must tell you it was a doctor that circumcised her. Thankfully, my other two sisters, now 28 and 24, were convinced and followed my advice. Since so many of you have spoken candidly about your experiences, I will too. The problem that we faced with my sisters was how to tell their prospective husbands that they were not circumcised after they had paid their dowry and a wedding date had been set. I had to face them and their families with this news. It was difficult for me as a Sudanese woman to discuss this topic with these men and ask them if they accept this. But it was easier than expected. Especially for the youngest sister, because her husband was religious and accepted the news without any difficulty. I also have a 14-year-old daughter who is not and will never be circumcised. As for my role as the Dean of the Nursing College, it is a position I have held since 1962. There is a program at the college that teaches the harmful effects of circumcision. I have to say it was difficult when I first started since I was close in age to my students, but I still teach the course today.

Throughout the first two days of the workshop, women of all ages from different backgrounds told their stories for the first time. Men and women alike were receptive to hearing what had been considered inappropriate to discuss just a few years earlier.

Over 150 participants at the closing session signed a plea that committed them to integrate education about female circumcision into their work and make eradication a priority in all future efforts. The organizing committee was to undertake the weighty task of launching a unified national campaign against female circumcision. The plea signed by all attendees read as follows:

Agreement to Eradicate Female Circumcision

Whereas, we have closely studied the impact of female circumcision and its harmful effects and heard the viewpoint of religious leaders, medical and psychosocial professionals, We the participants in the workshop, "Female Circumcision Mutilates and Endangers Women—Combat It!" organized by the Babiker Badri Scientific Association for Women's Studies, held in Khartoum from 8 to 10 March 1981, agree to fight this harmful tradition, which mutilates the appearance of what God has created and harms women both physically and mentally, thus putting their lives in danger. By unequivocally renouncing the practice of female circumcision, we commit ourselves to employ all the intellectual and physical resources available to us to fight this harmful tradition. We commit to becoming role models and educators for our families, neighbors, and communities. We pledge our commitment by signing this document. (BBSAWS 1981)

This declaration represented the inception of the mass campaign against female circumcision in the Sudan.

In October 1984, BBSAWS organized another, more structured workshop drawing participants from 24 African countries and international observers from the Netherlands, United Kingdom, Sweden, Germany, Switzerland, France, and Kuwait. The workshop was titled "African Women Speak on Female Circumcision." The published proceedings (BBSAWS 1984) identified its objectives:

1. To bring together all African women to share information and develop measures for the eradication of female circumcision.
2. To form a unified perspective on the issue.
3. To develop initiatives promoting self-esteem, confidence, independence and self-assertiveness to tackle this major issue.
4. To disseminate information on research and action.
5. To establish joint efforts and networks among African countries where female circumcision is practiced.

Another important objective of the workshop was to put together a unified and clear statement to the United Nations' Women's Decade Conference and the Nongovernmental Organizations Forum held in Nairobi in July 1985.

The workshop was lauded as a great success, providing a forum for African experts to come together to share information on the impact of female circumcision. At this important juncture, during the United Nations Decade for Women, there was growing international interest in efforts to eradicate the practice. Reports were presented by representatives from Djibouti, Egypt, Eritrea, Ethiopia, Gambia, Ghana, Kenya, Liberia, Mali, Nigeria, Sierra Leone, Somalia, Sudan, and Togo. Grassroots advocates and their international supporters were able to assess the types of circumcision practiced in each country, prevalence rates in different regions of each country, measures underway to eliminate the practice, and approaches that proved effective and could be adapted by other countries.

The recommendations and resolutions passed at these proceedings were groundbreaking. Participants "unanimously agreed that female circumcision is a violation of human rights, an encroachment on the dignity of women, a debasement of women's sexuality, and an unwarranted affront on the health of women" (BBSWAS 1984). At the end of the week, a detailed Plan of Action was drawn up that included recommendations for research, public awareness, integration of efforts addressing female circumcision into existing programs and projects, and mobilization at all levels to conduct comprehensive campaigns against the practice. Countries were urged to adapt the plan to fit local needs and conditions, and statements and letters were drafted to sensitize governments and regional and international agencies to support eradication campaigns. Participants unanimously passed a resolution asking African women to take the leading role in addressing the issue of female circumcision at the United Nations Nongovernmental Organizations' Forum. They recommended that non-African women's "contribution be incorporated as additional support to African women's campaigns on eradicating female circumcision. This statement followed the themes of the United Nations Decade for Women—Equality, Development and Peace" (BBSWAS 1984).

- It was recommended that the goal of all African women should be the *total eradication* of all types of female circumcision.
- Following the lack of evidence for a religious basis for practicing female circumcision, all religious connotations in the practice, such as referring to clitoridectomy as "Sunna" in some countries, should be abandoned. Campaigns should approach Islamic religious leaders to clarify this position to locals.
- Substitute events and rituals should be devised to replace practicing female circumcision as a rite of passage for girls into womanhood in the community. This is now commonly referred to as the "alternative rite of passage."
- Influential players at the local and international level should be drawn in to support eradication campaigns.
- Anti-female circumcision components should be integrated into all existing and new programs targeting women and development. Consequently, agencies involved in FGM and other women's issues should establish coordination and communication channels.
- A mass media campaign is critical for public awareness at all levels of the community.
- Approaches established should be sensitive to local and national needs. Thus it is critical to involve local circumcisionists, health workers, social workers, religious leaders, decision makers, educators, role models, parents, and members of the medical profession.
- Every attempt should be made to pass laws, or enforce existing ones, to ban the practice and penalize perpetrators.
- African women, under the umbrella of the Inter-African Committee, must mobilize international support for the eradication of female circumcision emphasizing the practice within a context of human rights, development, and well-being. The Inter-African Committee was assigned the task of monitoring and evaluating the progress of the various country campaigns. (BBSAWS 1984)

Media Campaigns and Advocacy Material Calling for Abolition of Female Circumcision

Through the years, BBSAWS has produced many posters, handouts, and booklets that target different segments of society to increase awareness of the negative physical, mental, and social effects of circumcision. These educational materials were written by local experts on female circumcision, and most were pilot-tested on students and medical professionals before being widely circulated in the capital city, Khartoum, and the surrounding regions.

The introduction to a popular question-and-answer booklet published by BBSAWS and UNICEF in 1997 reads:

Female circumcision is the most harmful practice adopted by Sudanese society throughout the ages. It is ironic how societies from which this custom was supposedly inherited from no longer practice female circumcision. Unfortunately, this harmful practice continues in our country even though its impact on the lives of women cannot be justified by religious, medical, or psychosocial arguments. It is therefore critical to conduct research and present studies to pinpoint the different contexts that interplay in promoting this harmful practice. Thus as part of a series of programs to fight female circumcision by the Babiker Badri Scientific Association for Women's Studies, this booklet is an effort to present the answers to frequently asked questions on the practice. This booklet is a product of a field study conducted in several urban and rural areas of the Sudan by the organization and the Ahfad University for Women, as part of its Reproductive Health program. The questions were collected during focus group discussions and the answers were prepared by experts in the field. ("You ask About Female Circumcision and the Babiker Badri Association responds," BBSAWS 1997)

In addition to printed materials, the organization successfully recruited influential local leaders and doctors to conduct public lectures and to appear on various media outlets.[6] Visual material was creatively produced which brought the realities of female circumcision and the challenges addressing it entails to an international audience.

The Campaign's Religious Perspective

Both the groundbreaking workshops conducted in the early 1980s by BBSAWS were characterized by a strong presence of Muslim and Christian clergy, which refuted common perceptions that female circumcision had a religious basis. Although some religious leaders had come out against the practice before, these workshops succeeded in merging the religious perspective with that of the health and psychosocial scientists, which proponents of female circumcision usually dismissed as too secular. Religious leaders began to corroborate their standpoints with evidence established by health and social experts.

The question-and-answer booklet published by BBSAWS and UNICEF ("You ask about Female Circumcision and the Babiker Badri Association responds," BBSAWS 1997) dealt extensively with the religious perspective:

Does a young man have the right to ask whether his prospective bride is circumcised or not?
Yes, it is acceptable for a young man to ask this question. Religious experts agree that since customs allow prospective couples to inquire about each other's physical and moral traits before marriage, this question would also be proper. The Prophet Muhammad has taught us that people should not be shy in asking about intimate issues that affect their lives. For example, a woman once asked the prophet, "Women have sensuous dreams just like men, so should they perform ablution?"[7] He answered that they should.

Is it true the uncircumcised young woman has insatiable sexual needs?
No, this is untrue. It is important to understand that sexual needs are not related to whether someone is circumcised or not. Sexual cravings originate from physiological and hormonal changes and the resulting behavior depends on this individual's environment, values, and upbringing. Therefore, female circumcision does not protect from infidelity.

Experts claim that female circumcision deforms a woman and have backed this up by referring to the verse from the Holy Qur'an that states, "And we have created man in the best form." On the contrary, they justify male circumcision. How can you explain this contradiction?
We don't see any contradictions. There are several sources that we can refer to, including the one mentioned in the question. Another verse states, "It is We Who created you and gave you shape,"[8] and the Prophet Muhammad said, "God is beautiful and loves all that is beautiful." The Prophet has also asked us not to do anything that will lead to suffering. These sources support the argument against female circumcision. But experts have not found similar bases to disallow male circumcision. Many studies have been done that prove the medical benefits of the practice and have shown it to have no harmful side effects on men.

Should opponents of female circumcision call for the prohibition of all forms of the practice?
Yes, all forms of female circumcision should be eradicated. Islamic teachings stipulate that if there is no Qur'an verse or Hadith[9] to elucidate an issue, then individuals and communities must decide what is in their best interests. The Prophet has said, "You

are more informed on the issues of your community." Thus, we have to use our judgment on female circumcision. If people strictly follow doctors' orders when they get sick, why should it be different for female circumcision, whose harmful effects have been distinctly identified?

Thus, along with refuting popular misconceptions regarding religious sanctions for the practice, religious arguments were used to support calls for its abolition.

The information in the educational materials produced by BBSAWS was composed from direct interviews with religious leaders or adapted from the discussions at meetings and workshops that the organization convened. As the following excerpts from workshop proceedings show, Muslim and Christian clerics and scholars consistently spoke out against female circumcision and provided evidence to dispel beliefs that religion endorses it. The excerpts are translated here in detail to present a thorough account of the different religious justifications used, which may be employed in future advocacy efforts.

Sheik Sideeq Abdul Hay, President of the Religious Legislation Council: By considering the different levels of Islamic thought, female circumcision is not a compulsory, duty-bound, or recommended practice in Islam. Therefore, abandoning female circumcision will not be considered as violating any religious laws or *shariah*.[10] On the contrary, it can be argued that God has created every organ for a specific purpose and mutilating any organ is defying the sacredness of God's creation.

Sheikh Khalaf Allah Omar Ibrahim, Head of Mosques and Religious Affairs: There are no Hadiths that prohibit male circumcision and research has proven there are valid medical reasons behind the practice. However, there is no similar research to show similar importance for women. But there are documented cases of female circumcision being used to hide infidelity. It has also been shown to be harmful to women during intercourse and delivery and this would thus contradict the Hadith stating, "Do not harm or reciprocate harm."

Father Fayloufous, Egyptian Priest: There is no reference whatsoever to female circumcision in the Bible, in both the Old and New Testaments. Jews and Christians in all parts of the world have not practiced female circumcision throughout the ages and civilizations. The early Egyptians, however, followed this practice and passed it on to their descendants, both Muslim and Christian, in the region. The practice has become deeply imbedded in the cultures of these communities regardless of their religion.

In the past several years there has been an awakening in international and national arenas to issues of women's and children's rights. Scientists and experts have taken on the critical agenda of eradicating female circumcision after being fully convinced of its many harmful effects. Research has to continue for further under-standing of its impact and ways to address them.

There is no justification for the practice in Christian teachings. Since it involves the removal of parts of or all the genital organs of the woman, this deforms the ap-pearance of what God has created. Genesis 34:1 states that God has created both males and females in their best forms. God has created all humans by His Will and each human being is complete in the form that he has been born with. So is it right for humans to then interfere with God's creation and deform it?

Another misconception is that female circumcision protects young women's chastity. This notion is not in alignment with Christian teachings that are based on morals and values. We do not gain virtue by bodily harm or oppression, but through our will and steadfastness to a life of moral integrity. Therefore a young woman's up-bringing in her home is what is important to guarantee chastity.

It is important to stress the non-Christian basis of female circumcision, noting that Christian cultures do not practice it in Europe, America, and most parts of Asia. In addition, none of the Arab Christians of Syria, Jordan, Iraq, Lebanon, and Pales-tine performs female circumcision.

To end, in following Christian teachings and beliefs, all Christian leaders have an obligation to contribute to the Egyptian national campaign to eradicate female circumcision. The Church should undertake this simultaneously with its programs in family planning. (BBSWAS 1981, 1984)

The Legal Perspective in Combating Female Circumcision

BBSAWS has engaged in the debate about the legal standpoints on and rami-fications of female circumcision. Many in the Sudan believe that setting up specific laws to criminalize and punish female circumcision may not be ef-fective. Some have, however, countered that applying current legislation and calling for new laws could be effective tools in abolishing the practice. A renowned legal expert and lawyer, Mahgouba Yassin, succinctly summarized the legal case in one of the association's educational booklets ("No to Female Circumcision," BBSAWS 1997). She states that female circumcision could be outlawed by applying the existing laws that protect against the "infliction of injury." Considering the evidence presented on the harmful effects of the practice on women's bodies, and supported by the lack of valid religious ju-risdictions, this constitutes an "infliction of injury" that should be punish-able by law. Dr. Yassin suggests using alternative legal and human rights norms and standards to make the case against female circumcision, such as arguing for the women's "right to consent" to any procedure done on her body.

The Psychological Impact of Female Circumcision

BBSAWS's eradication campaign attracted support from the most prominent psychologists and psychiatrists in the Sudan, leading to open discussions
about the harmful mental and social stresses of circumcision on women. Sudanese women gradually began to make connections between circumcision
and their previously unexplained symptoms and struggles. Kathira Yaseen of
the Sudanese Women's Union explained:

An important question that needs to be answered for us is "What do men want?"
Many Sudanese men have the wrong idea about their sexual roles. I have known
some of them who insist that their foreign wives be circumcised; this is absurd. Do
these men ask that their wives be circumcised just to increase their personal sexual
pleasure? Do these men not care about the feelings of their wives? Therefore, it is important that men are included in the awareness campaigns. It is important that they
understand the implications on women and how this can affect their relationships. I
believe that this lack of intimate harmony is the cause of much discord among Sudanese couples. And if Sudanese women had not been savvy and wise in dealing with
these situations, I think many would have broken marriages. Sudanese women have
struggled so much to deal with this problem. They often feign satisfaction just so
they can keep intact their identity, marriage, and social status.

Conclusion

BBSAWS's efforts have helped break the silence around the harmful effects of
female circumcision in Sudan and the region. The organization has succeeded in building trust and raising awareness among practitioners, parents,
religious leaders, and government officials, which is the first crucial step in
mobilizing communities to accept change. However, female circumcision
still continues to be practiced on the majority of girls in the Sudan (Abdel
Magied 2001). Much more work remains to be done. Women and men may
now be aware of the harmful effects of circumcision, but they must gain the
will and support to break away from social pressures and obligations in order to stop this practice.

    Nonprofit and nongovernmental organizations such as BBSAWS have a
central role to play in this process. In its action plan for the coming years,
BBSAWS has expanded its mission to implement a new strategy that will
adopt participatory approaches that will promote grassroots advocacy and
capacity building of local activists and practitioners. Programs working to

address female circumcision must adopt integrated and holistic approaches and be sensitive to local attitudes and sociocultural beliefs to meet with success. The information provided in this chapter highlights a positive evolution of attitudes taking place in the Sudan and, I hope, will encourage other local and international organizations to persevere in their efforts to help eradicate female circumcision.

Chapter 9

"My Grandmother Called It the Three Feminine Sorrows": The Struggle of Women Against Female Circumcision in Somalia

Raqiya D. Abdalla

My grandmother called it the three feminine sorrows.
The day of circumcision, the wedding night, and the birth of a baby
Are the three feminine sorrows!
I cry for help as my battered flesh tears.
No mercy. Push! They say,
It is only feminine pain,
And feminine pain perishes.
When the spouse decides to break the good tie,
Divorce and desertion,
I am left alone with my wounds.
Now hear my appeal!
Appeal for dreams broken
Appeal to all peace-loving people:
Protect and defend the innocent little girls,
So trusting and obedient,
To their parents and elders
Help them live in a world of love
Not a world of feminine sorrows!

—Dahabo Musa, 1988

"My Grandmother Called It the Three Feminine Sorrows" won first prize in a poetry competition for women from the Benadir region during the International Seminar on female circumcision (FC) held in Mogadishu, Somalia, in 1988. Dahabo Musa's poem captures the effects of circumcision on the mental as well as physical well-being of girls and women. Musa laments that, for those who are forced to endure it, the age-old tradition robs them of a carefree youth, deprives them of pleasure on their wedding night, and even denies them the experience of spiritual joy and wonderment at the miracle of childbirth. Their pain and suffering is so pervasive that it dominates all other feelings at the moments that define womanhood. Musa pleads with readers to honor the bodies and dreams of girl children, not to break their trust and turn their joy into sorrow.

Musa's poem is more than an outcry against circumcision; it voices an objection to the insidious social, political, and economic injustices that plague Somali women. In spite of the pervasive societal devaluation of women in Somalia, they have resisted oppression for as long as anyone can remember. Somali women make their feelings known through many forms of struggle against male authority. Even though there is a strong societal consensus on the importance of circumcision, women who aspire to positive transformation in their communities protest the practice.

This essay discusses the social context of female circumcision and the ideology that supports it and describes the efforts women are making to end the unnecessary pain that afflicts their lives. It presents selected personal narratives of Somali women reflecting upon their experiences in order to illuminate the shifting perceptions and attitudes toward the ancient tradition. Finally, I provide some suggestions for a sensible campaign that takes into account the social and political environment in Somalia, which produces ideas and values venerating FC. Indeed, the task of eliminating FC requires both a better understanding of its social origins and a cross-cultural approach based on mutual respect and collegiality.

Context

No one knows exactly the origins of circumcision in Somalia, although there is some speculation that the practice was emanated from Ancient Egypt (see Abusharaf, this volume). Whatever its source, the practice of circumcision is nearly universal and has a profound impact on Somali women (Nitir 1993). Somalia has one of the highest FC prevalence rates in the world. Almost 100 percent of its female population has undergone some form of circumcision. The majority of girls undergo the operation irrespective of economic class, education, or urban/rural background. The most drastic form, known as Pharaonic circumcision or infibulation, is the most prevalent type, and its practice is justified by numerous explanations similar to those of the Kenuz

Nubians (see El Guindi, this volume). Somali girls are circumcised when they are quite young; the average age of circumcision is between six and ten years.

Understanding a complex ideology like the one surrounding circumcision requires a strong grasp of the historical, political, religious, economic, and social context. Somali society is patrilineal, patriarchal, and patrilocal; kinship is traced through the male line, older men hold dominant positions, and newly married couples reside with the husband's family. Somalia is a pastoral society with an economy based on raising livestock; 80 percent of the population lives in rural areas and follows a nomadic way of life. The primary social unit is the family, which places great emphasis on clans and communal social organization. Male superiority is intricately woven into customs and local interpretations of Islamic traditions. The ideal woman should be able and strong, but never challenging to men's authority. Orthodox Islam has made its mark on this society, defining to a remarkable degree its basic codes of moral and personal behavior and regulating gender relations in matters pertaining to women's modesty, virginity, and chastity. Somali women's personality and behavior is shaped by a combination of the Qur'an and Muslim teachings with indigenous customs and beliefs. Paradoxically, local interpretations of Islamic percepts have contributed to both improvement and deterioration in the status of women with respect to legal matters such as custody of children, polygamy, and rights to property. Fear of women's sexuality has led to the imposition of strict codes of virginity and chastity as appropriate standards of conduct. This explanation begs a basic question: why does society place this emphasis on the virginity and modesty of women for reasons of family honor? This question cannot be addressed without understanding the interconnections between societal attitudes toward women's sexuality and men's political and economic interests. Virginity as a gendered attribute is intimately tied to men's economic interests and property rights over cattle, land, camels, and other wealth.

Given this political economy of chastity in Somali society, strict measures are placed on women before and after marriage. For example, married women caught committing adultery may be divorced and condemned by society. Failure to punish the woman results in loss of honor for the husband and his clan. Although modesty is exhorted for both men and women, society stresses its worth in women's lives more than it does for men; women are expected to tolerate adultery or polygamy when committed by their men folk. It can be argued that, among the main factors influencing female circumcision, girls are circumcised to guarantee their virginity and to prevent their independent sexual pleasure and excitability. The clitoris is cut off because it has no procreative utility or utility to men. Infibulation assures the man that he is the first to have sexual intercourse with the woman. Young girls are likely to hear about the circumcision operation before they endure it, creating anxiety about sex and sexuality from a young age. Although inhibition of women's sexual desires figures prominently in the decision to circumcise, this justification has no religious basis. There is ample evidence that Islam takes a positive rather than a negative attitude toward the sexual pleasure and enjoyment of both sexes. In sum, control of women's sexuality, the pursuit of purity and cleanliness, and religiosity are the main justifications perpetuated in Somali society. Until recently, they have been accepted wholeheartedly.

The infibulation operation in Somalia has two stages. The first, excision, consists of the total removal of the clitoris and the labia minora. Called *xalaalays* or *gudniin* in Somali terms, this is considered an act of purification. The second stage consists of the excision of various parts of the labia majora and fastening together the raw edges of the vulva, with vegetable thorns in the traditional setting or with catgut if the operation is done by a trained midwife. The circumciser inserts thorns across the "lips" of the vulva, thereby obliterating the vaginal entrance except for a small opening to allow the passage of urine and menstrual flow. In Somalia, this procedure is known as *qodob*, which means to sew up. If the operation is not up to the traditional standard, if the opening left for the flow of urine and menstrual blood is considered too big, or if the extent of the removal of the clitoris and adjacent tissues is unsatisfactory, the girl is usually operated on a second or even a third time.

Risks to Women's Health

Although FC is widely condemned by health practitioners, almost all Somali females have been subjected to it. The health hazards and psychological dangers of circumcision are both immediate and long-lasting. The operation has consequences that can appear right afterwards and create complications throughout women's lives. A study carried out in Benadir Women and Children's Hospital in Mogadishu in 1984–1985 found that 493 women and girls treated as outpatients or admitted to hospital during that time complained of 686 gynecological and obstetrical complications related to FC. The most common immediate complications reported were wound infections, hemorrhage, the formation of scar tissue and cysts, and urine retention. The most common long-term complication was chronic urinary tract infection caused by the pooling of urine because of the tight infibulation, a common complaint of young girls. Dysmenorrhoea is also prevalent; most Somali girls suffer lower abdominal pain during their monthly period because the very small opening prevents the normal, easy flow of vaginal secretions and menstrual fluid (Warsame 1989). In a study concerning the risks of medical complications after female circumcision, which was based on interviews with women in Mogadishu conducted by M. A. Dirie and G. Lindmark (1992; see also Dirie and Lindmark 1991a, b), a significant number of women complained of both immediate and long-term complications, including hemorrhage, infection, urine retention, pelvic inflammatory disease, infertility, and obstructed labor. Newly married women complained of pain during sexual intercourse, since penetration is difficult if de-infibulation—a short incision along the former suture line to facilitate sexual intercourse—is not performed at marriage. In Somaliland and Djibouti, a midwife often does the de-infibulation at the time of marriage. In southern Somalia and in the Sudan, the husband is expected to perform this task by penile penetration. The attempt to de-infibulate the woman in this manner causes great pain, carries a risk of infection, and causes frustration for the couple. Sometimes the bride becomes pregnant while still completely infibulated, preventing vaginal exams and prenatal care and leading to further difficulties at the time of delivery. Many infibulated women experience prolonged labor at the second stage, which increases the risk to the mother and may harm the fetus. According to the Benadir Hospital study, the second-stage labor of the infibulated woman normally lasts 5 times longer than the average time of the uncircumcised woman. The report mentions other complications related to prolonged labor, such as laceration and perineal tears. Medical personnel dealing with infibulated women indicate that the scarred area obstructs the delivery of the baby and in many cases severe perineal tears take place even if an anterior episiotomy is done. Serious complications include vesico-vaginal and recto-vaginal fistulae, abnormal openings between the vagina and the bladder or the vagina and the rectum that can cause urinary and fecal incontinence. These conditions may occur as a result of the prolonged and obstructed labor caused by infibulation (Warsame 1989).

Infibulated women face these health hazards in every stage of their lives. The constant worries of painful monthly menstruation; the painful de-infibulation just before marriage; the forcible penetration and even physical assault during intercourse; the excruciating pain of de-infibulation and re-infibulation imposed during every childbirth—all these memories have serious effects not only on the physical health of women but on their mental well-being as well. Because this practice is deeply rooted in the value system of Somali society and evokes deeply felt sentiments and strong emotions, concern about its health risks does not find the validation it deserves.

A Community Study

In my book, *Sisters in Affliction* (1982), I attempted to raise awareness and to stimulate action against the harmful practice of female circumcision. This study was the first of its kind in Somalia, gathering comprehensive information and presenting it in a coordinated form, taking into account the socio-cultural and historical features of the practice instead of looking at the practice in isolation. In 1980, I conducted a pilot study in Mogadishu with 110 people, 70 women and 40 men, to investigate attitudes towards circumcision. My main objectives were to explore important aspects of circumcision, to examine the magnitude of the practice and its perpetuation, to discover the attitudes of women, and to discover the views of men. A 62-question survey was administered to women and a 23-question survey was administered to men. Female respondents were selected at an outpatient gynecology clinic and at government ministries and agencies; male respondents were selected at government ministries and agencies. Respondents were between the ages of twenty and sixty years and were born in various regions of Somalia. They had varying educational levels, occupational statuses, and socioeconomic backgrounds. The study revealed that all 70 women interviewed had been circumcised: 57 had been infibulated, 9 had been circumcised, and 4 had a clitoridectomy. All were circumcised when they were quite young: 35 percent by their seventh year, 65 percent by their ninth year, and 100 percent by age 13. Nineteen of the women had had their daughters infibulated and six had had their daughters circumcised. Midwives performed 54 percent of the operations. Forty of the women reported being excited and frightened before the operation, 14 women reported feeling joy and worry, 11 women reported feeling curiosity and eagerness to know what would happen, and 5 women could not remember their feelings prior to the operation. In total, 40 of the 70 women (57 percent) reported experiencing significant complications, while 30 reported experiencing minor or no postoperative complications. Male opinions on infibulated and uncircumcised women varied: 12 out of 40 men said they enjoyed intercourse with non-circumcised partners;

14 reported no difference; and 14 had not experienced intercourse with a non-circumcised woman. Twenty-three men (57 percent) showed some awareness of women's feelings related to sex.

Respondents' perceptions of public attitudes toward circumcision centered on negative opinions of un-circumcised women. The majority of both women and men (40 women and 25 men) believed that "society would not accept them because people would consider them loose and oversexed and would question their sexual morals and fidelity." A smaller proportion (18 women and 7 men) believed that "society would not accept them because people would regard them as unpurified Muslims." A similar proportion (12 women and 8 men) believed that "uncircumcised females are not accepted by the society because people would look at them as a shame to the Somali culture and traditions."

The study showed that higher levels of employment and educational attainment are associated with more liberal feelings about the practice. Respondents were also more likely to favor discontinuing the practice if they were in the youngest age group (twenty–thirty years). Most of the women interviewed considered it a prerequisite for marriage and important for their daughters. At the same time, a majority (42 women and 23 men) thought that the custom should be abolished. This contradiction arises because even those who do not support the practice are unwilling to give it up under current social obligations. Next, I explore the reasons people give for continuing the practice.

Three Somali Women Speak

There is great value in hearing the voices of women who are directly affected by FC. The case studies presented here are an attempt to help the reader engage directly with the fears, values, and aspirations of Somali women who are struggling with the experience of circumcision. Somali women have never been submissive in accepting the subordinate status imposed upon them by their culture and traditions. They have always made their feelings known in a society that is male-dominated and highly chauvinistic. Women expressed their grievance and resistance against any form of oppression and subjugation in many ways. My study confirmed a general impression that there is a growing feeling against this ancient custom in Somalia. These three case studies document the different experiences of these women and express their sense of how it affected them personally.

Faduma

Faduma was a forty-five-year-old widow with four children at the time of the interview. She had no formal education and worked as a cleaner in a government agency. She had been married at the age of fourteen to a nomad. She bore six children; two daughters and two sons are still living. Faduma described her circumcision as a painful ordeal, after which she bled for three days. She suffered during her wedding and ran away from her husband several times; she does not enjoy sexual relations. Although her daughters were infibulated, she would eagerly support government and religious leaders if they were to abolish the practice.

When asked if she still remembered the circumcision operation, Faduma retorted: "How can I forget such an ordeal? I remember everything as if it happened yesterday. When asked to give the details, she said:

Circumcision is a common practice for Somali girls and I was expecting it when it was my turn. Little girls always look forward to this operation since they learn about it early in life. I knew about the event two days earlier and was feeling happy and excited until the eve of the operation when I felt worried and could not sleep well the whole night. It was an early, cool morning that the circumcision took place. I was the first one to be circumcised among the three, because I was the youngest and my mother did not want me to see what would happen to the other girls. Girls are not supposed to be cowards according to the nomadic custom and should tolerate the pain, but unfortunately I could not stand the severe pain of the circumcision. I screamed when the woman performed the operation and cut my clitoris and ran away bleeding before she could sew me with the thorns. My mother and the midwife caught me and all the women around held me tight and pressed me down until the woman operator finished sewing me up.

When asked what kind of instruments had been used for the cutting and sewing, she recalled that a sharp knife was used for cutting and, as customary, thorns were used for joining up the two sides of the wound. Different herbs were used for the treatment of the wound. In the rural areas, she said: "they always dig a hole in the ground, light a fire and burn certain herbs and circumcised girls sit over it. It helps the wound become dry and also its aromatic smell kills the unpleasant odor of urine and blood."

After Faduma had bled intermittently for three days, her mother decided to take her to the nearest village outpatient clinic. "My mother remained with me in that village for about two weeks, where we stayed with some relatives until I was able to go back to the nomadic area with my mother. My mother was nursing me all the time and the village male nurse came to check on me every second day. I was fed with special foods during the time I was sick, in order to make up for my lost blood. I was given liver, milk, and meat."

Faduma related how she suffered even after she had healed from the operation. "Girls can hardly urinate when they are virgins because they are tightly sewn up. They have the same problem with their monthly periods." She explained:

It used to take us hours to finish our morning urine. We girls used to get up very early, before the rest of the family were awake, and go to the forest in groups, but it was always hard to get rid of all the urine because it came in drops and never finished properly. We envied our mothers and grandmothers when they went to urinate in the forest in their turn and came back quickly. We looked forward to the day when we could do this, and when menstruation would come and finish without pain and difficulty. Marriage was a new problem and a solution at the same time.

Faduma was then asked about her experiences during her wedding. She replied:

I was afraid and worried about everything because I was young, and my father made all the arrangements for my marriage to a man 20 years older than myself. Later I discovered that he had given a large number of camels to my family as a bride-price. I suffered during my wedding time. The custom in my region was, and still is, that the man de-infibulates his bride. My husband used a knife to cut the infibulation and when I tried to run away and struggled, he accidentally cut the sides of my legs and the whole area was messed up with blood. I lost a lot of blood and then developed a constant fever and my vagina became swollen. I was terribly sick when my mother came and took me home. After that I was taken to the regional hospital where I stayed for a week.

My family decided to keep me with them until I regained my strength and grew mature enough for the marriage burden and responsibilities. I stayed with them for two complete years before they took me back to my husband.

But she did not remain with him long the second time, either.

After I stayed with my husband for two nights of painful intercourse and fear, I decided to run away and I went back to my family. I did not listen to all their persuasions and did not go back. This time also I was separated from my husband for another two years. At the age of 18 years, I was returned to my husband, still against my will. When I stayed there for a few weeks, tolerating my dislike of the man and his sexual desires for the sake of pleasing my family, I discovered that I was pregnant and I stayed with him and stopped running away.

Her pregnancy sealed her fate; Faduma stayed with her husband.

Faduma was asked if she enjoyed her sexual relations with her husband after that. She replied with obvious disgust: "I do not remember ever enjoying such a relationship. Even when the pain and difficult times were over, I used to feel terribly frightened. I always used to submit to it out of duty and just to have children." Each pregnancy resulted in prolonged labor, sometimes for two days, and each time she suffered some infection. All her children were born at home in the rural area with the assistance of a traditional midwife.

Both Faduma's daughters were circumcised and infibulated at the age of eight and nine years. She said, "Although I had suffered so much because of circumcision, it is a traditional custom and I had to have it done." When asked why women are circumcised, Faduma said that it is shameful not to be circumcised and men derive pleasure only from circumcised women. "Of course, no woman can marry without circumcision in our country. I heard only recently that non-Muslim women are not circumcised, but I have not heard of any people in Somalia who do not circumcise their daughters." Faduma was then asked if she thought the practice should be abolished. She said that if religious and government leaders decided that girls should not be circumcised, she would be the first one to support them because of her own experiences of its serious, harmful effects. "Women suffer a lot from this operation, from childhood until their old age."

Ardo

Ardo was a thirty-two-year-old graduate of an intermediate school with secretarial training and works as a typist in one of the government ministries. She was born and raised in Mogadishu; her father was a religious leader, and her mother was a housewife with no formal schooling. Ardo was circumcised and infibulated at the age of seven along with several other girls. She suffered complications and had thorns taken out; days later she was returned to the midwife and re-sewn. She also had a bad experience when she first married. She later remarried, but still did not enjoy sexual intercourse.

When asked how she was circumcised and whose decision it was, Ardo replied:

I was the one who initiated my circumcision when I saw some of my friends in the neighborhood were being circumcised. My mother was delighted to see my eagerness and agreed to include me with the group. I was then circumcised at the same time as these girls. I was excited and happy when my mother agreed, but when I saw the woman operator and her razor blade, I felt frightened. When it was my turn I was al-ready trembling but forced myself to sit down so that my mother would not see that I was afraid. When the women there held me tight and the midwife parted my legs, I was full of fear, and when she started the cutting, I screamed loudly and fought to free myself. One of the women filled my mouth with cloth, another one closed my eyes, and they kept me tight and suffocated me with their bottoms until I nearly ran out of air. By the time the operation was over, I was exhausted and hardly breathing. My mother told me that the operator used six thorns to sew up my wound, three on each side. I did not know what was happening to me except that I was feeling severe pain. I also felt the rough, strong fingers of the woman operator.

After the operation, I stayed in bed for two days without moving, as I was afraid to do so. I refused to urinate as well, but even when I tried to on the second day, I could not as it was so painful. My bladder was so full and hard and I was crying. Be-cause of this my father decided that I should be taken to the hospital. When the doc-tor examined me, he took the thorns out of the wound and then helped me to urinate. After all the urine was out I felt relieved of my pain. After two days, my mother insisted that I should be sewn again and called another midwife. I cried and resisted, but they were stronger than I was and the midwife sewed me up again. This time I felt pain but it was not as painful as the cutting of the clitoris. On the fourth day after my second operation, the midwife came and took out the thorns. My legs were tied up for several days and I was walking with the support of a stick for another few days. It took me about two weeks to resume any other activities. My mother nursed me, cleaned the wound, applied herbs, burned some incense under my legs, and used to feed me with traditional *mug mad* [dried meat], porridge, and milk.

Seven years after I found that I had something hard and big on the scar of the infibulation. It was like a small ball. I went to see a doctor. He told me it was nothing serious and was a common complaint with infibulation, which could be remedied by a minor operation. I was admitted to hospital, underwent the operation from which it took me a week to recover.

Ardo explained that she knew many girls and women who suffered from cir-cumcision and had heard of sad cases of young girls who bled to death as a result of the operation, particularly in rural areas. "You see," she said, "people always hide such incidents."

When Ardo was asked why she thought women undergo these tortures, she replied:

It is a deep-rooted custom in our culture and people think it is an important opera-tion for women because it prevents them from being oversexed. Uncircumcised girls are not accepted among our society. As you know, infibulation is a prerequisite for marriage because no man wants to have an oversexed woman who becomes unfaith-ful after marriage. No family wants their daughter to have "loose" ways and bring shame to the family. Because of this, mothers make sure that their daughters are properly circumcised and infibulated.

The force of social expectations seemed overwhelming to her.

Ardo believed that her difficult experiences in her early married life resulted in part from her infibulation.

Well, I got married to my first husband when I was 15 years old and I never liked that man; he was too old for me, about 40 years old. Only my father decided that I should marry him. He was always a stranger to me. At that time, nobody told me anything about marriage and how to deal with such a situation. On my wedding night there was a big ceremony and all my friends and my relatives and my husband's were present. I was given many presents and beautiful things. But it was the most terrible evening of my life. When I was left alone with this strange man for the first time, I felt shy and afraid at the same time and did not know what to expect from this strange man. The first nights of my wedding were really awful and filled with fear. The custom in Benadir region is for the men to de-infibulate their brides with their penis. Except in very rare cases it is an insult if they use an instrument or if (as in the northern region) the midwife de-infibulates. Anyway, I refused to submit or cooperate with my husband. I shouted and fought with him, and bit him seriously. Five days after my wedding, the man was still not able to have intercourse with me. Then I was forced to go to the hospital where they opened my infibulation. After that I got an infection and was sick for a few days before the man forced me again. I was never happy with that first husband and I continued to hate him and fought with him in every sexual contact. I finally left him, and refused to go back, until he agreed to divorce me.

Her second marriage was better, but still marked by discomfort with sexual relations. "With my second husband, I can say that I am happy, because he was my own choice this time. I rarely enjoy sex with him because I still have some reservations and bad memories about it."

Ardo had two children, a daughter and a son, at the time she was interviewed. She said that she would not have her daughter infibulated, but would have a sunna circumcision for her instead. She said that her husband also preferred the sunna circumcision, but would not agree with her not to have their daughter circumcised at all. She concluded, "As long as we are Muslims, I do not know why we do not use only sunna, which does not involve the same difficulties and complications as infibulation." Ardo condemned the practice of infibulation but supported the milder form of circumcision, which she believed is a religious obligation.

Sahra

Sahra, a thirty-five-year-old mother of six children (four daughters and two sons), was a housewife with no formal education who was born and brought up in town. Her father was a policeman and her mother a housewife with no formal schooling. Sahra married a literate civil servant who has since become a successful businessman. She was circumcised alone at the age of seven years. She said, "It was my aunt's decision as my mother died when I was four years old." When asked to tell us something about her circumcision experience, Sahra said:

I have so much to tell as I had to undergo that horrible operation three times. It was an early morning when the traditional midwife came with her instrument bag and performed the operation. I knew I was going to be circumcised because my aunt kept telling me that it was time that I should, as I must be clean and that it would help me to grow up quickly into a fine big girl like my sister. I was very much afraid of the woman operator when she opened her dirty bag and produced the knife. (I was told later it was a razor blade.) I was held very firmly and tightly and my back was pressed back by some women friends of my aunt and some relatives. When my legs were parted and the midwife started to perform the operation, I felt great pain and I screamed and fought wildly, but it was not possible to free myself. After all these years, I still remember the pain and how frightened I was. When it was over, I could hear the ululations of the women, and then they broke an egg on the wound, which they said would cool down the sharp pain. They also used *melmel* and other traditional herbs. In spite of this I started to bleed and they were not able to stop it until the midwife took out the thorns. Then the bleeding stopped and she put more herbs on the wound. I was left like that for four days. They did not take me to hospital but my aunt and the operator were nursing me at home. The fourth day after my first operation, the midwife came again with her knife; I was held tightly again and then re-infibulated with several thorns. I was very shocked and shivering with fear and pain.

At the age of 12, I was told that my infibulation was not proper (i.e., not tight enough) and therefore, I had to have another operation. I was very unhappy about it, but I was told I would not be regarded as a decent girl if I were not tightly infibulated. Other girls of my age would laugh at me and gossip about me and also there would be no hope for me to marry if I was not infibulated well and according to the customary standard. It was a horrible, painful and sickening experience for me but I had to force myself to undergo it.

That third operation was successful. This time I was very careful with my movements even when I was allowed to walk. My aunt also nursed me very carefully. I was fed with little fluids and plain white rice and porridge with very little butter for the first three days, so that I would not urinate and defecate frequently during the first few days after the operation. After the first week, circumcised girls are usually given better foods, like meat, milk, etc., to help them regain their health.

Although Sahra healed from this third surgery, it had other complications. Sahra told us that menstruation was very painful, particularly before she was married. "I used to vomit and feel terrible abdominal pain and backache but I am much relieved since I got married and especially after I had children."

The initiation of her married life was as difficult as her circumcision. Sahra said:

My wedding was another unpleasant period of my life. On the second day of my wedding around 5 o'clock in the afternoon, the midwife came to de-infibulate me. Of course I knew what was going to happen to me because my married friends had told me about the sufferings and torture of the wedding night. When I saw the midwife and the other women waiting for me, I pretended I was going to the bathroom, I locked myself in and refused to come out. This spoiled everything that evening, and the appointment with the operator was postponed to the next day. I refused to open the door until the next morning. That day I was warned that if I refused to submit to the midwife, they would call men to de-infibulate me by force. So after resisting for a few hours I gave up and submitted myself to the operation because I was more afraid of the men cutting me up. I had heard some cases of girls who ran away during their wedding time and then were caught and cut by strong men.

Sahra described her wedding nights as difficult, miserable nights, full of fear, worries, sleeplessness, and sometimes even physical struggle and fights with my husband to prevent frequent, painful intercourse.

"I am happy with my husband now, but even after 15 years of marriage I still hate the sexual act," Sahra said. "I have strange feelings about it, but I could never explain them. I do not know whether my cold feelings are due to circumcision or to other factors. I thought every woman had the same feelings, until I discussed them with a friend of mine." Childbirth, too, was always difficult, with much suffering before and after.

When asked if her daughters were infibulated, Sahra answered, "I did have my two elder daughters infibulated, but I will not have my younger daughters infibulated." She said that she still regrets having had her daughters infibulated and blames this on the influence of her husband. She said, "My husband is in favor of girls being circumcised and infibulated. I know he will not agree that our younger daughters shall not be infibulated, but I will insist regardless of what happens to them in the future." Sahra strongly opposed the continuation of the practice: "It is really a brutal practice which makes women suffer all their lives. I believe it is not a religious obligation but was just intended by men to control women's sexuality like animals. I think it is time now that women should stand together and fight against this useless old custom."

The Struggle of Somali Women Against Circumcision

For the last three decades, women's movement in Africa has given much attention to promoting the status and well-being of women by protecting them from harmful traditional practices. African women's NGOs played a crucial role in highlighting the battle against the practice at the international, national, regional, and local levels (see Ahmed, this volume). The Inter-African Committee (IAC) on Traditional Practices Affecting the Health of Women and Children and its 26 national affiliates in Africa and 4 groups in Europe, the Research, Action and Information Network for Bodily Integrity of Women (Rainb ♀), and FORWARD are well-known African NGOs working on this issue. In almost every African country, national and local organizations are working on the elimination of FC from their communities, while many international organizations and individuals have devoted themselves, with considerable support and commitment, to combating the practice. Progress in recent years has been marked by sensitization and awareness-raising campaigns; an increase in the flow of information, the funding of research and educational programs aimed at behavioral and attitudinal changes, and the empowerment of women to combat the practice in affected communities. In addition, many countries have introduced legislation and regulations to halt the spread of the practice.

Beyond the important roles played by these organizations, it is the responsibility of women themselves to challenge the multiplicity of interpretation of religions and legends that are deliberately employed to sanction practices which mutilate them physically and damage them psychologically. Somali women activists have been part of this movement to combat circumcision as a traditional practice harmful to the health of women and children for more than three decades. Somali women first voiced their concerns about the practice on the occasion of the establishment of the Somali Women's Democratic Organization (SWDO) in 1977 in Mogadishu. A workshop was organized for women delegates from all the regions of the country; reproductive health was among the topics addressed. Edna Adan Ismail, a former WHO Representative in Djibouti, an activist in women's health issues and the Director of Training in the Ministry of Health in Somalia at that time, presented this new theme to the workshop participants. Ismail insisted that issues pertaining to reproductive health should address the health consequences of FC, which was a persistent problem that adversely affected almost all Somali women. Women delegates showed a keen interest in the practice as an issue of great concern to them. The Central Committee of SWDO agreed to Ismail's proposal, although with caution that no one could foresee what the reaction of women delegates would be. This initiative was the first breakthrough for women to speak openly of this practice, discussion of which had been taboo. In that historic meeting, an urgent need to challenge this deeply rooted value system was felt and articulated. Participants realized that it is only women themselves who can create awareness in our society to fight against the practice. In order to convince the public of the need to abolish FC, it is essential to gather useful information to attain a better understanding of factors contributing to the continuation of the custom in our society.

My book *Sisters in Affliction* was an effort to break the veil of silence around this deeply entrenched tradition. Subsequently, a National Committee was formed from concerned ministries and institutions (the ministries of Health, Education, Religious Affairs, and Information; the Somali Women's Democratic Organization; and the Youth Organization) to carry out various activities such as training programs, dissemination of information and educational materials, research studies, outreach workshops, and the fostering of dialogue with groups of women and youth. Advocacy for the rights of female children and women was increased through lobbying and networking to raise awareness among women, decision-makers, doctors and health care workers, and religious leaders, as well as the society at large. Certain circumcision campaign activities, such as group discussions, the sharing of information, and reflection on individual experiences, opened the door for women to have the courage to discuss the issue more vigorously. Increasingly, the major concern for Somali parents is the question of how to maintain religious and traditional norms regarding the sexual behavior of women and girls once this tradition is abolished. Many mothers worry that, if they abandon the circumcision and infibulation of young girls, they cannot predict the consequences for their daughters. What if they are rendered unmarriageable? Parents agonize over the potential sexual activities of their daughters and are concerned about the pressure from the older members of the family to continue the practice. This issue continues to have a profound impact on Somali society, and those of us who have grown up with this brutal practice are still struggling to find lasting and acceptable solutions. As Somali women activists, we have always stressed the importance of persuading people the government of the need to eradicate circumcision by showing factual evidence of its harmful character. Legislation and other preventive actions to eliminate the practice were also advanced as important symbols for change. Today, the fact that 21 February is recognized annually as FGM Day with a Somali hospital, the Edna Adan Maternity, serving as the center of cooperation for the Horn of Africa on FGM-related problems represents a remarkable step forward.

When we decide as concerned women, Africans, and Somalis, to fight against FC, we demonstrate the courage and determination necessary to put an end to this deliberate, man-made affliction of women. Experience has shown us that long-standing beliefs and practices cannot change easily; it requires long-term effort and commitment. We endeavor to work closely with traditional communities so as to gain their confidence and trust and to demonstrate to them the existence of viable options. Our approach to the eradication of the practice should embrace the guiding principles of dialogue and conviction with the aim of building bridges that support the desired behavior and attitudinal modifications. In my opinion, the most important catalysts for change are the education and support programs created by the affected women and their communities. The fight against FC is more effective and lasting when communities are empowered to raise the issue themselves, reject the practice, and establish their own preventive strategies as we have seen in many parts of Africa (see Abdel Hadi, this volume).

With this understanding, the Somali Women's Democratic Organization's recommendations attempted to provide a comprehensive vision as to how to address FC in our society. Government action was the first measure to combat the practice at the national level. This action should involve development of a national policy, formulating legislation forbidding the practice, forming a national commission including ministries and agencies, and enlisting the Ministry of Health and Women's organizations to work with midwives who support the practice. This national campaign proved to be a critical component of the eradication effort because it helped arouse consciousness, mobilize important stakeholders, encourage religious leaders to participate, get women's organizations to take on the cause, and mobilize groups such as trade unions and youth organizations to educate their members. Other equally significant recommendations that women's groups helped shape include making education on the effects of the practice part of medical training, educating doctors and other medical staff about its complications, and enlisting the Ministry of Education to include information on the damage caused by the practice in school curricula. The Somali women's organization was well aware that educating the public about the facts of the detrimental health consequences and human rights issues involved will ultimately yield long-lasting results. With this message, greater attitudinal shifts are likely to occur—and, indeed, are already starting to take shape. Somali women's groups understand that achieving cultural change is not a simple task. Indeed the comprehensive proposals of Somali women groups call for social, economic, and political improvement in the status of women. This improvement is not only key to eliminating traditions that affect their well-being and prosperity but also for the sustainability of attitudinal shifts towards the abolition of female circumcision.

PART III

Debates in Immigrant-Receiving Societies

Chapter 10

The Double-Edged Sword: Using the Criminal Law Against Female Genital Mutilation in Canada

Audrey Macklin

The question that preoccupies most Western academics when they address female genital mutilation (FGM) is whether the national or international community should tolerate the practice. Yet the salient issue for most human rights activists working from within the communities where FGM has been prevalent is not *whether*, but *how*, to eradicate the practice. This problem has attracted less interest among Western academics, legal scholars, and feminist intellectuals. It poses both practical and theoretical challenges, because any strategy depends for success on its ability to harmonize with the social, political, legal, and cultural formations in which it is deployed.

This essay focuses on policies adopted in one country of immigration—Canada—in order to explore the complex positioning of women within diasporic communities. What are the risks and the benefits of using the legal system of the host country to redress one particularly stark manifestation of gender inequality within immigrant and refugee communities? Who is in the best position to make this assessment? What does the evidence to date suggest?

Canada officially considers itself a multicultural state in both a positive and a normative sense: We are multicultural, and we like it that way (or so we claim). Canada is also committed to the principle of equality. Indeed, both values are constitutionally entrenched in the Canadian Charter of Rights and Freedoms:

s.15(1) Every individual is equal before and under the law and has the right to the equal protection and equal benefit of the law without discrimination and, in particular, without discrimination based on race, national or ethnic origin, colour, religion, sex, age or mental or physical disability.

s.27 This Charter shall be interpreted in a manner consistent with the preservation and the enhancement of the multicultural heritage of Canadians.

Theoretical discussions of multicultural citizenship often begin with a question that goes something like this: "How can a liberal democracy accord equal respect to the autonomy of all individuals in a way that acknowledges and respects the formative significance of people's membership in particular communities?" A conventional framing of the issue of FGM within liberal debate about multiculturalism typically involves querying whether respect for cultural differences requires toleration of a practice which appears fundamentally and irredeemably violent, debilitating, and misogynistic (see, for example, Okin 1999). Or, to put the question in the language of the Charter, does s.27 trump s.15? The answer is almost invariably an emphatic *no*: FGM represents the limit of liberal tolerance for cultural diversity.

I will not wade into that debate as currently framed, except to note in passing that several countries where FGM is prevalent and endorsed by the dominant culture have also taken formal, legal steps to prohibit it, with varying—but usually lesser—degrees of practical success. Many commentators acknowledge that the practice is contested within the communities where it has been practiced, but most treat this as a contingent fact of little theoretical significance. Instead, they revert to the notion of "cultures in collision," which juxtaposes a monolithic minority culture with the dominant culture and thereby reifies the essentialized conception of culture that liberal critics profess to reject. The case study I present here takes as its starting point the fact that FGM is opposed by many members of the communities where it has been practiced.

My interest lies in examining FGM through another theoretical lens that appears in the literature. Instead of formulating a substantive theory of what multicultural citizenship requires, this alternative approach emphasizes the procedural aspect of citizenship and promotes the participation of members of various identity groups in the political, social, and judicial institutions that shape the national community. The virtues of representation exceed the soundness or quality of the resulting policies. Inclusion in the process of formulating, interpreting, and enforcing the laws and policies that affect citizens is itself a critical indicator of citizenship, independent of particular outcomes.

The extensive literature on deliberative democracy and communicative ethics challenges the instrumentalism of interest-based politics and promotes the ideal of a political community where participants achieve consensus on fundamental norms through reasoned argument among equal citizens. Both internal and external critiques have grappled with the abstract and utopian quality of this procedural framework. At present, the formal equality of legal citizenship masks profound social, political, and economic inequalities between citizens and among groups of citizens, which affects not only participation in the polity but also the extent to which participation is meaningful. In other words, representation is not only about having a seat at the table, but also about speaking and being heard.

Melissa Williams articulates the importance of representation in terms of equal citizenship: "the full and equal citizenship of members of marginalized groups depends upon their participation in processes of political decision-making, and these processes must be conducted in a manner that is open to the reasons that marginalized groups bring to them" (Williams 2000: 145). An element of bootstrapping inheres in marginalized groups' strategy of mobilizing politically and attempting to enter the formal channels of political discourse. By this I mean that members of disadvantaged communities recognize that while they may possess formal, legal citizenship, they do not enjoy the benefits of respect, access to resources, and networks that accompany substantive citizenship. These groups deploy the incidents of enfranchisement to participate in the political process as a means of advancing and securing the substantive recognition that formal citizenship itself fails to provide. Herein lies the paradox: mobilizing in a way consistent with membership is undertaken precisely in order to redress the lack of genuine membership.

In the context of criminal law, immigrants and refugees are frequently reminded that they are lucky to be here and that they are expected to adapt to, and obey, Canadian law as a condition of membership. The suspicion that they will not do so is frequently manifested in over-policing, inadequate protection, and insensitive and/or discriminatory treatment at all stages of the criminal process, both as accused and as victims.[1] This situation creates a dilemma for those who occupy a disadvantaged status in the particular ethnocultural community. For instance, many racial-ethnic minority and immigrant women who are subject to domestic violence fear that seeking protection from the state will expose their partners to a racist criminal justice system, reinforce negative stereotypes about the violent, sexist, and primitive nature of their community, and leave them even more marginalized and vulnerable than before. Small wonder many members of minority ethnocultural communities distrust and feel alienated from the legal system. Their reluctance to access the legal system becomes another symptom of their exclusion from membership and the protections that citizenship is meant to provide.

Notwithstanding the hazards of engagement, certain woman-centred African immigrant groups decided to undertake law reform advocacy in relation to female genital mutilation. Although powerful segments within these various communities defend the practice as a religiously based and/or culturally mandated tradition, many women and men from within the same communities reject the validity of the religious and/or cultural rationales invoked in its favor.

The extent to which FGM occurs in Canada is unknown, but anecdotal reports suggest that the procedure is performed here. Most operations are probably done by health care professionals, since in Canada, unlike Britain or France, few young women show up at hospitals suffering from botched procedures. Activists within immigrant communities attempt to discourage FGM through education about its adverse medical and psychological consequences. They also engage in consciousness-raising to dispel the cultural or religious justifications for the practice. At the same time, these activists are keenly aware that publicity about FGM often elicits revulsion from the mainstream culture and further stigmatizes immigrants from these communities as backward or uncivilized.

One factor that seems relevant in weighing the consequences of criminalization as a strategy for eradicating FGM is the relative size of the community that allegedly engages in the practice. Where virtually everyone imposes FGM on their daughters (for example, in Somalia or northern Sudan), enforcing a criminal law against the entire population is not feasible. Selective prosecutions with highly publicized convictions may provide general deterrence, but the more likely outcome will be widespread nonenforcement that in turn breeds contempt and disregard for the law. Where the community that practices FGM is a national minority, such as the Maasai in Kenya, the efficacy of the criminal law may turn on who has jurisdiction to enact and enforce criminal law, the extent to which communal autonomy prevails, and the relationship of elites within the national minority to the dominant elites. Parallel situations involving gender relations illuminate the issue. For example, feminist Palestinian citizens of the State of Israel complain that, although murder is a crime throughout Israel, Israeli police sometimes decline to enforce the law against men accused of "honor killings" within the Palestinian citizen community out of alleged deference to the norms of

Palestinian culture. This tolerance redounds to the benefit of Palestinian men and reinforces the subordination of Palestinian women. Where the community in question is a small, nonnational minority, such as recent immigrants to Canada, the effects of criminalization extend beyond the incidence of arrests, prosecutions, and convictions and encompass the status of group and others' perceptions of its members.

The Canadian Department of Justice first considered the desirability of amending the Criminal Code to make FGM a criminal offense in 1991. In its report, the Department of Justice recommended against amendment, concluding that FGM already constitutes a criminal offense under existing laws prohibiting aggravated assault (Government of Canada, Criminal Code s.268), assault causing bodily harm (s.267), and failure to provide the necessaries of life to a child. Just as amputating a child's hand without medical reason would fall within the general definition of aggravated assault as wounding, maiming, disfiguring, or endangering life, so too would excising a girl's clitoris and/or labia. Based on this advice, no action was taken to criminalize FGM explicitly.

However, in 1993 the Criminal Code (ch.45, s.3) was amended to add the offense of removing a child under the age of 18 from Canada with the intention of committing outside Canada an act which would be an aggravated assault or an assault causing bodily harm in Canada (s.273.3). The effect of the amendment was to criminalize taking a girl out of Canada with the intent of subjecting her to FGM elsewhere, conduct which would not have been criminal absent the amendment. Presumably, the objective was to dissuade parents from evading Canadian law by taking their daughters to be circumcised overseas. In effect, Canadian criminal law's jurisdiction was extended extraterritorially to take precedence over competing normative frameworks elsewhere that permit FGM. For purposes of the criminal law, Canada claimed as its own those girls "ordinarily resident" in Canada, whatever other nationality they might possess.

A few years later, in 1997, the government reversed its earlier position and amended the Criminal Code to define FGM explicitly as a form of aggravated assault to which no person could consent.[2] Why did this happen, and what message did the government intend to convey through the explicit criminalization of FGM? The practice had already been pronounced illegal under the general law prohibiting various forms of assault. From a purely doctrinal perspective, it would have made more sense to create an exemption from the law of assault for male circumcision, a common cultural and religious practice in North America; technically, male circumcision also constitutes an aggravated assault. The fact that no one seriously fears criminal prosecution for circumcising a male child speaks to the power of dominant cultural norms to supersede the letter of the law and determine what the law is "really" about.

My first reaction to the criminalization of FGM was to wonder if singling out the practice for special mention in the Criminal Code announces to Canadian society that the practices of some members of particular communities are so heinous and the members of those communities so unruly that they warrant special targeting for criminal sanctions. Such action could reinforce stereotypical negative associations between immigrants, minority cultures, and criminality, accentuating their status as outlaws to Canada and reinforcing native-born Canadians' self-perception as enlightened, liberated, and law-abiding. In a compelling article, David Fraser uses legislative debate in Australia to support this critique of the criminalization of FGM in that country (1995; see also Fraser 1994). Similar analyses have been advanced regarding the criminalization of FGM in Britain, France, and the U.S.

Indeed, I feared that it would be a short step from singling out those who commit FGM as outside the law of the state to demanding that people from countries where FGM is practiced should literally remain outside the state and be denied entry to Canada as "undesirable" or "criminal" types. One particularly invidious strand of anti-immigrant backlash appropriates migrant women's activism around domestic violence to argue for restrictions on immigration from so-called nontraditional source countries because men from those countries do not respect women's human rights. In short, my concern was that explicit criminalization of FGM adds nothing to the existing law except more stigma.

Although I was prepared to hold up the explicit criminalization of FGM in Canada as an object lesson in how the dominant culture, through the power of naming, gratuitously marginalizes members of minority cultural communities, I decided to investigate how the law actually came into existence. To my surprise, I discovered that the political pressure to criminalize FGM in Canada emanated from women in immigrant communities who inserted themselves directly into the legislative process. Their assertiveness contrasts directly with the process reported in other jurisdictions, where the affected women themselves rarely participated or, when they did so, were selectively recruited by more broadly based organizations to perform the role of exoticized victim of primitive misogyny.

In speaking with activists from immigrant communities and from immigrant women's groups in Canada,[3] I learned that while there was no consensus among opponents of the practice, a number of anti-FGM activists within those communities actively supported explicit criminalization. What ensued was a sophisticated campaign that conducted grassroots organizing and built coalitions with mainstream feminist groups. A major impetus for the 1997 amendment was a 5,000-person petition launched by Sadia Gassim, an immigrant from a country where FGM is prevalent, which was presented to the Minister of Justice. Signatories included people within and outside communities where FGM was culturally sanctioned.

In late 1996, the House of Commons Standing Committee on Justice and Legal Affairs invited submissions on a draft amendment to the Criminal Code regarding child prostitution, child sex tourism, criminal harassment, and FGM (Bill C-27). Community-based organizations such as Women's Health in Women's Hands, the Female Genital Mutilation Legal Community Committee, the African Canadian Legal Clinic, and the National Action Committee on the Status of Women (among others) weighed in, favoring explicit criminalization.

The FGM Legal Community Committee explicitly asserted its interest in participating in law reform as a democratic right flowing from citizenship: "as part of our movement to eradicate female genital mutilation and in fulfilling our duty and responsibility as citizens, [we] demand our right as citizens of this country, to be part of the decision making process, using our expertise and experience in the determination of female genital mutilation legislation that so vitally affects our lives" (Canadian FGM Legal Committee 1996). The lack of consultation prior to the initial draft of Bill C-27 elicited angry objections from many of the NGO participants, which explains the strong tone of this passage.

Supporters of the amendment claimed that naming FGM as a criminal offense would convey the message of its illegality more unequivocally, thereby providing a more powerful deterrent (Baya 1996: 23). However, all the anti-FGM briefs I examined gave precedence to education and consciousness-raising within the community as the means to eradicating the practice.[4] The form and substance of the criminal sanction was assessed in accordance with its heuristic value (Baya 1996: 23; Canadian FGM Legal Committee 1996: 29; African Canadian Legal Clinic 1996: 13). When I asked one advocate, Khamisa Baya, if she was concerned about the stigmatizing effect of specifically targeting FGM in the Criminal Code, she surmised that the affected communities are already so maligned by mainstream Canadian society that criminalizing a particular cultural practice associated with these communities would hardly make a difference. In other words, given the current degraded status of these immigrant communities, they had little to lose in terms of group reputation, but something to gain in terms of protecting vulnerable members of the community.

Like all actual instances, the process through which African immigrant women asserted themselves as political subjects is a highly imperfect representation of deliberative democracy in action. It would be futile to launch a critique of ideal theory based on its impracticality. Nevertheless, I believe there is merit in examining real situations as a means of identifying some of the complexities that must eventually be confronted when the theoretical rubber hits the empirical road. Presumably, each case presents some issues that are idiosyncratic, and others that are more generalizable.

Many scholars have commented on the applicability of the principles of deliberative democracy in contexts of multiculturalism and inequality of power, noting that norms of communication may privilege groups who practice certain kinds of speech. Let me add to this the following concern: Once we recognize the existence of minority communities from which participants in public deliberation may emerge, we must confront the implications of the fact that these communities may establish their internal norms according to processes do not conform to the tenets of communicative ethics. That is not to say that norms are uncontested within those communities; it means that power dynamics between members within particular communities may be constituted and negotiated differently than the power dynamics between members and the mainstream.

How does the story of the criminalization of FGM in Canada illuminate these issues? As racialized, Muslim, immigrant women, the Somali and Sudanese women who led the advocacy campaign occupy a disadvantaged position in Canada. Although some commentators query the exclusionary effects of the formal structures of public deliberation, from my reading of the submissions of the FGM Legal Community Committee and Women's Health in Women's Hands, these groups were manifestly able to articulate their objectives and their reasons by reference to normative claims—equality, citizenship, participation—that would be cognizable in the arena of political debate. I do not know whether this required distortion of their preferred mode of argumentation in order to accommodate the formal requirements of participation, but my point is simply that the mode of discourse was not an insurmountable barrier. Moreover, they were also successful in recruiting support and forming coalitions with overlapping communities. In particular, the African Canadian Legal Clinic and the National Action Committee on the Status of Women lent their support to explicit criminalization. The level of cooperation was evident not only in the general content of the various sub-missions but also in the exact reproduction of key passages of text. I doubt very much that defenders of FGM, however powerful within their respective communities, would have as easy access to the mainstream language of political discourse, or to potential allies.

The strategic choice to collaborate with the mainstream justice system and call for a law as an instrument that would speak directly to immigrant communities was made by the advocacy groups with foreknowledge of the risks attendant in engaging with a criminal justice system known to be indifferent, uncomprehending, or outright hostile to racialized and ethnic minorities. The submissions reflect this awareness. For example, the FGM Legal Community Committee, the African Canadian Legal Clinic, and Women's Health in Women's Hands all advocated a two-tier sentencing system which would expose those who actually perform and profit from the operation to more serious penalties than the parents of the girl. In particular, they were concerned that the imprisonment of parents would not be in the best interests of the child. Each group explicitly linked its position to concerns about racial bias in sentencing. As Women's Health in Women's Hands put it: "These concerns regarding overly lengthy incarceration of parents and/or guardians are neither unfounded nor exaggerated, and are strengthened by documented reports of endemic systemic ethno-racial discrimination in the criminal justice system and similar biases in the sentencing process of the judicial system. The result of such institutionalized discrimination is not only higher than average conviction rates but also relatively lengthier incarceration periods for Canadians from ethno-racial communities" (Baya 1996: 14).

Other specific responses to the draft legislation related to inserting a more comprehensive definition of FGM that would expressly cover re-infibulation, which may be performed after childbirth. The groups opposed the inclusion of a "therapeutic defence" for procedures performed for the sake of physical health, reproductive function, or "normal sexual appearance." Some argued that FGM never has a therapeutic benefit, and that current notions that altering women's genitalia can be "therapeutic" is a Western conceit that can be traced back to the Victorian era, when clitoridectomy and the removal of ovaries were performed to "cure" nymphomania, promiscuity, lesbianism, and masturbation. As Baya put it: "Female genital surgeries continue to be practised today in the West that have questionable or no medical benefits for the woman herself—for example, 'father's stitches' (extra stitches during episiotomy repair) to make the vaginal opening tighter after vaginal delivery, vaginoplasty for cosmetic purposes to 'snug' the vagina to enhance male sexual pleasure, or so-called 'labia reductions' and 'female circumcisions'" (Baya 1996: 7). These submissions deftly invert the lens back on the ideology and practices of the dominant culture to critique the therapeutic defense contained in the draft legislation, disrupting the conventional dichotomy of the "liberated First World woman" and the "oppressed Third World woman." Finally, the groups complained that, by precluding the possibility of consent to FGM by a person under age eighteen, the draft law implicitly left available a defense of consent when the act was performed on a female over eighteen. These advocacy groups rejected any defense of consent, regardless of age.

While these organizations successfully promoted explicit criminalization of FGM, they were only partially successful with respect to the consent defence. The final law states that no consent is to FGM is valid unless "the person is at least eighteen years of age and there is no resulting bodily harm" (Government of Canada, Criminal Code, s.268.3, s.268.4). The therapeutic defence remains. Similarly, the two-tier sentencing scheme was rejected. The law prohibiting FGM in Canada carries a maximum fourteen-year sentence for parents and for those who perform the procedure.[5] The measures proposed by the advocacy groups to balance the need to protect vulnerable girls and women against the racist tendencies of the criminal justice system failed to win acceptance.

It is also important to bear in mind that the statute has potential consequences beyond criminal liability. If the parents are not Canadian citizens, deportation is a possible consequence of conviction for a serious criminal offence such as aggravated assault. In fact, no one has ever been charged with an offence related to FGM, either before or after the 1997 amendment. We can only speculate on the significance of this fact. Maybe FGM is not being done in Canada, maybe it is not being done any longer, or maybe it is goes unreported by members of immigrant communities and undetected by teachers, health care professionals, and social workers.

Trying to criminalize a practice associated with particular ethnocultural groups without playing into racist conceptions of that group is a daunting and delicate task, and the briefs I reviewed self-consciously attempted to negotiate the terrain between a dismissive rejection of law as an institution sustaining racialized oppression versus a naive faith in law as a transparent instrument of social change.

At one level, the narrative I present here may be criticized as an "easy" case for liberals concerned about multiculturalism to the extent that everyone involved was publicly committed to eradicating FGM. None of the scholarly analyses of FGM from within the literature on multiculturalism cite public defenses of the practice from members of immigrant communities. The nearest to a public endorsement I have seen is in Doriane Lambelet Coleman's description of the "Seattle Compromise," in which a hospital in Seattle, Washington, agreed to perform a symbolic circumcision by nicking the labia of female infants and drawing blood. Her article describes Somalis who warned that they would subject their daughters to traditional, debilitating circumcision in the absence of the proposed alternative (Coleman 1998: 740). In general, it appears that while scholarly debate has been preoccupied with the question of whether FGM should be tolerated, the actual debate in immigrant communities has turned on how best to bring about its demise.

Some might suggest that this academic fixation is politically harmless, but I do not agree. I contend that it is a marginalizing narrative[6] which reifies and perpetuates a depiction of Africans as lawless, disordered, and primitive. Imagine that Canadians were a minority community in the state of Nirvana where there existed true equality between the sexes. Observers from Nirvana noticed that some Canadian men sexually harassed Canadian women. Earnest debate erupted in Nirvana, continuing for years, about whether Nirvana should tolerate the Canadian cultural practice of sexually harassing women. And that's all they talked about, over and over and over. It is probably safe to say that some Canadians do see sexual harassment as relatively innocuous behaviour, implicitly sanctioned by prevailing cultural norms. However, I venture to suggest (perhaps optimistically) that for most Canadians, the question is not whether sexual harassment is a culturally defensible practice, but rather how best to identify and end it. Yet if all the Nirvana press talks about and reports on, and all that Nirvanan scholars write about, is whether Nirvana should tolerate Canadians' cultural practice of sexual harassment, ordinary Nirvanans might be forgiven for thinking of all Canadian men as cads who either harass or conspire to protect harassers, and of all Canadian women as pathetic victims who meekly submit to their fate. Not only is it an unflattering picture of Canadian culture, it also demeans Canadian women while purporting to express concern about them.

According to the advocates of criminalizing FGM, the law was intended primarily as another instrument of persuasion to convince resistant sectors of the community that FGM was wrong. In other words, law reform operated as a mechanism for reconfiguring intragroup power. Those who opposed FGM evidently felt that they had not been able to prevail on the strength of existing legal, medical, cultural, feminist, and religious arguments against the practice. Whether this was due to their status within their communities as women and as feminists and/or to the perceived weakness of their arguments is not clear. Passage of a specific law prohibiting FGM accorded them a tactical advantage over those who had disregarded them until that point, improving their access to norm-generating discourse within their community. In other words, it enhanced their intragroup recognition as women.

Outside of their communities, the form of recognition gained through the criminal law must be assessed as highly problematic. Visibility as perpetrators and victims of a culturally distinct crime is hardly the type of recognition ethnic communities usually seek. The mixed record of advocacy on this matter underscores how cultural and racialized minorities take a gamble when they decide to engage with law, even for limited, strategic purposes. Activists within the community can control the form and content of internal grassroots education, and they may believe that the role of law should be confined to deterrence. They may carefully craft a balanced approach to legislative reform, only to see one side of the balance discarded by legislators. After a criminal law is passed, they cannot control (though they may try to intercede) how the power of the law will be exercised by the dominant society's police, prosecutors, and judges against members of their community who transgress the law. Nor can they determine how the law will be read by mainstream culture and the impact this will have on their communities.

I suspect—as do activists in other nation-states who opposed criminalization—that the law will in fact be interpreted as a matter of white, Judeo-Christian Canadians inscribing their moral superiority on African Muslim bodies through the text of the criminal law. The fact that the proponents of the law came from the communities who are the law's object will likely remain unknown to the vast majority of Canadians. The marginalized status of Canadians of African origin means that they rarely are, and are even more rarely seen, as law makers. Instead, they are more frequently characterized as law breakers, a perception that the criminalization of FGM can only exacerbate.

Once a new criminal offence is added to the Criminal Code, it is rarely removed.[7] Even if cultural norms in all sectors of these immigrant communities evolve away from the practice of FGM in the next five, ten, or twenty years, I suspect that an offence named FGM will continue to send out a message to and about certain Canadians for a very long time.

In her thoughtful article on deliberative democracy and minority representation, Melissa Williams attempts to articulate certain procedural norms to ameliorate the multiple effects of marginalization on disadvantaged groups' ability to participate meaningfully in political decision-making. She concludes that

> For relatively privileged citizens engaging in a discourse with marginalized citizens, [democratic deliberation] requires a willingness to interrogate one's own judgements about the unreasonableness of others' arguments, particularly where recognizing the validity of those arguments would jeopardize one's material or cultural interests. One might even go so far as to say that a spirit of impartial discourse sometimes requires a sort of "difference principle as applied to reasons." By this I mean a willingness to regard the reasons offered by marginalized groups as the reasons that sustain a collective decision even when those reasons are not immediately available from within one's own social or cultural experience. (Williams 2000: 145)

Williams's proposal seems to presume that marginalized groups speak with one voice.

Where such a situation obtains, this approach may indeed be appropriate.[8] However, sometimes the appearance of consensus results from the suppression of dissenting views within a community; in other instances, lack of consensus may surface publicly. I must admit that I disagree with the position taken by the various groups that advocated explicit criminalization of FGM. I find myself more persuaded by the critique articulated by similarly situated groups in other nation-states. Although I cannot explain why similar groups did not coalesce in Canada to oppose explicit criminalization, I would not readily assume that the arguments used by groups elsewhere are inapplicable to Canada. I doubt that the differences between the justice systems in Canada and elsewhere inspire sufficient confidence in Canadian institutions to warrant taking the risks entailed in resorting to the criminal law to deal with the problem of FGM as it exists here. Moreover, I am sceptical that deferral to the reasons offered by marginalized groups can substitute for persuasion on the substantive norms at issue. It will clearly not work where members of marginalized groups express divergent opinions. We might, of course, still struggle to achieve an "enlarged perspective" that makes us more receptive to persuasion by unfamiliar arguments, but such a stance is not reducible to deference. My point is that once we take intragroup diversity seriously, the availability of deference as a method of resolving intergroup differences in perspective is constrained by the absence of a formal mechanism for prioritizing the different voices within a specified community. We must return to argument and persuasion, whether expressed through logocentric analysis, in narrative, or by other means.

If we assume that there were no voices from within immigrant communities who were willing to speak against explicit criminalization as a necessary means of deterring FGM in Canada, I concede that it would be highly problematic for those who are not members of these communities to oppose the advocates, especially on the grounds that legislative action would not be in the best interests of their own community. Such a stance would appear patronizing at best. Both the desired benefits and the potential costs of explicitly criminalizing FGM will redound to the advocates' respective communities. If there is a compelling reason for deference, it arises less from a difference principle as applied to reasons, and more from the empirical uncertainty regarding the effects of the legislation, as well as the fact that those who will feel those effects are in the better position to assess which risks they prefer to assume.

The theoretical conundrum is clear: negotiating intragroup power relations within marginalized communities through resort to an apparatus of the state may help redress inequalities within the group, but may simultaneously push the group as a whole further to the margins. Assuming such contradictory results are sometimes unavoidable, perhaps the normative question that should inform action should be: Where will this leave the most vulnerable members within those disfranchised communities—further ahead, or further behind?

Consequences

In January 2002, almost five years after the law was amended to criminalize FGM specifically, a Sudanese couple were charged with having the procedure done to their adolescent daughter while in Canada. The charges were based on the daughter's allegation that she was subjected to FGM at the age of eleven, while in Canada, by an unidentified "practitioner." The accused insist that the girl was infibulated in Sudan more than ten years earlier, at a time and place where the practice was inflicted on about 90 percent of females. The family left the country before the youngest daughter reached the age where the procedure is customarily performed, and the accused explained that they harbor no intention or desire to inflict it on her in Canada. The family currently live in St. Catharines, a small southern Ontario city close to Toronto. The alleged practitioner has not been identified, apprehended, or charged. Notably, in none of the media coverage has any member of the Sudanese community stepped forward to justify the practice. Some tried to provide a contextual explanation of why it happens, but all opposed its perpetuation.

Based on my conversations with the prosecutor and a defence counsel, as well as a female community leader, it seems clear that neither police, nor child welfare authorities, nor the lawyers involved approached the case with any real attentiveness to the complex cultural, social, and gender dimensions of the issue. This not to suggest that these actors were ill-intentioned. Rather, it appears that none of the actors consulted with anyone from the affected community, whether locally in the city or in Toronto, for advice on how to approach the situation in a culturally sensitive manner. Perhaps they simply did not recognize a need to do so.

The family has been torn apart physically through the various state interventions, including detention of the parents in custody and apprehension of two children by child welfare authorities. Given the small size and precarious position of the community, culturally appropriate foster care is not available. The Sudanese community in the city is deeply concerned, but uncertain about where and how best to channel this concern. The family is traumatized, as individual members and as a unit. The long-term emotional and social damage to the complainant, the accused, the other children, and the family as a whole is probably incalculable even before the case is resolved.

Whatever else happens, the experience of this family will serve as an object lesson and a deterrent to any other parents in Canada who might contemplate subjecting their daughters to FGM. If they did not know before that FGM was a criminal offence in Canada, they will know now. But this is not the scenario envisaged by those who advocated the new law. They saw the law primarily as an educational tool, not as a punitive cudgel. However, public funding to subsidize anti-FGM education by volunteers within immigrant communities was not forthcoming at the time.[9] Of course, ignorance of the law is no excuse, but the fact remains that FGM is de jure or de facto legal in many countries of origin, and the Canadian government has never made a concerted effort to advise newcomers that the practice is prohibited and will not be tolerated in Canada.

Persons in positions of authority in the criminal justice and child welfare systems do not necessarily recognize when, why, and how to seek assistance in grappling with complex intercultural issues. In smaller communities, such persons may not possess all the requisite tools themselves, but an awareness of the need for consultation with those who might be better prepared and the mechanisms for seeking out such assistance also appear to be lacking.

Finally, as is so often the case, events do not unfold in real life in accordance with expectation. In the St. Catharines case, the accused did not attempt to justify the commission of FGM on their daughter by claiming ignorance of Canadian law or the primacy of cultural traditions over Canadian law. The sole issue was one of credibility as to facts, which revolves around when and where the FGM occurred. The daughter alleged that she was subjected to FGM in Canada approximately two years prior to the charges being laid. The parents maintained that the procedure had been performed in Sudan a decade before, and the complainant and her two older sisters were infibulated at the behest of their grandmother. The father claimed he was out of the country at the time and did not consent. The accused acknowledge that that the practice is illegal in Canada, they do not presently condone it, and they have consistently stated that they neither wish nor intend to inflict it on their remaining uncircumcised daughter.

It is clear that the facts do not fit the pattern that political theorists typically assume, wherein parents or perpetrators of FGM attempt to justify their actions by reference to cultural traditions. In the present case, media accounts of the case tended to ignore or gloss over the actual issue, and instead use the prosecution as a springboard to the stereotypical and entirely hypothetical scenario of parents who wilfully subject their daughters to FGM in Canada.

Some ten months after this case came to the attention of state authorities, after numerous sensationalist media accounts, detention of the parents in custody, child apprehension, and the continued state wardship of the complainant, the Crown decided to withdraw the charges against the parents. The prosecution's case depended entirely on the credibility of the complainant about when and where the FGM occurred, and after various intervening events, the Crown concluded that it could not obtain a conviction based on the complainant's testimony.[10]

Of course, even if the FGM occurred in Sudan a decade earlier, the fact that their daughter made a complaint of this nature surely signals seriously unhealthy dynamics within the family, the sources of which are likely inseparable from the intense intergenerational stress many immigrant families experience as they struggle with the upheaval that migration precipitates. But this is a different story about immigrants, culture, and gender than the dominant narrative about FGM. Regrettably, I suspect that the encounter of this family with the criminal justice and welfare system to date has probably only made a bad situation worse. The complainant remained a ward of the court from December 2001 until late 2002, before returning to live with her family at the age of fifteen.

One challenge posed by this scenario about the state and diasporic communities is directed at scholars of multiculturalism. Academic opportunism, much like media sensationalism, tends toward selection of micro-level "real world" examples for instrumental objectives, be it the advancement of a theoretical argument or the selling of newspapers. Yet scholars often present themselves as sincerely inspired by macro-level "real world" dilemmas that matter deeply to the persons affected, and they offer well-intentioned, sophisticated normative roadmaps toward a solution of those problems. Sometimes, the examples match the priorities of those whom the example depicts, but sometimes they do not. In the case of FGM, perhaps, the time has arrived to shift attention away from the normative question that so preoccupies scholars—should this practice be tolerated?—to the normative, as well as critical and programmatic, question that preoccupies women and men from these communities—how can this practice be eradicated in a way that that will promote and enhance the dignity of individuals and of the community as a whole?

It is, of course, left to the community itself—as individual members and as a collective comprising common and disjunctive interests—to reflect on the risks and benefits of engaging the criminal apparatus of the state as part of a strategy of manifesting and advancing citizenship claims by marginalized members.

Chapter 11

Representing Africa in the Kasinga Asylum Case

Charles Piot

This essay focuses on the landmark 1996 case in which Fauziya Kasinga (Kassindja[1]), a Togolese woman, sought and won political asylum in the United States in order to escape genital cutting and forced marriage in Africa. The arguments advanced by the lawyers involved in the Kasinga case and the images in the media reporting on it circulated widely and came to define much more than Kasinga's travails or the practice of female genital cutting itself. Like Robert Kaplan's demonizing piece in the February 1994 *Atlantic Monthly*, "The Coming Anarchy," they evoked and inserted themselves into a genealogy of racist stereotypes about Africa that have long mediated the West's relationship to the continent. In so doing, they glossed over complex local realities and once again fictionalized and fetishized Africa as the West's Other.

In what follows, I examine two principal sites: first, the court transcripts of the arguments presented by Kasinga's lawyer and by the lead attorney for the Immigration and Naturalization Service (INS) before the Board of Immigration Appeals (BIA) on 2 May 1996; and, second, the articles about the case that appeared on the front page of the *New York Times* throughout the spring, summer, and fall of 1996. These two sites were intimately tied together, indeed fed off one another, and provided mutually reinforcing "truths" about Kasinga and FGM for the wider public. I then contrast the portrayal of Kasinga and her ordeal in these two venues with those details of her story I came to know through discussions with one of her lawyers and with an official at the American Embassy in Togo whom I met in July 1996 just after the case had been decided, at a time when the State Department was trying to decide whether it should take a stand on genital cutting and reporters from both the *New York Times* and the *Washington Post* were in Togo to do after-the-fact background stories on Kasinga's family. This American official had been charged with investigating the case so that the Embassy could not only respond to adverse publicity surrounding it but also generate new policy that would bring pressure to bear on the Togolese government to pass a law against the practice. His involvement indicates the global reach of this debate; a hearing before the INS was connected not only to a Western public through the media and the Internet but also to an embassy in a backwater region in West Africa and, thence, to the intimacies of life in rural Togolese villages.

I should mention at the outset that I myself played a minor role in the Kasinga case. Since I had conducted ethnographic fieldwork in northern Togo, near the homeland of Kasinga's ethnic group, the Tchamba, I was contacted early on by one of her lawyers to see whether I might be willing to serve as an expert witness during her initial hearing at the Immigration and Naturalization Service. After listening to the facts of the case, however, I was reluctant to become involved. While I was sympathetic to Kasinga's plight, I had never been to the area Kasinga was from, and the people I have worked with do not practice female genital cutting (Piot 1999). Moreover, I sensed that, if I testified at her hearing, I would be forced to seriously compromise my own views and, in the process, reify those images about Africa that many of us work hard to undo in our classrooms and in our writing, or else I would do damage to her case. Nevertheless, I agreed to file a letter with the court based on a reading of the ethnographic literature which affirmed that the Tchamba of northern Togo practiced clitoridectomy and that it was likely that a Tchamba woman would be expected to undergo the procedure before she married. Much to my astonishment—for I had said nothing of substance about Kasinga herself, and I had used anthropological scholarship that was a half-century old—my letter was used right through the trial process and cited in the BIA's final opinion on the case as expert testimony that reinforced the case Kasinga's lawyers were trying to make (see U.S. Dept. of Justice 1996). This gives some indication of the house of cards on which this legal case was built.

Kasinga's Story

I begin by describing some of the facts of Fauziya Kasinga's life and transnational ordeal. She grew up in a Muslim family in the town of Kpalimé in southern Togo. Her mother was a petty trader and her father a successful businessman. Her father's income from the transportation business enabled him to build a spacious eight-bedroom house, which Kasinga described as "one of the finest" in Kpalimé (Kassindja and Bashir 1998: 12), and to send his daughter to boarding school in neighboring Ghana during her high school years. However, when she was sixteen, her father died. She returned to Togo to find that her mother had been banished to her natal home in Benin and that she was now under the guardianship of her father's sister. Unable, or unwilling, to pay the school fees, Kasinga's aunt kept her home and arranged for her to marry a local man with three wives.[2] She was also expected to undergo clitoridectomy at the time of marriage. Opposed both to the marriage and to being cut, Kasinga fled with the help of an older sister. They borrowed money from their mother and crossed the border to Ghana. Kasinga purchased a plane ticket and flew to Germany. She spent two months in Germany, and then, with the aid of a Nigerian man she met on the street, obtained a British passport and flew to Newark, New Jersey.[3]

Upon arrival in the U.S., she told immigration officials that she was fleeing forced genital mutilation in her home country and wished to seek political asylum. As is routine for someone entering without a visa, she was detained. She spent the next sixteen months in detention facilities in New Jersey and Pennsylvania, where she not only shared cells with hardened criminals and murderers but also was repeatedly strip-searched, shackled, denied sanitary napkins, put in isolation as punishment for washing herself at dawn before her morning prayers, and beaten and tear-gassed during a prison riot. A cousin of Kasinga's found an attorney who was willing to take her case and pressed for an asylum hearing. At this hearing in August 1995, for which I submitted my letter, her claim was denied by an immigration judge who found her story "inconsistent" and "irrational." At that point, Layli Miller Bashir, then a law student at American University in Washington, D.C., took up Kasinga's cause and contacted Karen Musalo, a lawyer at American University's International Human Rights Clinic. Musalo agreed to take the case and appealed the earlier decision. On 2 May 1996, she and the INS presented arguments before seven members of the Board of Immigration Appeals. The appeals board, unlike the earlier judge, found Kasinga's story credible and the arguments of the lawyer who presented her case compelling, and granted her political asylum on June 13, 1996. The case before the board was made easier for Kasinga and her lawyers by the fact that INS general counsel David Martin was himself willing to grant asylum to Kasinga if it was based on sufficiently narrow grounds so as to ensure that the INS would not be flooded with FGM asylum requests. During the spring and into the summer and fall of 1996, Kasinga's case was publicized throughout the media and by human rights and feminist organizations on the Internet. This attention focused not only on Kasinga's flight from forced FGM but also on the horrific treatment she had been subjected to while detained in this country. Though this publicity was never mentioned by the lawyers during their arguments, or by the judges in their ruling, it clearly played a major role in the case's outcome.

The Case Before the Board of Immigration Appeals

The case heard by the BIA in May 1996 turned on five sets of arguments. First, whether or not Kasinga was a credible witness—that is, whether the inconsistencies in earlier accounts she had given to INS officials and at her earlier hearing[4] were serious enough to impugn her testimony about what had happened. Second, whether the Board itself should rule on the case or whether, in light of new evidence, they should remand it to the lower court judge who had heard the case previously. Third, whether or not Kasinga's situation (and FGM more generally) fit within the framework of political asylum law. Asylum law requires that an individual establish a well-founded fear of harm or persecution involving "a threat to life or freedom" because of his or her race, religion, nationality, politics, or membership in a social group. Fourth, whether, if returned to Togo, Kasinga would be forcibly subjected to FGM, or whether she could find safe haven elsewhere in the country. And fifth, whether in deciding this specific case, the board should restrict its ruling to the narrow facts of the case at hand or attempt to establish a broad framework for future cases as well.

Much of the discussion by both of the lawyers and between lawyers and judges revolved around the third of these issues: whether Kasinga had been subjected to harm based on her membership in a "social group."[5] For me as an anthropologist, this was the most interesting part of the debate. The pressing issue here was that gender—unlike race, religion, nationality, and politics—is not a recognized group category under asylum law. As INS general counsel Martin put it, classic asylum cases focus on a person "who is the political opponent of a dictator and has fled for fear of his/her life" or "a minority group subjected to a life-threatening campaign of ethnic/racial hatred." Thus, the board had to decide whether a gender-based claim was covered by the vague residual category of membership in a "social group." In arcane discussions that called to mind a certain Fortesian anthropology but were notable for their inattention to any of the anthropological literature, both lawyers and judges were drawn into debate about what social group category into which to place Kasinga. Kasinga's lawyer, Karen Musalo, suggested that the group in question was defined by "gender and tribe": the social group of women of the Tchamba people of northern Togo. INS attorney David Martin wanted to narrow the definition of the group in question to include only Tchamba women who were uncircumcised: "young women of the Tchamba Kusuntu tribe who have not been circumcised in accordance with tribal custom." Martin's concern was that legal precedent would be established by a favorable ruling and that such precedent might enable thousands of women to make asylum claims in the future. Furthermore, he wanted to narrow the group to those uncircumcised Tchamba women who had *resisted* cutting and who had a "country-wide fear of persecution" for their resistance. This last point was key, for mere social ostracism or economic hardship that might result from noncompliance could not, he argued, constitute grounds for asylum. Kasinga's lawyer protested the INS's attempt to narrow the definition of the social group in question, although not too vigorously, for Musalo was caught between her desire to establish a general framework for FGM jurisprudence that could be applied to future cases and her more immediate desire to win this case for her client.

But, one of the judges asked Martin, is this a "true social group"? Another asked: is it a "cognizable group" that has any reality outside of this context? "For what other societal purpose does the particular social group exist?" asked a third. These questions were motivated by the fact that individuals cannot bring asylum claims unless they can show that they are members of social groups. It is ironic that human rights law, from which asylum law derives, is based on the rights of the individual. In this case the INS could not accede to a definition of group—women of the Tchamba tribe—that is arguably the only definition that might correspond to some locally "cognizable" social grouping, precisely because it was so broad as to invite thousands of asylum petitions. By narrowing the definition to uncircumcised Tchamba women who resist cutting and justly fear they will be persecuted country-wide, the INS was proposing an invented social category—indeed, a group that might only consist of a single person, Kasinga herself. The contradictions at play here were never resolved, for both lawyers were under time constraints (each had only a half-hour for argument) and wanted to return to other arguments they needed to make. Finally, what was remarkable to me as an anthropologist, who worries about such esoteric questions as the nature of group identity in a place like West

Africa, was that there was no expert testimony adduced to help decide the issue. None of the standard scholarly questions about group identity were raised: how homogeneous it might be? is there universal compliance with ritual practice? with genital cutting? and so on.

In addition to the central matter of defining group identity, other interesting issues were raised during the hearing which I only allude to here. The question of the *motive* of the so-called persecutors came under discussion, for in classic asylum cases involving persecution for religious or political beliefs the claimant must show malicious and punitive intent on the part of his or her persecutors. Thus, the issue raised in this context was whether the "harm of mutilation" was carried out with *malignant* intent. INS attorney Martin suggested that not only was it difficult to divine the nature of a person's subjective beliefs but also it was probable that those responsible for the practice of genital cutting had "benign" motives—that is, that they were likely merely carrying out the dictates of their culture. In order to get around this stumbling block, he proposed what one of the judges referred to as the "novel" idea that there might be certain cultural practices that, whatever the motives of those involved, were so appalling as to "shock the conscience of a great part of the world community," and that should therefore be considered a form of persecution. Notice, however, as with the discussion of group identity, the notion of intent that is key for asylum law is here dismantled: persecution might be unintentional and "benign." But the implications of this deconstructive move, again for lack of time, were left unresolved.

The judges briefly raised the question as to why genital cutting is practiced in the first place. INS attorney Martin responded, "I don't know . . . we are at a loss to come up with a reason that would explain it . . . it's part of a cultural practice. . . ." Musalo objected to this vacuous response by stating, "FGM is performed purely for the purpose of gender subjugation . . . to control women's sexuality and reproduction. . . ." Martin then conceded that "some sociologists" describe it that way." Here, too, none of the anthropological literature on genital cutting was invoked.

The issue as to whether Kasinga would be subjected to a country-wide threat of persecution was key, because a claimant who could meet all of the other criteria for asylum would still be deported back to her home country if she could find a safe haven anywhere in that country. On this matter, the lawyers argued that in a country with a 50 percent rate of female circumcision, finding a safe haven would be well-nigh impossible. How they arrived at this figure, I do not know. State Department statistics for Togo in 1996 reported a

12 percent rate country-wide,[6] though even this is likely inflated; I have heard from more reliable Togolese sources that the figure is closer to 5 percent.

Given the momentous nature of this hearing, the silences in this text are mind-boggling and the list of anthropological howlers long. There is no discussion whatsoever of Tchamba and what they are like (the nature of groups, of ritual, of how they might respond to those who resist ritual practice), no testimony by anyone familiar with present-day Togo,[7] no inkling that two decades of discussion by Africanist scholars has established as orthodoxy that homogeneous social groups do not exist and that group identity is often fluid and shifting, and no reference to any anthropological literature on female genital cutting.

Moreover, these silences are filled by the crudest, most essentializing images and stereotypes. Kasinga was assumed by all in attendance to be a member of a "patriarchal tribe" with "immutable cultural norms" that practices "forced polygamy" and "mutilates" its women. Women of the tribe, it was suggested, "are brainwashed into believing that mutilation is good for them." These terms and images cycled through the entire discussion like shadows in the background, remaining utterly uncontested and uninterrogated, and providing a bedrock of understanding and a set of normalizing assumptions that filled the void of incomprehensibility, the utter inability of anyone in the room to conceive of anyone anywhere engaging in a practice like genital cutting. The only uncertainty during this courtroom hearing was whether the particulars of Kasinga's case would enable her to fit into the rigid, albeit ill-defined, categories of asylum law.

The Media

My larger concern as a scholar of West Africa is with the fact that this reification of false image and stereotype about Togo, and metonymically about all of Africa, is not confined to a hearing in a federal courtroom with a handful of attorneys and judges in Falls Church, Virginia. Meanings were created in this courtroom for a larger public, and this opinion was (and is) widely cited in the press and beyond. Its demonizing images have become hegemonic, and so normalized in the print media, on the radio, and on the Internet that counter-discourse about the meaning of female genital cutting is today for most Westerners utterly unthinkable.[8]

Moreover, the fact that the same, self-iterating narrative emerges across all these sites is no accident. In the spring of 1996, Kasinga's lawyers sought help from a media-savvy New York-based feminist human rights group, Equality Now, which put them in touch with *New York Times* metro-area correspondent Celia Dugger. Immediately the lawyers realized they had a sympathetic ear and arranged for Dugger to interview Kasinga in her Pennsylvania detention facility. The article that emerged from this interview was published on the front page of the *Times* on 15 April. It not only brought the case to the attention of a wider public (which the intense petitioning and Internet activity of human rights organizations throughout the spring had been unable to achieve) but also significantly influenced the INS and the BIA.[9] Within ten days Kasinga was released from detention (an event that produced another Dugger article on the front page of the *Times* on 25 April 1996), and within two months she was granted asylum. I do not have the space here to analyze all four of Dugger's *Times* articles on Kasinga and her case, published on 15 April, 25 April, 14 June, and 11 September 1996, but they are fascinating, powerful narratives and mimetic (albeit more fully fleshed out) iterations of the same story told in the courtroom. They move from Kasinga's treatment under detention to her flight from arranged marriage and forced FGM in Togo, and finally, in the article that appeared after the BIA ruling and following a trip Dugger made to Togo (11 September 1996), all the way back to the courtyard of the family "patriarch" chastising Kasinga's mother for facilitating her escape. This piece was emblazoned with pictures of dirt roads and submissive women, with heads bowed before male patriarchs; it was punctuated by such subheadings as "The Tradition," "The Escape," "The Patriarch," "The Apology," "The Village." The article is peppered with phrases like "*for millennia*, girls across Africa . . ." and "it has been the custom *since antiquity* . . ."—all suggesting backwardness and stasis. Its evocation of images of the immutable nature of patriarchal tradition in a timeless Africa was extraordinary. Dugger had never been to Africa before her July trip, spoke neither French nor Tchamba, and spent only a few days in the country. Yet she wrote an article read by millions that spoke the "truth" not only about Kasinga's personal odyssey and Tchamba culture but also about an entire continent. It seemed to validate the BIA ruling retroactively.

Re-Telling Kasinga's Story

But how otherwise to portray Kasinga's travail? Based on what I heard about the case from one of her lawyers and from the U.S. Embassy official I met in Togo in the summer of 1996, I am fully prepared to believe that Kasinga was being coerced into a marriage and into a ritual practice that she did not want to undergo. However, I read this coercion in a different register, for it took place within a long family history of jealousy and exclusion, of strained relations between her well-to-do father and his brothers and sisters with whom he refused to share his wealth. This family conflict was characterized by the sort of snobbery and greed that typifies many struggles on the edges of the bourgeoisie in African cities today, in which self-interest is disguised behind a proclaimed rejection of tradition. "I don't do those rituals any longer because I am modern and no longer believe in Tchamba tradition" is the refrain, when the underlying reality is often "I have money and don't want to share it with you." The coercion to which Kasinga was subjected after her father died and her mother was banished was the family's indirect revenge on Kasinga's father.[10] Her refusal to submit to their wishes to marry further incited their anger. This is not in any way to justify what they did; indeed, I am deeply compelled by Kasinga's situation. Rather, it is an attempt to renarrativize Kasinga's story as one that is not about a timeless tradition of mutilating rituals and unyielding patriarchy in remote rural villages but rather about a nasty family dispute and about issues of class and modernity in Togo today.

But here's the rub. In the United States, an applicant cannot get asylum based on his or her status and claims as an individual. Kasinga's lawyers could not have argued that their petitioner was caught in an ugly family dispute and was being coerced into an arranged marriage and into engaging in a ritual act against her wishes. The law requires that asylum claims be based on membership in a cognizable social group that comes under persecution. This contradiction is the proximate cause of the demonizing imagery that Kasinga's lawyers were forced to draw on. To win their case, they *had* to portray her as coming from an unchanging patriarchal society of mutilators. And because the lawyers got Celia Dugger to write the story they had scripted and the human rights organizations to reiterate this narrative endlessly on the Internet, it is this contradiction that I see as responsible for producing this global discourse. Needless to say, this cultural script transcends the courtroom, and borrows racist, imperialist, and missionary images of Africa that are centuries old. Nevertheless, it was here produced in a new register, and with a focus and visibility that is unprecedented. This traveling narrative and truth-telling is hegemonic and thoroughly fetishized, in both Marxian and Freudian senses of that term, a story which utterly erases its origins in a past and different family history.

Whose Politics?

I end by raising a question about the role of the anthropologist in writing about this overdetermined issue. It is clear, at least to me, that before long anthropologists will be more fully brought into the FGM asylum process, if not by the lawyers of those seeking asylum, then certainly by an INS that worries about being deluged with asylum claims. A more robust and nuanced literature is beginning to emerge (Walley 1997; Boddy 1998 and 1998; Shell-Duncan and Hernlund 2000; Gruenbaum 2001) that, while not supporting genital cutting, complicates any simple-minded reading of the practice. This literature will surely be cited and invoked by the INS. Thus, we will risk finding ourselves in the uncomfortable position of being used by, even of being complicitous with, what many of us regard as a deeply conservative arm of the U.S. government. Indeed, I imagine that when this emerging literature begins to circulate and comes to the attention of the INS, few women will be able to get asylum under current definitions of the law. How, then, as anthropologists *and* feminists, are we to think about our role in this debate? Is there, as Marilyn Strathern (1986, 1988) suggested over a decade ago, an irreconcilable difference between feminist and anthropological agendas, between a global, universalistic feminism and an anthropology committed to communicating the nuance and meaning of local cultural worlds? And at what cost?

Afterword: Safe Harbor and Homage

L. Amede Obiora

*The story when we were young was that you could not have a child, unless you were circumcised in a cleansing ceremony (*iwu ahu*). The occasion used to be quite festive and, because the betrothed girls were thoroughly pampered in the process, many anticipated it with enthusiasm. Women who were exposed to the tenets of Christianity and formal education, however, often ended up escaping it. When one of my friends was getting married, the groom's family requested that she undergo the ceremony. In order not to engender strife with the prospective in-laws, her guardian conceded and performed elaborate preliminary ceremonials in apparent preparation. The circumciser came as scheduled, but she had received prior instruction not to perform the actual procedure; so they busied themselves with other stuff behind closed doors to give the impression that the procedure was taking place. My friend was to role-play by lying in bed for a couple of days. Funnily enough, she would forget the role at times and try to jump around with her mates as usual, to the embarrassment of her aunt who had claimed she was circumcised.*

—Flora Nwakuche (née Nwapa)

In an autobiographical interview, Africa's first published female novelist described this intriguing case of subversion.[1] Although this incident transpired during the 1940s, it shares some parallels with the process of change that is taking place in coming-of-age rituals for girls and young women in Africa today, and vividly underscores the complex dynamics of a society in transition.

A more recent experience in Oguta, the community in southeastern Nigeria where this incident took place, illuminates the possibilities for change that inhere in culture. Apparently, members of the community used to incur inordinate expenses to underwrite funeral rites. Both the state and the church pontificated against this practice for a long time, but to no avail, especially when the deceased's family had considerable wealth and influence. As a last resort, the church elected to set a time limit for funerals and reserved the right to refuse to participate in any burial that transgressed its decree. The test of the new order came on the occasion of the death of a notable figure whose demise was metaphorically equated to the falling "Iroko," which is a tree of considerable significance, to convey the magnitude of the loss it signified for the community. Despite the paramount place the deceased had enjoyed and the corollary expectation that the church would make an exception and lift the time constraint to accommodate an elaborate burial ceremony, the church exercised its prerogative, remained adamant, and actually prevailed. The burial was expedited, to the chagrin of the bereaved and to the amazement of the community. This turn of events would have been inconceivable in the past, especially given the socioeconomic status of the deceased and the importance attached to burial rites in the prevailing worldview. Presumably, the key decision makers in the family of the deceased had to weigh their commitment to elaborate funeral rites against other compelling considerations and interests, including the risks of compromising the integrity of the deceased's faith by denying her the Christian burial she so deeply desired. Like the observation made by Flora Nwakuche, this experience is an apt reminder of the fact that culture is not unyielding, but constantly evolving and amenable to change.

So much has been made of the triumph of custom over reform initiatives and of the stranglehold of culture as a constraint on gender equity. At an intuitive level, many agree that culture is dynamic. Yet, the challenges it poses to the implementation of reform tend to mystify this understanding. Drawing on these examples from Oguta, it is plausible to postulate that the overarching task for advocates of transformation in culturally embedded gender practices such as female circumcision is to identify fruitful pressure points in order to cultivate countercultures that affirm women's rights. Evidence of such points is not far from the view of the culturally competent who are able to appreciate culture as a holistic entity and to assess it within the context of its political economy. In this light, this collection edited by Rogaia Abusharaf is an important addition to existing literature. These contributions offer many windows on ways and means of constructively challenging and changing gender-biased aspects of indigenous cultural practices. The fascinating documentation of ongoing and wide-ranging efforts to eradicate female circumcision at the grassroots level across Africa yields insights into the determinants and logic of transformation. In the same vein, these contributions delineate the confluence of cultural and structural variables that is instrumental in reversing patterns of allegiance to the practice. From the evidence uncovered in these studies, it is clear that due attention to these factors is critical for the effective orchestration of systematic reform measures.

Emerging consensus about the health hazards of radical forms of genital cutting, together with substantial shifts in the level of commitment to these age-old traditions, are narrowing the gap in opinions regarding the imperative for change. Notwithstanding this convergence, ascertaining and harnessing the most viable means for its achievement remains an abiding challenge. The emphasis on the means is not to suggest that there are not persons who are opposed to the end itself. Some defenders of tradition emphasize the value of female circumcision more assertively because the practice has been called into question and its perpetuation is, indeed, in doubt. The findings of contemporary research which demonstrate that change is inevitable suggest the expedience of deliberations over what vectors can best contribute to the transformative process and maximize the benefits of change for all concerned. The exemplary programs analyzed in this book have motivated women to interrogate their priorities systematically and opened up the space for vigorous critiques of female circumcision to be voiced and heard. How these critiques were effectively deployed to orchestrate measurable change is a remarkable tale that illuminates the conditions on which social change depends.

The cases discussed here point up persisting methodological challenges and enrich our understanding about how to enhance the viability of correctives. Exploring the ramifications of using criminal law in a host country against female circumcision practiced by immigrants, Audrey Macklin sheds light on the complex positioning of women within Diaspora communities. Macklin extols the procedural aspect of citizenship, highlighting the paradox that manifests when marginalized groups exercise the prerogatives of citizenship to mobilize in protest against the poverty of their formal enfranchisement. She argues that the virtues of representation are considerable, since those who are subject to law and policy are included in the process of formulating and interpreting them. Macklin's consideration of the implications of deliberative democracy captures a core theme of this collection and speaks to the constructive role of the deliberative process in the creation of gender-sensitive norms.

Much of the collection underscores the inescapable importance of meaningful opportunities for participation in opening up vistas of change in gender practices. While these practices are rooted in shared norms and social values, their conceptualizations are in turn influenced by dialogue and debate. Several scholars have forcefully illuminated the pivotal place of public discussions in facilitating careful scrutiny of and, if necessary, retreat from embedded practices. For example, Anthony Giddens defines what he calls "dialogic democracy" as the recognition of the authenticity of the other, whose views and ideas one is prepared to listen to and debate. According to Giddens, this mutual process is the only alternative to violence in many areas of the social order where disengagement is no longer a feasible option (Giddens 1994). Amartya Sen articulates the centrality of participation for the critical, informed, and unregimented evaluation of what aspects of culture and tradition should be maintained or abandoned. Arguing the need for people affected to participate in deciding what they want and what they have reason to accept, Sen contends that "the legitimacy of adhering today to views enunciated in the sixth century B.C. has to be decided by those who live today" (Sen 1999: 31). To buttress his viewpoint, Sen earmarks education as a basic condition for the substantive exercise of participatory freedom. The findings of several contributions in this volume offer empirical support for such arguments.

Amal Abdel Hadi recounts the fascinating example of an Egyptian Christian village that stopped the practice of female circumcision, without the assistance or intervention of policymakers, politicians, or the medical community. Village leaders entered a compact with local midwives, traditional birth attendants, and barbers enjoining them to refrain from performing the procedure. Particularly instructive is the identification of a statistically significant positive correlation between respondents' involvement in development activities and their fulfillment of the undertaking not to circumcise girls. In Abdel Hadi's analysis, the main reason for the authoritative shift and cultural transformation is that the village has been a site of consistent development efforts that promoted women's participation and noticeably reconfigured gender roles. Primarily under the auspices of the Coptic Evangelical Organization for Social Services (CEOSS), the village established portable water network and sewage systems, professional training for youth, revolving loans and capacity building for income-generating activities, agricultural and environmental protection projects, community-wide education programs with special emphasis on women and girls, and health literacy programs focusing on nutrition, hygiene, disease prevention, family planning, reproductive health, and mother and child health care services.

The central importance of the empowerment of women to the successful elimination of female circumcision is consistent with findings about factors that account for the indisputable decline of the practice in other arenas.

A number of contributions pay varied forms of homage to gains made by Tostan. This Senegalese NGO offers a widely celebrated best practice model that uses development or capacity-building outreach for women as the key means of eroding the attractions of female circumcision. Tostan provides participants from the target population with resources to improve their standard of living, while helping them to acquire and effectively put to use the tools required to tackle culturally sensitive issues such as female circumcision. The positive results of Tostan's programs demonstrate that with increased socioeconomic assets, people can assert a stronger commitment to gender equity objectives and they are better equipped to undertake various tasks to advance the agenda.[2]

A broad spectrum of strategies has been implemented to modify knowledge, beliefs, attitudes, and behavior about the practice. However, until recently these strategies had not been adequately documented to demonstrate how they work or to evaluate their impact. The paucity of empirical evidence that characterized earlier anti-circumcision interventions gave the impression that it took the international denunciations that peaked during the 1990s for cognizable shifts in the practice to occur. The emergence of operations research about female circumcision has been useful on many fronts. Such studies advance understanding about promising methodologies and provide information on how to design effective interventions, as well as enabling advocates to identify and integrate factors that support success, control drawbacks, and facilitate continuous monitoring and evaluation of program effectiveness. More and more, these studies are calling attention to the scope and force of African agency and initiative for the curtailment and eradication of the practice.

The illumination of African voices and choices is a particular strength of this collection. The essays span a wide reach geographically, ranging from grassroots activities on the continent to efforts in the Diaspora. The essays offer objective accounts of African women creatively traversing an array of terrains to define their own destinies and further the well-being of their communities. These studies are a welcome corrective for a genre of writings and approaches that has portrayed African women in circumcising communities as passive, if not unthinking sadists and masochists, who required international outcry to confront the ravages of circumcision. Since historically many of the relevant traditions were oral rather than recorded in writing, dissent from the practice may have existed since time immemorial, even if there is no concrete testament to that effect and even if organized mobilization against the practice is more typically a contemporary phenomenon.

Positioned against insights from this volume, the global anti-circumcision campaign is best seen as a collaborative effort synchronizing momentum within Africa with the facilitative support of an international alliance. While the importance of external support must be acknowledged, it would be unfortunate to construe it as indispensable.

Hamid El Bashir quotes an African proverb: "No matter how slow, a caravan that moves steadily ultimately reaches its distant destination." The invocation of this and other folk sayings in this book underscores a distinctive contribution of this collection: it exemplifies a rare attempt to investigate and feature a series of concerted efforts undertaken by Africans for Africans to champion the struggle against female circumcision. The success of recent coordination and sensitization has at once obscured and enhanced this long tradition of dissent and accountability. The acknowledgment of indigenous knowledge and the conscious embrace of its value in solving local problems is a key explanation for the growing success of organized activism against female circumcision. Conversely, the cultural change that is taking place without programmed intervention reflects the force of indigenous change agents. In fact, the top-down imposition of criminal penalties is not an effective deterrent in the absence of endemic processes that catalyze reorientation against female circumcision.

Asha Mohamud, Samson Radeny, and Karin Ringheim examine a three-pronged strategy aimed at helping parents who have already stopped circumcising to come out of the closet, provide a way out to families who are undecided or inhibited by social pressure, and establish a strong non-circumcising community as an alternative to the community of adherents to the practice. Focusing on a pioneering initiative to integrate health, legal, psychological, and religious concerns, Shahira Ahmed discusses a program to combat female circumcision in the Sudan that is now in its third decade of existence. Advisedly, she notes that the prevalence of the practice today is still high and that campaigners have a lot to accomplish before they can abolish the practice in all its forms. In this context, she takes solace in the reminder that the journey of a thousand miles begins with a single step. In reckoning the steps that constitute the miles, some of the studies historicize activism against female circumcision and by implication articulate overdue credit for the unsung heroes and heroines who were brave enough to speak out against the practice when it was not just unfashionable but actually dangerous to confront it.

The great strides made by eradication programs engender resentment, if not outright hostility, among persons who perceive unfairness in the refusal to acknowledge preexisting activism and the failure to situate the newer programs that are being introduced on a continuum with the activism that incubated and laid the groundwork for them. Not even a program as popular as Tostan's escapes criticism in this respect. Interestingly, campaigners who once bore the scourge of deviance persevered, undaunted by the arduous path and such humiliating treatment as having pebbles thrown at them; ultimately they gained respect as standard bearers and now enjoy the pleasure of fielding requests for assistance. These studies bear witness to the gradual proliferation of local groups who seek to regulate the incidence and form of the practice and do not hesitate to enlist the coercive power of the state to enforce restraint. Another significant trend documented in the studies is the substitution of a range of symbolic gestures, such as *Lazga* (the placement of a plaster around the labia majora), for the actual cutting. Fadwa El Guindi furnishes further evidence of such cultural dynamism and self-refashioning, suggesting that the corrective use of the clitoral procedure in the Anglo-American context influenced its reading in African context and relating the preoccupation with its sexual ramifications to a restrictive ethos and Christian traditions of penance. El Guindi notes that among the Mettokki-speaking Kenuz of Nubia, the less severe form called "nylon" circumcision came into use during the late 1950s or early 1960s as a fashionable innovation. This trend was not a result of planned international intervention. In her view, the Nubian case demonstrates that the form of female circumcision has been changing to accommodate local women's choices. The determination of cause and effect in complex relationships is a task that calls for tremendous care. These authors' deliberate attempts to assign credit to local initiative highlights concerns about the role of outsiders in countering the sway of circumcision.

The characteristic messages of good hope in the book are tempered by some discouraging findings. For example, El Bashir's study documents the recent adoption of female circumcision in Mayerno, a predominantly Hausa-Fulani settlement in central Sudan. A local health worker reports a marked departure from this ethnocultural group's indigenous tradition, in which women are not circumcised, and an upsurge in demand for the most severe form of Pharaonic circumcision; younger women are accommodating to the surrounding culture, even as campaigns against the practice are gaining strength there. Nafissatou J. Diop and Ian Askew offer another sobering report that counterbalances heartening reports of successful interventions. Reviewing projects aimed at converting excisors, they conclude that these programs have not been effective in actually deterring the performance of female circumcision. Even those who had been sensitized in an effort to persuade them to desist from the practice persisted in cutting girls in response to families' requests and were not convinced that what they do is wrong. They explained that they continue to perform circumcisions because they were not provided with the alternative means for income generation they had been promised. The dilemma posed by the situation of the excisors demonstrates the difficulty of insisting on unequivocal positions when a situation calls for more nuanced responses. This caveat is reinforced by Tostan. In catering to the socioeconomic needs of the participants, the initiative addresses the context that enables practices such as female circumcision. Tostan's effectiveness supports a more nuanced reading of the structure of authority and suggests that a top-down analysis fails to capture the payoffs of integration. Indeed, Diop and Askew caution against isolated interventions and establish the value of comprehensive approaches that address female circumcision as an integral component of human rights and community development. By the same token, instructive insights from some winning strategies presented in this book illuminate what works and the artificiality of merely abstract attacks.

Another key lesson of the models discussed in this volume relates to the centrality of a community-based focus. Several contributions underscore the costs of noninclusion and warn that not enlisting the participation of traditional authorities risks undermining the success of the anti-circumcision campaign. The so-called code of silence or reticence that marks the practice in certain places underlines the fact that a meaningful reform agenda entails exploring creative, sincere, and nonthreatening ways to enlist the support and mediation of the larger community, especially local religious authorities, village elders, and youth. This approach may take the form of actively courting, reorienting, and coopting formal indigenous institutions and apparatus of governance. It is not unusual in the development community to disregard these tried and proven institutions. This outright neglect or underutilization is especially ironic in light of the emphasis on capacity building and the resources invested in the formation of new institutions. If indeed the practice at issue is embedded in cultural traditions, it stands to reason that traditional entities are potential forces of resistance and opposition. However, there is nothing inherently or invariably oppositional about them.

In the final analysis, it is plausible to argue that anti-circumcision campaign is an idea whose time has come. On this score, Dimba Diwara's assertion is apt: "We keep doing things most of the time without thinking about them. I say, this is what my father did and what my grandfather left me. But

I do not keep everything they left me. I am dressed differently, I travel by cars and trains and sometimes planes that they never saw. If they were here they would tell me to be a good man and a good Muslim and that is what I am being right now."[3] His perspective captures the organic and dynamic dimensions of indigenous cultures and social structures. The shifts in the practices of female circumcision highlighted in this book offer powerful empirical rationale for fostering an enabling environment for the dynamic transformation of culture.

Notes

Chapter 2. *"Had This Been Your Face, Would You Leave It as Is?" Female Circumcision Among the Nubians of Egypt*

This essay is dedicated to the memory of Charles C. Callender, exemplary ethnographer, colleague, and friend. I also gratefully acknowledge the assistance of Dr. Laila Shukry El Hamamsy, former director of the Social Research Center of the American University in Cairo; Robert Fernea, director of the Ethnological Survey, and B. J. Fernea; Jake Homiak and Robert Leopold, at the Smithsonian National Anthropological Archives; and Kari Sprowl, for background research on the history of clitoridectomy in Europe and the United States.

1 For a detailed discussion of historical background, see Fernea and Fernea 1991: 123–53.

2 Sudanese Nubians displaced by the dam were resettled at Kashim el-Ghurba in the Sudan.

3 If this conclusion is correct, then the question arises of how the Kenuz ended up in the region of Aswan in Egypt. The only reliable information available is linguistic. It has been suggested that the Kenuz were originally a trading colony sent by a Dongolawi kingdom to oversee trade at the First Cataract at Aswan, the old port city on the border between Egypt and the early Christian kingdoms of Nubia (Fernea and Fernea 1991: 137). Their business would have been to oversee overland shipments of goods by camel caravans between Egypt and Dongola, avoiding going through the region south of the Kenuz area which was then populated by ancestors of the Fedija Nubians. This idea of early trade colonies would account for the Kenuz presence in a number of villages south of the Esno-Kom-Ombo region, across the old dam and the First Cataract, long before their final resettlement in Kom-Ombo in 1963. It might also "explain the Kenuzi domination of most of the commerce that (until recently) took place between Aswan, the Kenuzi villages, and the Fedija Nubian villages all the way to Wadi Halfa" (Fernea and Fernea 1991: 137). The Dongolawi ancestors of the present-day Kenuz may have relied more heavily on trade than on agriculture for their livelihood.

4 In the eleventh century, the Rabi'a tribe, an Arabian tribe from Yamama (in Yemen) who had entered Egypt in the ninth century, finally settled in the Nubian region around Aswan. They would have become numerically and linguistically strong by the time the nomadic Bani Kanz came from the desert and took over the area in the eleventh century. The Rabi'a brought with them their language (Arabic), religion (Islam), and sociopolitical organization (patrilineal descent), but they eventually adopted the local language and culture by mixing with Nubians and marrying their

daughters. This mixed group came to be called Bani Kanz, and later Kenuz, the name used until today for the northern Nubian groups. Bani Kanz and Kenuz were terms derived from the "Kanz el-Dawla," a title bestowed on the chief of this group in late Fatimid times (Fernea and Fernea 1991: 135, n. 2).

5 In a matrilineal system, kinship ties are traced through mothers rather than fathers. The Nubians are also exogamous, which means that people find spouses outside their own group. In this instance, the matrilineal kinship system, when combined with exogamous marriage patterns, was responsible for the transfer of corporate wealth outside the group, but the same principles worked to preserve group identity through the women. Women transmitted the culture down through their children and cemented tradition despite exogamous marriage, change of religious affiliation, and corporate wealth transfer.

6 In a recent synthesis, Gruenbaum (2001) concurs, although she accords too much importance to what a pious Muslim male guest lecturer said regarding the Islamic basis of female circumcision (65–66).

7 It is significant that this term is widely used by American men and women to refer to the sex act; it is considered a performance, rather than an experience.

8 Viagra and similar medications increase blood flow to the genitals, treating the sex act as a physical problem. While Viagra does increase blood flow to women's genitals, the sex therapist Laura Berman, director of the Berman Center in Chicago, has emphasized that this factor alone is insufficient to enable women to achieve orgasm.

9 I intentionally use the term mutilation here, although I am critical of its being deployed to describe customary traditions that are embedded in culture, in order to add comparative perspective.

10 This conference was held on February 22–28, 1978, at Al-Ahfad, the first girls' school in Khartoum, to commemorate the school's 75th anniversary. As a participant in the conference, I was struck by the level of candor and openness expressed in the papers presented and in the remarks commenting on them. The American Embassy personnel and diplomats were very nervous about this session. The ambience was of total shock that this "secret" phenomenon was being publicly exposed. Women participants and local commentators did not give the impression that it was considered secret in this sense; rather, it was only private, and it was primarily a concern of women.

11 The Nubian Ethnographic Survey covered the entire region of Egyptian Nubia from the southern border of Aswan to the northern border of the Sudan. The survey consisted of an extensive study with intensive fieldwork by three teams of anthropologists, research assistants, and local associates. It comprised three linguistic areas: the Mettokki-speaking Kenuz, the Arabic-speaking central area, and the Fedija of the south. This major project was funded by the Ford Foundation and was sponsored by the Social Research Center of the American University in Cairo, fieldwork was carried out by teams of researchers from the SRC with full consent and official approval of the Ministry of Social Affairs in Egypt.

12 *Hegab* is Egyptian spoken Arabic for *hijab*, which is an Arabic word encompassing multiple meanings. For more on the multivocality of Hijab, see El Guindi 1995, 1999, 2005.

Chapter 3. Male and Female Circumcision: The Myth of the Difference

1 Mrs. Al-Warzazi referred to our correspondence in her report on the 1997 conference on traditional practices: UN Economic and Social Council, 25.6, par. 18.

2 For the Old Testament, I use Samuel Raphael Hirsch's German version, as translated into English by Gertrude Hirschler (New York: Judaica Press, 1990).

3 I was confronted with the position of Edmond Kaiser on this subject in the Swiss newspapers. See my letter in *Le Nouveau quotidien*, 8 July 1997, and the answer of Edmond Kaiser in the same newspaper, 18 July 1997.

4 For such a ritual, see Goldman 1995.

5 Message on Internet, 30 May 1997, from Ari Zighelboim, akp@communique .net. See also *London Daily Telegraph*, 5 May 1997.

6 For the New Testament, I use the New Revised Standard Version (Nashville: Thomas Nelson, 1990).

7 Quotation from Cyril of Alexandria are my translations from

8 For the Qur'an, I use the translation by Rahsad Khalifa at http://www .submission.org/Q-T.html.

9 See the two Saudi fatwas in *Magallat al-buhuth al-islamiyyah, Riyadh*: no. 20 (1987), 161, and no. 25 (1989), 62.

10 See http://www.moslem.org/khatne.htm, which refers to my article, "To Mutilate in the Name of Jehovah or Allah."

11 See Qur'an 3:191; 13:8; 25:2; 30:30; 32:7; 38:27; 40:64; 54:49; 64:3; 95:4.

12 Verses 4:118–19 say: "[The Devil] said, 'I will surely recruit a definite share of Your worshipers. I will mislead them, I will entice them, I will command them to mark the ears of livestock, and I will command them to distort the creation of GOD.' Anyone who accepts the devil as a lord, instead of GOD, has incurred a profound loss."

13 Jad-al-Haq reiterated his position in another fatwa in October 1994, which repeats three times the sentence relating to the declaration of war against those who abandon male and female circumcision.

14 Al-Tantari quoted in *Al-Ahram*, Arabic-language daily newspaper (Cairo), 9 October 1994, p. 8.

15 See "Circumcision," *Encyclopedia Judaica* 1978, vol 5.

16 Aquinas, *Summa Theologica*, IaIIae, q. 102, a. 5, ad 1. See also IIIa, q. 70, a. 3, arg. 1, ad 1.

17 Editor, "Circumcision vs. Cancer," *Newsweek* 21 (1943): 110–11.

18 Email sent by owner-intact-1@cirp.org le 25.6.1997, signed by Miral Fahmy.

19 See United Press International, 29 October 1986.

20 http://www.axt.org.uk/antisem/archive/archive1/switzerland/switzerland.htm.

21 American Convention, Art. 4 par. 2: "Every person has the right to have his life respected. This right shall be protected by law and, in general, from the moment of conception. No one shall be arbitrarily deprived of his life." Art. 5 par. 1: "Every person has the right to have his physical, mental, and moral integrity respected." African Charter, Art. 4: "Human beings are inviolable. Every human being shall be entitled to respect for his life and the integrity of his person. No one may be arbitrarily deprived of this right."

Chapter 4. Community-Based Efforts to End Female Genital Mutilation in Kenya: Raising Awareness and Organizing Alternative Rites of Passage

The three coauthors collaborated on the MYWO/PATH project discussed in this essay. At the time this work was conducted, Asha Mohamud was a Senior Program Officer with PATH in Washington, D.C. A physician and reproductive health specialist, she served as Project Director for the MYWO/PATH collaboration, responsible for conceptualizing and overseeing the project, providing technical assistance, and fundraising. Samson Radeny, a sociologist, was a Senior Program Officer in charge of the culture, gender, and health programs under which these activities were implemented. He was the PATH-Kenya point person for FGM eradication projects, overseeing technical assistance to the project partners and working directly with MYWO coordinators in the field. Karin Ringheim, a sociologist, was a Senior Program Officer with PATH; she was responsible for evaluating the project, using data collected during the 1992–1993 baseline survey and the 1999 end-line survey conducted by Joyce Olenja of the University of Nairobi.

Leah Muuya, whose words stand as the epigraph for this chapter, made this statement in September 1995; her comments were captured in the first MYWO/PATH video, "Secret and Sacred." Muuya was MYWO's program manager for the project from its inception to her untimely death in 2000. In addition to her inspiring and untiring work, we want to acknowledge the contributions of the MYWO district coordinators: Nancy Ogega and Jerusha Mubishi in Meru; Agnes Pareiyo and Agnes Yapan in Narok; Michelina Lengewa in Samburu; and Jeria Kerubo Moragia in Kisii. Ancieta C. Kiriga and Flora Kaweanja Nthiga of the NGO Ntanira Na Mugambo ("Circumcision with Words") provided leadership for the development of the alternative rite of passage.

This project received support from many sources, including the Wallace Global Fund, the Public Welfare Foundation, the Moriah Fund, the Ford Foundation, the Threshold Foundation, Save the Children Fund, Australian Aid, and UNIFEM, the United Nations Development Fund for Women.

1 The largest women's organization in Kenya, the Maendeleo Ya Wanawake Organization (MYWO) promotes women's human rights, political participation, and economic security. With branches all over the country, the organization works to achieve gender equality primarily by sponsoring programs in women's reproductive health, including HIV/AIDS and STD prevention, family planning, and maternal and infant health, as well as to eliminate female genital mutilation and substitute alternative rites of passage. Other MYWO initiatives include income generation, environment and energy conservation, and women's leadership development and training.

2 This survey was carried out with the technical and financial assistance of the Population Crisis committee, now called Population Action International.

3 The Program for Appropriate Technology in Health (PATH), an international organization, focuses on improving women's health by developing technologies and programs that support women during pregnancy and childbirth; increase women's access to family planning methods; and provide women with services related to disease detection, prevention, and treatment. Other major programs focus on children's

health and the prevention of communicable diseases. By collaborating with governmental and nongovernmental agencies in developing countries, PATH works to develop infrastructures to supply essential health services and bridge technology gaps in the delivery of appropriate health care.

4 The unpublished and published documents on which this essay is based include MYWO/PATH project reports. The baseline survey, titled "A Report on Harmful Traditional Practices that Affect the Health of Women and Their Children in Kenya," was published circa 1992 by MYWO. Its findings were reported in MYWO/PATH's "Qualitative Research Report on Female Circumcision in Four Districts in Kenya," February 1993. The end-line survey is presented in Joyce Olenja's "Evaluation Report on Eliminating the Practice of Female Genital Mutilation: Awareness Raising and Community Change in Four Districts of Kenya," submitted to PATH and MYWO in October 2000. This report summarizes data from the baseline survey for purposes of comparison. Data from this report was used in PATH's *Evaluating Efforts to Eliminate the Practice of FGM: Raising Awareness and Changing Harmful Norms in Kenya* (2000).

5 The 1998 Demographic and Health Survey, while national in scope, did not include districts in the northeast, where FGM is thought to remain nearly universal. Thus the figure of 38 percent seriously underestimated the national prevalence of this practice.

6 Kisii and Gusii are closely related languages which are mutually comprehensible. During the period covered by the project reports, the district of Kisii, which takes its name from the town of Kisii, was divided in two, Kisii and Gucha; the subdistrict of Nyamira is just north of Kisii. The national DHS, which identified this ethnocultural group as Kisii, included all Ekegusii speakers wherever they lived in Kenya. Most resided in these adjacent districts, but some had moved to other rural regions, and some to the capital.

7 During the period covered by the MYWO/PATH report, the district of Meru was divided; its districts and subdistricts include Nyambene or South Meru, and Tharaka Nithi. The ethnic groups who live there all speak Meru, but there are some cultural differences among them.

8 The Samburu language is related to Maa, but the Maasai are a very distinctive ethnocultural group. The district of Samburu is poorer and less stable than Narok; in addition to suffering from drought, the people have been affected by the civil war that spilled over from neighboring Somalia.

Chapter 6. Strategies for Encouraging the Abandonment of Female Genital Cutting: Experiences from Senegal, Burkina Faso, and Mali

This essay is based a series of research studies undertaken by the Population Council through its operations research program in sub-Saharan Africa. Funding for these studies was provided by USAID under Contract number CCC-3030-C-00-3008-00 and Cooperative Agreement number HRN-A-00-98-00012-00. The opinions expressed in this essay are those of the authors and do not necessarily reflect the views of USAID.

1 The Population Council is an international nonprofit NGO that conducts biomedical and social science research, and provides technical expertise in response to requests from national and local groups that undertake projects to improve public health, with a particular emphasis on reproductive health and rights and gender equity.

2 Tostan, which means "breakthrough" in the Wolof language spoken by the majority of the population in Senegal, is an international NGO based in Senegal. "Tostan: Women's Health and Human Rights" can be found on the web at <www .tostan.org>.

Chapter 8. The Babiker Badri Scientific Association for Women's Studies and the Eradication of Female Circumcision in the Sudan

1 See the introduction to this volume for an explanation of the various types of female circumcision. Although the terms used to refer to this array of practices vary and are a matter of debate, I use female circumcision consistently here, as BBSAWS itself does.

2 Although BBSAWS's programs address the medical and legal aspects of the practice, I have addressed these subjects only briefly because the literature on these topics is extensive. See, for example, Abdel Magied and Ahmed (2002); El Nagar et al. (1994).

3 Sheik is the title given to a leader, particularly a spiritual leader, of a community.

4 Omdurman is one of three towns constituting the national capital area of Sudan. One of the oldest cities in Sudan, it has been the site of many decisive political events throughout Sudanese history.

5 The WHO Regional Office for the Eastern Mediterranean in Khartoum, in collaboration with the WHO Regional Office for Africa, sponsored what became known as the Khartoum Seminar. This gathering formulated recommendations for governments to eliminate female circumcision, including setting up national commissions for the coordination of activities and the intensification of education. See WHO (1979).

6 Those speaking on behalf of the eradication campaign included the religious leader Sheikh Hassan Abu Sabib; midwife Hawa Ali El-Baseer; psychiatrists Dr. Ahmed Sirrag and Taj El-Sir Doleeb; and gynecologists Dr. Abdal-Salam Gerees, Dr. Tawfig El-Deeb, Dr. El-Hadi El-Nahas, Dr. Abbo Hassan Abbo, and Dr. Mohamed Hassaneen.

7 Ablution here refers to the Muslim ritual cleansing of the body.

8 Qur'an 7:11.

9 Unlike the verses contained in the Qur'an, Hadith are the sayings and traditions of Prophet Muhammad himself, and form part of the record of the Prophet's

Sunna, way of life and example. The Hadith record the words and deeds, explanations, and interpretations of the Prophet concerning all aspects of life. Hadith are found in various collections compiled by Muslim scholars in the early centuries of the Muslim civilization. Six such collections are considered most authentic. See Islamicity's website: <http://www.islamicity.com/IslamicGlossary>.

10 The Shari'a, the revealed and the canonical laws of the religion of Islam.

Chapter 10. The Double-Edged Sword: Using the Criminal Law Against Female Genital Mutilation in Canada

1 For analyses of pervasive racial discrimination in the justice system, see the reports from the Government of Ontario (1994) and the Government of Canada (1996).

2 The Canadian Criminal Code s.268.3 states that to wound or maim includes to "excise, infibulate or mutilate, in whole or in part, the labia majora, labia minora or clitoris of a person." The statute allows exceptions only for medical necessity, or if the woman was over 18 years of age and no bodily harm resulted.

3 My thanks to Sadia Gassim, who organized the petition, and to Lucya Spencer of the National Organization of Immigrant and Visible Minority Women of Canada (NOIVMWC) and Khamisa Baya of Women's Health in Women's Hands, who discussed their involvement in the legislative process with me. Sadia Gassim, telephone interview, 16 June 1999; Khamisa Baya, telephone interviews, 10 June 1999, 14 June 2002. Khamisa Baya also shared her collection of petitions and briefs presented to the government in 1996 by Women's Health in Women's Hands, which are cited herein as Baya 1996.

4 The NOIVMWC created a comprehensive and nuanced workshop manual on FGM as a resource for organizations and groups interested in educating their communities. The objectives of the workshops are to correct misconceptions and fallacies about FGM; give information about the negative health and legal consequences of FGM; help participants think about ways to prevent FGM; help participants find the self-confidence to face the social pressure to continue FGM prevalent among certain communities; and prepare participants to educate others in their communities about the need to eradicate female genital mutilation. See National Organization of Immigrant and Visible Minority Women of Canada (1998).

5 In Baya's view, because parents are motivated by a misplaced belief about what is in the best interests of their daughter, they ought not to be punished, and the family ought not to be dismembered, by a possible prison term. The person who performs the procedure for profit warrants a more severe sentence. Baya interview, 1999.

6 I thank Ruth Rubio-Marin for this helpful phrase.

7 Even laws declared unconstitutional may remain on the statute books for many years before they are finally removed. Outmoded laws often remain even though they are never enforced. For example, s.71 of the Criminal Code still proscribes dueling. Apparently, dueling was made an offense because people accused of assault or murder consequent to a duel were routinely acquitted by juries. Explicit

criminalization was required to overcome the "cultural defense" of avenging an insult to honor.

8 The episode Williams describes involved an application to the U.S. Senate Judiciary Committee to approve the renewal of the special design insignia of the United Daughters of the Confederacy, which included an image of the Confederate flag. Carol Moseley-Braun (D.-Ill.), the sole African American on the committee, strongly objected the renewal of the patent because of the association of the Confederate flag with the institution of slavery. Although the application was initially approved, a majority of Committee members reversed their decision after listening to Senator Moseley-Braun's objection.

9 A televised report about the St. Catharines case indicated that requests for government funding to assist in running educational programs have been unsuccessful to date.

10 James Ramsay, Crown Prosecutor, St. Catharines, Ontario, telephone interview with author, 18 June 2002.

Chapter 11. Representing Africa in the Kasinga Asylum Case

1 In her 1998 autobiography written with Layli Miller Bashir, *Do They Hear You When You Cry*, she spelled her surname "Kassindja." In the press at the time, and often still today, she was referred to as "Kasinga," a misspelling (and mispronunciation) that apparently resulted from an Immigration and Naturalization Service official's error. Since this essay deals with documents that use the erroneous spelling, I retain it here.

2 Accounts of the identity of Kasinga's "husband" are confused and contradictory. Kasinga claimed during trial that he was forty-five years old, although he told two American journalists that he was 28 (Dugger, 11 September 1996; Coleman 1997). Kasinga claimed that he was a well-to-do builder and politician with connections to local police, while he claimed to be a petty trader who didn't even "know what a district assemblyman is" (Coleman 1997).

3 To add one more twist to a complicated personal story, the embassy official I spoke with (see also Coleman 1997) told me that during his investigative work, he had sought out a woman in the Togolese government who had always been a reliable source of information. Upon hearing his description of the facts of Kasinga's case (about which she was previously unaware), she said it was likely (since she knew others similarly situated) that Kasinga was part of an international prostitution ring that worked the Togo-Germany-U.S. triangle. "They are told that if they are caught without papers, they should say they are fleeing FGM," he repeated her having said.

4 There was some ambiguity in Kasinga's earlier statements concerning her marital status (whether or not she was *already* married to the man in question), whether or not her father was still alive, who performed genital cutting among Tchamba (an old man or an old woman), and exactly what had happened when she was in Germany. There was also concern about the fact that portions of the taped transcript

from the earlier hearing were inaudible, and that the record included an untranslated document (in French) from the Togolese police.

5 All the other issues, except for whether the Board of Immigration Appeals should establish a broad framework for future policy, were dealt with briefly, both during the hearing and in the court's final opinion.

6 U.S. Department of State, *Togo Country Report on Human Rights Practices for 1996.*

7 Kasinga's lawyers submitted an affidavit by Merrick Posnansky, an archeologist, which asserted that FGM was common in Tchamba, that Tchamba women who chose not to undergo the procedure would be forced to do so, that because "Togo is a very patriarchal society" young women Kasinga's age would have no say in their marital fates, and that if returned to Togo she would be subjected to country-wide persecution. Although he conducted archeological work in Togo, Posnansky has never to my knowledge conducted ethnographic work there, speaks none of the local languages, and has never lived among Tchamba.

8 See Grewal and Kaplan (1996) for a postcolonial feminist critique of the Orientalist assumptions that similarly inform Pratibha Parmar and Alice Walker's 1993 film *Warrior Marks.*

9 Other articles published during spring 1996 include those by Judy Mann and Linda Burstyn in the *Washington Post* (19 January, 17 March), by Ellen Goodman in the *Boston Globe* (10 April); and by A. M. Rosenthal on the Op-Ed page of the *New York Times* (12 April).

10 Even Dugger's account suggests such a retelling: "Mr. Kasinga's decisions [to not have his daughters cut, and to educate Fauziya] brought stinging disapproval from his own extended family. They accused him of trying to act like a white man. His girls would never be considered full Tchamba women until their genitals had been excised, the elders said, and he was wasting money by sending them to high school. But Mr. Kassindja kept a distance from his relatives, including his cousin, who lived a few blocks away. 'He was a rich man, so the family couldn't tell him anything', said the cousin, Mouhamadou Kassindja, now the family patriarch."

Afterword: Safe Harbor and Homage

1 Flora Nwakuche (née Nwapa), interviewed by L. Amede Obiora, Lagos, Nigeria, July 1991.

2 See Obiora (2003).

3 Quoted by Asma Mohamed Abdel Halim in her unpublished conference paper, "From Bagadadji to Abu Hashim: New Approaches to Combat Female Circumcision."

References

Abdalla, Raqiya H. D. *Sisters in Affliction: Circumcision and Infibulation of Women in Africa.* London: Zed Books, 1982.

Abd-al-Raziq, Abu-Bakr. *Al-khitan, ra'y al-din wal-'ilm fi khitan al-awlad wal-banat* (Circumcision: Perspective of Religion on Male and Female Circumcision). Cairo: Dar Al-i'tissam, 1989.

Abdel Hadi, Amal. "Female Genital Mutilation in Egypt." In *African Women's Health*, ed. Meredith Turshen. Trenton, N.J.: Africa World Press, 2000.

———. "Islam, Law, and Reproductive Health in Egypt." In *Islam, Reproductive Health, and Women's Rights*, ed. Sisters in Islam. Kuala Lampur: Sisters in Islam, 2000.

———. *We Are Decided: The Struggle of an Egyptian Village to Eradicate Female Circumcision.* Cairo: Cairo Institute for Human Rights Studies, 1999.

Abdel Hadi, Amal and Seham Abdel-Salam. *Attitudes of Egyptian Physicians Towards FGM.* Cairo: Cairo Institute for Human Rights Studies, 1998.

Abdel Hadi, Amal and Nadia Abdel Wabah, eds. *The Feminist Movement in the Arab World.* Cairo: New Woman Research Centre, 1995.

Abdel Halim, Asma Mohamud. "Claiming Our Bodies and Our Rights: Exploring Female Circumcision as an Act of Violence." In *Freedom from Violence: Women's Strategies from Around the World*, ed. Margaret Schuler. New York: United Nations Development Fund for Women, 1992.

———. "Rituals and Angels: A Case Study of Female Circumcision in the Sudan." In *From Basic Needs to Basic Rights*, ed. Margaret Schuler. Washington, D.C.: Institute of Women, Law, and Development, 1995.

Abdel Magied, Ahmed. *Overview and Assessment of Efforts Against Female Genital Mutilation (FGM) in Sudan.* Khartoum: UNICEF-SCO, July 2001.

Abdel Magied, Ahmed and Suad Musa Ahmed. "Sexual Experiences and the Psychosocial Effects of Female Genital Mutilation or Female Circumcision on Sudanese Women." *Ahfad Journal* 19, 1 (2002). In *International Feminist Perspectives: Women and Violence*, ed. Vanessa Farr, special issue of *Atlantis* (Halifax), 2002.

Abdel Magied, Ahmed and Amna M. Badri. "Problems That Face Genitally Mutilated Immigrant Sudanese Women and Their Awareness of Available Relevant Health Services in London (A Case Study)." *Ahfad Journal* 17, 2 (2000): 29–37.

Abdel-Salam, Seham and Magdy Helmy. *Mafahim gadida li hayat afdal: dalil al seha al ingabeyah* (New Concepts for a Better Life: A Reproductive Health Manual). Cairo: Egyptian Task Force Against Female Genital Mutilation, 1998.

Abduh, Muhammad. *Tafsir al-Qur'an al-karim: tafsir al-manar* (Interpretations of the Qur'an: Manar Interpretations). Vol. 1. 2nd ed. Beirut: Dar al-ma'rifah, 1980.

Abul Fadl, Mona. "Revisiting the Woman Question: An Islamic Perspective." *Chicago Theological Seminary Register* 83, 1 (1994): 28–64.

Abusharaf, Rogaia Mustafa. "Local Knowledge and Ritual Reproduction in Village Societies: Educating Young African Women to 'Succeed in a World Authored by Men.'" *Radical Philosophy Review* 5, 1 and 2 (2002–2003): 126–40.

———. "Revisiting Feminist Discourses on Infibulation: Responses from Sudanese Feminists." In *Female "Circumcision" in Africa: Culture, Controversy and Change*, ed. Bettina Shell-Duncan and Ylva Hernlund. Boulder, Colo.: Lynne Rienner, 2000.

———. "Unmasking Tradition." *The Sciences* 38, 2 (1998): 22–27.

———. "Virtuous Cuts: Female Genital Circumcision in an African Ontology." *Differences: Journal of Feminist Cultural Studies* 12, 1 (2001): 112–40.

———. *Wanderings: Sudanese Migrants and Exiles in North America.* Ithaca, N.Y.: Cornell University Press, 2002.

Accad, Evylene. *L'exisée.* Paris: L'Harmattan, 1982. *The Excised*, trans. David K. Bruner. Colorado Springs: Three Continents Press, 1989.

Ahfad University. *History of the Ahfad University for Women.* <http://www.ahfad.org /history/> (accessed 12 May 2005).

Al-Asbahani. *Kitab dala'il al-nubuwwah* (Reports on Prophetic Evidence). Riyadh: Alam al-kutub, 1988.

Aldeeb Abu-Sahlieh, Sami Awad. *Male and Female Circumcision Among Jews, Christians, and Muslims: Religious, Medical, Social and Legal Debate.* Warren Center, Pa.: Shangri-La Publications, 2001.

———. *Khitan al-dhukur wal-inath al-yahud wal-masihiyyin wal-muslimin, al-jadal al-dini.* Riyadh and Beirut: El-Rayyes, 2000.

Alexander, Jacqui M. and Chandra T. Mohanty, eds. *Feminist Genealogies, Colonial Legacies, Democratic Futures.* New York: Routledge, 1997.

Al-Ghawwabi, Hamid, *Khitan al-banat bayn al-tib wal-islam*, in *Majallat liwa al-islam*, nos. 7, 8, and 11 (1951). In Abu-Bakr Abd-al-Raziq, *Al-khitan: ra'y al-din wal-'ilm fi khitan al-awlad wal-banat* (Circumcision: Perspective of Religion on Male and Female Circumcision). Cairo: Dar Al-i'tissam, 1989.

Al-Jamal, Abu-al-Ala Kamal Ali. *Nihayat al-bayan fi ahkam al-khitan* (Conclusive Evidence on the Laws of Circumcision). In *Maktabat al-iman.* Cairo: Al-Mansurah, 1995.

Al-Jamri, Abd al-Amir Mansur. *Al-mar'ah fi zil al-islam* (The Woman in Islam). 4th ed. Beirut: Dar al-hilal, 1986.

Al-Mahdawi, Mustafa Kamal. *Al-Bayan bil-Qur'an* (Evidence from the Qur'an). Vol. 1, *Al-dar al-gamahiriyyah.* Casablanca, Morocco: Misratah and Dar al-afaq al-Jadidah, 1990. In Sami A. Aldeeb Abu-Sahlieh, *Khitan al-dhukur wal-inath ind al-yahud wal-masihiyyin wal-muslimin, al-jadal al-dini.* Riyadh and Beirut: El-Rayyes, 2000. Annex 22.

Al-Mannawi, Muhammad. *Fayd al-qadir sharh al-jami al-saghir* (Fayid Al Qadir: Explanations from Short Compilations). Vol. 3. Beirut: Dar al-ma'rifah, 1995.

Al-Sukkari, Abd-al-Salam Abd-al-Rahim. *Khitan al-dhakar wa-khifad al-untha min mandhur islami* (Male and Female Circumcision from an Islamic Viewpoint). Héliopolis, Egypt: Dar al-manar, 1988.

Al-Tabari. *Tarikh Al-Tabari* (History by Al-Tabari). Vol. 1. 3rd ed. Beirut: Iz-ad-Din, 1992.

Aman, Virginia Lee Barnes and Janice Boddy. *Aman: The Story of a Somali Girl—as Told to Virginia Lee Barnes and Janice Boddy.* Toronto: Knopf; London: Bloomsbury; New York: Pantheon, 1994.

American Academy of Pediatrics. "Report of the Ad Hoc Task Force on Circumcision." *Pediatrics* 103, 3 (1 March 1999): 686–93. <www.cirp.org/library/statements/aap1999> (accessed 10 May 2005).

Amin, Ahmad. *Qamus al-adat wal-taqalid wal-ta'abir al-masriyyah* (Encyclopedia of Egyptian Customs and Language). Cairo: Maktabat al-nahdah al-masriyyah, 1992.

Ammar, Rushdi. *Al-adrar al-sihhiyyah al-natijah an khitan al-banat* (The Health Impacts of Female Circumcision). In *Al-halaqah al-dirasiyyah an al-intihak al-badani li-sighar al-inath,* 14–15 October 1979. Cairo: Jam'iyyat tandhim al-usrah, 1979.

Amnesty International. *Female Genital Mutilation: A Human Rights Issue.* 1997. <www/amnesty.org/alib/intcam/femgen/fgm.htm> (accessed 25 April 2005).

Annaud, Mathilde. *Aborigènes: la loi du sexe.* Paris: L'Harmattan, 2000.

Aquinas, Thomas. *The Summa Theologica.* Benziger Bros. edition, 1947. Trans. Fathers of the English Dominican Province. <www.ccel.org/a/aquinas/summa/home.html> (accessed 12 May 2005).

As'ad, Maurice. *Khitan al-banat min manzur massihi.* Cairo: Al-jam'iyyah al-masriyyah lil-wiqayah min al-mumarasat al-darah, n.d. (circa 1998).

Askew, Ian, Jane Chege, Carolyne Njue, and Samson Radeny. "A Multi-sectoral Approach to Providing Reproductive Health Information and Services to Young People in Western Kenya: The Kenya Adolescent Reproductive Health Project," *Frontiers Final Report.* Washington, D.C.: Population Council, 2004.

Assaad, Marie Bassili. "Female Circumcision in Egypt: Social Implications, Current Research, and Prospects for Change." *Studies in Family Planning* 11, 1 (1980): 3–16.

Awaken: A Voice for the Eradication of Female Genital Mutilation. Journal and online discussion forum published in London, Nairobi, and New York, by Equality Now, since 1997. <http://www.equalitynow.org/campaigns.fgm/awaken_en.html> (accessed 12 May 2005).

Babiker Badri Scientific Association for Women Studies (BBSAWS). *Alkhifad l'aka wa tashweeh fa haribo* (Report on papers and discussions of the workshop, "Female Circumcision Mutilates and Endangers Women—Combat It!"). Khartoum: BBSAWS, 1981.

———. *Anta tas'al 'an al-Kifad wa jami'yat Babiker Badri tujeeb* (You ask about Female Circumcision and the Babiker Badri Association responds). Khartoum, Sudan: BBSAWS and UNICEF, 1997.

———. Brochure on the association's activities. Khartoum: BBSAWS, 2002.

———. *La lil Kifad* (No to Female Circumcision). Khartoum, Sudan: BBSAWS and UNICEF, 1997.

———. *Proceedings of workshop "African Women Speak on Female Circumcision."* Khartoum: BBSAWS, 1984.

———. *The Story of Bakheeta* (a booklet on the harmful effects of female circumcision, in Arabic). Khartoum: BBSAWS and UNICEF, 1997.

Badawi, Jamal. "The Issue of Female Circumcision." Appendix to Jamal Badawi, *Gender Equity in Islam: Basic Principles*. 1995. Burr Ridge, Ill.: American Trust, 2003. Available at <http://www.soundvision.com/gender/female circumcision .html> (accessed 12 May 2005).

Barstow, Anne Llewellyn. *Witchcraze: A New History of the European Witch Hunts. Our Legacy of Violence Against Women*. San Francisco: Pandora/HarperCollins, 1994.

Barth, Lewis M., ed. *Berit Mila in the Reform Context*. New York: Berit Mila Board of Reform Judaism, 1990.

Basu, Amrita, ed. *The Challenge to Local Feminisms*. Boulder, Colo.: Westview, 1995.

Benedict, Ruth. *Patterns of Culture*. Boston: Houghton Mifflin, 1934.

Bhabha, Homi. *The Location of Culture*. New York: Routledge, 1994.

Bigelow, Jim. *The Joy of Uncircumcising: Restore Your Birthright and Maximize Sexual Pleasure*. 2nd ed. Aptos, Calif.: Hourglass, 1995.

Boddy, Janice. "Body Politics: Continuing the Anticircumcision Crusade." *Medical Anthropology Quarterly* n.s. 5, 1 (1991): 15–17.

———. "Remembering Amal: On Birth and the British in Northern Sudan." In *Pragmatic Women and Body Politics*, ed. Margaret Lock and Patricia Kaufert. Cambridge: Cambridge University Press, 1998.

———. "Violence Embodied? Female Circumcision, Gender Politics, and Cultural Aesthetics." In *Rethinking Violence Against Women*, ed. R. Emerson Dobash and Russell P. Dobash. Thousand Oaks, Calif.: Sage, 1998.

———. "Womb as Oasis: The Symbolic Context of Pharaonic Circumcision in Rural Northern Sudan." *American Ethnologist* 9, 4 (1982): 682–98.

Bop, Codou. *Rapport de consultation sur les mutilations génitales féminines*. Dakar: CESSI, 1999.

Boulware-Miller, Kay. "Female Circumcision: Challenges to the Practice as a Human Rights Violation." *Harvard Women's Law Journal* 8 (1985): 155–77.

Bourdieu, Pierre. *The Logic of Practice*. Trans. Richard Nice. Stanford, Calif.: Stanford University Press, 1990.

Bruce, James. *Travels to Discover the Source of the Nile in the Years 1768–1773*. Vol. 3. London: Robinson, 1790.

Brunet, Michel and Pierre Vidal. *Garcons et filles*. Film, 1986.

Bryk, Felix. *Circumcision in Man and Woman: Its History, Psychology, and Ethnology*. New York: American Ethnological Press, 1943.

Callender, Charles and Fadwa El Guindi. *Life-Crisis Rituals Among the Kenuz*. Case Western Reserve University Studies in Anthropology 3. Cleveland: Press of Case Western Reserve University, 1971.

Canadian Charter of Rights and Freedoms, Part I of the Constitution Act, 1982, being Schedule B to the Canada Act 1982 (UK), 1982, c.11.

Canadian Female Genital Mutilation Legal Community Committee. "Brief to the Parliamentary Standing Committee on Justice and Legal Affairs Re: Bill C-27 Section 268 subsections (3) & (4)." 26 November 1996.

Carr, Dara. *Female Genital Cutting. Findings from the Demographic and Health Surveys Program*. Calverton, Md.: Macro International, September 1997.

Cellule de Coordination sur les Pratiques Traditionelles Affectant la Santé des Femmes et des Enfants, Guinea (CPTAFE), and PATH (for CPTAFE: Morissanda Kouyat, Mandjou Sylla, and M. Djan Diallo; for PATH: Carol Hooks, Asha Mohamud, Kristina Gryboski, Carolyn Jefferson, Donna Sutton, and Nicole Warren). *Female Genital Mutilation: Identifying Factors Leading to Its Perpetuation in Two Regions in Guinea, 1996–1998.* Mothercare Project, 1998. <www.mothercare.jsi.com/RHF/guinea.pdf> (accessed 10 May 2005).

———. *Survey on Female Genital Mutilation in Upper and Middle Guinea. Discussion of Principal Findings.* Arlington, Va.: John Snow/MotherCare, 1998.

Cellule de Planification et de Statistique du Ministère de la Santé (CPS/MS), Direction Nationale de la Statistique et de l'Informatique (DNSI), et Opinion Research Corporation Macro. *Enquête démographique et de santé au Mali 2001.* Calverton, Md.: CPS/MS, DNSI, and Macro International, 2002.

Center for Development and Population Activities (CEDPA). *Positive Deviance: An Introduction to FGM Eradication.* Cairo: CEDPA, 1999.

Center for Reproductive Law and Policy (CRLP). *Beijing at 10: Reviewing a Decade of Progress.* New York: CRLP, 2005.

———. *Bringing Rights to Bear: An Analysis of the Work of UN Treaty Monitoring Bodies on Reproductive and Sexual Rights.* New York: CRLP, November 2002.

———. Factsheet on the Illegal Immigration Reform and Responsibility Act of 1996. New York: CRLP, 1997.

Chabukswar, Y. V. "A Barbaric Method of Circumcision Amongst Some of the Arab Tribes of Yemen." *Indian Medical Gazette* 56, 2 (February 1921): 48–49.

Chanock, Martin. "Culture and Human Rights: Orientalising, Occedentalising and Authenticity." In *Beyond Rights Talk and Culture Talk: Comparative Essays on the Politics of Rights and Culture,* ed. Mahmood Mamdani. Cape Town: David Phillips; New York: St. Martin's Press, 2000.

Charlesworth, Hillary. "What Are Women's International Human Rights"? In *Human Rights of Women: National and International Perspectives,* ed. Rebecca J. Cook. Philadelphia: University of Pennsylvania Press, 1993.

Chege, Jane Njeri, Ian Askew, Susan Igras, and Jacinta K. Mutesh. *Testing the Effectiveness of Integrating Community-Based Approaches for Encouraging Abandonment of Female Genital Cutting into CARE's Reproductive Health Program in Ethiopia and Kenya.* Washington, D.C.: Frontiers in Reproductive Health, Population Council, and CARE International, December 2004.

Chege, Jane Njeri, Ian Askew, and Jennifer Liku. "An Assessment of the Alternative Rites Approach for Encouraging Abandonment of Female Genital Mutilation in Kenya." *Frontiers in Reproductive Health* final report. Washington, D.C.: Population Council, September 2001. <www.popcouncil.org.> (accessed 17 April 2005).

Cohen, Eugene J. *Guide to Ritual Circumcision and Redemption of the First-Born Son.* New York: Ktav, 1984.

Cold, C. J. and J. Taylor. "The Prepuce." *British Journal of Urology* 83, suppl. 1 (January 1999): 36–44.

Cole, Johnetta. "Women in Cuba: The Revolution Within the Revolution." In *Comparative Perspectives of Third World Women: The Impact of Race, Sex, and Class,* ed. Beverly Lindsay. New York: Praeger, 1980.

Coleman, Carter. "The Fight Against Female Genital Mutilation." *Self* (January 1997): 126–42.

Coleman, Doriane Lambelet. "The Seattle Compromise: Multicultural Sensitivity and Americanization." *Duke Law Journal* 47 (1998): 717–83.

Comité d'Action pour les Droits de la Femme et de l'Enfant (CADEF). *Report sur l'enquête menée par le CADEF sur les mutilations génitales féminines dans les régions de Kayes, Sikasso, Segou, et le district de Bamako.* Bamako, Mali: CADEF, 1994.

Comité National de Lutte contre la Pratique de l'Excision (CNLPE). *Enquête national sur l'excision au Burkina Faso.* Ouagadougou, Burkina Faso: CNLPE, 1997.

Cook, Rebecca J., ed. *Human Rights of Women: National and International Perspectives.* Philadelphia: University of Pennsylvania Press, 1993.

Davis, Elizabeth Gould. *The First Sex.* New York: Penguin Books, 1972.

Denniston, George C. "Circumcision: An Iatrogenic Epidemic." In *Sexual Mutilations: A Human Tragedy,* ed. George C. Denniston and Marilyn Fayre Milos. New York: Plenum Press, 1997.

Denniston, George C. and Marilyn Fayre Milos. *Sexual Mutilations: A Human Tragedy.* New York: Plenum Press, 1997.

Dera, Lassane, et al. *Enquête nationale sur l'excision au Burkina Faso: rapport d'analyse.* Ouagadougou, Burkina Faso: Institut National de la Statistique et de la Démographie, 1997.

Diallo, Assitan. *Mutilations génitales féminines au Mali: revue de la littérature et des actions menées.* Bamako, Mali: Population Council, 1997.

Diamond, Stanley. *In Search of the Primitive: A Critique of Civilization.* Piscataway, N.J.: Transaction Publishers, 1989.

Diop, Nafissatou J. et al. *Efficacité de la formation du personnel de santé dans l'éducation des clientes sur l'excision et la prise en charge des complications.* Bamako, Mali: Population Council, 1998.

Diop, Nafissatou J. et al. *Expérimentation d'un programme d'éducation de base au Burkina Faso, le programme Tostan, rapport final.* Dakar: Population Council, September 2004.

Diop, Nafissatou J. et al. *Female Genital Cutting.* Program Briefs. Frontiers in Reproductive Health. New York: Population Council, 2001.

Diop, Nafissatou J. et al. *La stratégie de Tostan: évaluation du programme d'éducation à base communautaire, rapport intermédiaire.* Dakar, Population Council, 2002.

Diop, Nafissatou J., Edmond Bagdé, Djingri Ouoba, and Molly Melching. *How 23 Villages Participated in a Human Rights-Based Education Programme and Abandoned the Practice of Female Genital Cutting in Burkina Faso.* Synthesis Document of the Tostan Programme Implementation in Burkina Faso by Mwangaza Action Association. Dakar: Frontiers in Reproductive Health, Population Council, April 2003.

Dirie, Mahdi Ali and Gunilla Lindmark. "Female Circumcision in Somalia and Women's Motives." *Acta Obstetrica Gynecolica Scandanavica* 50 (1991): 581–85. 1991a.

———. "A Hospital Study of the Complications of Female Circumcision." *Tropical Doctor* 21 (1991): 146–48. 1991b.

———. "The Risk of Medical Complications After Female Circumcision." *East African Medical Journal* 69, 9 (September 1992): 479–82.

Dorkenoo, Efua. *Cutting the Rose: Female Genital Mutilation: The Practice and Its Prevention*. London: Minority Rights Publications, 1994.

Dugger, Celia. "A Refugee's Body Is Intact But Her Family Is Torn." *New York Times*, 11 September 1996.

———. "U.S. Frees African Fleeing Ritual Mutilation." *New York Times*, 25 April 1996.

———. "U.S. Grants Asylum to Woman Fleeing Genital Mutilation Rite." *New York Times*, 14 June 1996.

———. "Woman's Plea for Asylum Puts Tribal Ritual on Trial." *New York Times*, 15 April 1996.

Early, Evelyn A. *Baladi Women of Cairo: Playing with an Egg and a Stone*. Boulder. Colo.: Lynne Rienner, 1993.

Eisler, Riane. *Sacred Pleasure: Sex, Myth, and the Politics of the Body*. New York: HarperCollins, 1995.

El Bashir, Hamid. *Women and the Agony of Culture: Strategies for the Eradication of Female Genital Mutilation in Sudan*. Khartoum: SNCTP and UNICEF, n.d.

El Dareer, Asma. "Attitudes of Sudanese People to the Practice of Female Circumcision." *International Journal of Epidemiology* 12, 2 (1983): 138–44.

———. "Complications of Female Circumcision in the Sudan." *Tropical Doctor* 13, 3 (July 1983): 131–33.

———. "Epidemiology of Female Circumcision in the Sudan." *Tropical Doctor* 13, 1 (January 1983): 41–45.

———. *Woman, Why Do You Weep? Circumcision and Its Consequences*. London: Zed Books, 1983, 1992.

El-Gibaly, Omaima et al. "The Decline of Female Circumcision in Egypt: Evidence and Interpretation." *Social Science and Medicine* 54 (2002): 205–20.

El Guindi, Fadwa. "The Angels in the Nile: A Theme in Nubian Ritual." In *Nubian Ceremonial Life: Studies in Islamic Syncretism and Cultural Change*, ed. John G. Kennedy. Berkeley and Cairo: University of California Press and American University in Cairo Press, 1978.

———. "Beyond Picturing Culture: A Critique of a Critique." *American Anthropologist* 103, 2 (2001): 1–6.

El Guindi, Fadwa. El Guindi Nubian Kenuz Papers. Los Angeles: El Nil Research, 1962–1965.

———. *El Sebou': Egyptian Birth Ritual*. Film. Los Angeles: El Nil Research, 1986.

———. "From Pictorializing to Visual Anthropology." In *Handbook of Methods in Cultural Anthropology*, ed. H. Russell Bernard. Lanham, Md.: AltaMira Press, Sage, 1998.

———. *The Myth of Ritual: A Native's Ethnography of Zapotec Life-Crisis Rituals*. Tucson: University of Arizona Press, 1986.

———. "Ritual and the River in Dahmit, Nubia." In *Contemporary Egyptian Nubia: A Symposium of the Social Research Center, the American University in Cairo* (Aswan, Egypt: Dar el-Thaqafa, 1964), vol. 2, ed. Robert A. Fernea. New Haven, Conn.: Human Relations Area Files, 1966.

———. *Veil: Modesty, Privacy, and Resistance*. Oxford: Berg, 1999.

———. "Veiling Infitah with Muslim Ethic: Egypt's Contemporary Islamic Movement." *Social Problems* 28, 4 (1981): 465–85.

El Guindi, Fadwa and Charles Callender (co-creators). Charles Callender Papers. Collection of ethnographic materials from field project among Kenuz Nubians. Anthropology Archives. Washington, D.C., and Cairo: Smithsonian Institution and Ethnological Survey, Social Research Center, American University in Cairo, 1962–1963.

El Katsha, Samiha, Sherine Ibrahim, and Noha Sedky. *Experiences of Nongovernmental Organizations Working Towards the Elimination of Female Genital Mutilation in Egypt.* Cairo: Center for Development and Population Activities (CEDPA), 1997.

El Nagar, Samia, Sunita Pitamber, and I. Nouh. *Synopsis of the Female Circumcision Research Findings.* Khartoum: Babiker Badri Scientific Association for Women's Studies (BBSAWS), 1994.

El-Masry, Youssef. *Le drame sexuel de la femme dans l'orient arabe.* Paris: Laffont, 1962.

El-Messiri, Sawsan. "Self-Images of Traditional Urban Women in Cairo." In *Women in the Muslim World,* ed. Lois Beck and Nikki Keddie. Cambridge, Mass.: Harvard University Press, 1978.

El Saadawi, Nawal. *The Hidden Face of Eve: Women in the Arab World.* London: Zed Books, 1980.

Encyclopaedia Judaica. 4th ed. Jerusalem: Keter, 1978.

Fernea, Elizabeth Warnock and Robert A. Fernea. *Nubian Ethnographies.* Prospect Heights, Ill.: Waveland Press, 1991.

Fink, Aaron J. "Circumcision and Heterosexual Transmission of HIV Infection to Men." Letter, *New England Journal of Medicine* 316 (1987): 1546–47.

———. "A Possible Explanation for Heterosexual Male Infection with AIDS." Letter, *New England Journal of Medicine* 315 (1986): 1167.

Fisher, Andrew et al. *Designing HIV/AIDS Intervention Studies: An Operations Research Handbook.* New York: Population Council, 2002.

Fleiss, Paul M. "An Analysis of Bias Regarding Circumcision in American Medical Literature." In *Male and Female Circumcision: Medical, Legal, and Ethical Considerations in Pediatric Practice,* ed. George C. Denniston, Frederick Mansfield Hodges, and Marilyn Fayre Milos. London: Kluwer Academic; New York: Plenum, 1999.

———. "Where Is My Foreskin? The Case Against Circumcision." *Mothering: The Magazine of Natural Family Living* (Winter 1997): 36–45.

Fraser, David. "The First Cut Is (Not) the Deepest: Deconstructing 'Female Genital Mutilation' and the Criminalization of the Other." *Dalhousie Law Journal* 18, 2 (1995): 310–79.

———. "Heart of Darkness: The Criminalisation of Female Genital Circumcision." *Current Issues in Criminal Justice* 6, 1 (July 1994): 148–51.

Gairdner, D. "The Fate of the Foreskin, a Study of Circumcision." *British Medical Journal* 2 (1949): 1433–37.

Gayman, Dan. *Lo, Children . . . Our Heritage from God.* Schell City, Mo.: Church of Israel, 1991.

Geertz, Clifford. *Local Knowledge: Further Essays in Interpretive Anthropology.* New York: Basic Books, 1983.

Giddens, Anthony. "Living in a Post-Traditional Society." In *Reflexive Modernization: Politics, Traditions, and Aesthetics in the Modern Social Order,* ed. Ulrich Beck, Anthony Giddens, and Scott Lash. Stanford, Calif.: Stanford University Press, 1994.

Ginzberg, Louis. *The Legends of the Jews.* 12th ed. Philadelphia: Jewish Publication Society, 1937.

Goldman, Ronald. *Circumcision, the Hidden Trauma: How an American Cultural Practice Affects Infants and Ultimately Us All.* Boston: Vanguard, 1997.

———. *Questioning Circumcision: A Jewish Perspective.* Boston: Circumcision Resource Center, 1995.

Gollaher, David. *Circumcision: A History of the World's Most Controversial Surgery.* New York: Basic Books, 2000.

Gordon, Daniel. "Female Circumcision and Genital Operations in Egypt and Sudan: A Dilemma for Medical Anthropology." *Medical Anthropology Quarterly* 5 (1991): 3–14.

Government of Canada. *Criminal Code of Canada,* RSC 1985, as amended.

Government of Canada, Department of Justice. *Ethnocultural Groups and the Justice System in Canada.* Ottawa, 1996.

Government of Ontario. *Commission on Systematic Racism in the Ontario Criminal Justice System.* Toronto, 1994.

Gregorius, Anba. *Al-khitan fil-massihiyyah* (Circumcision in Christianity). Faggalah, Cairo: Lajnat al-nashr lil-thaqafah al-qubtiyyah, 1988.

Grewal, Inderpal and Caren Kaplan. "Postcolonial Studies and Transnational Feminist Practices." *Jouvert: A Journal of Postcolonial Studies* 5, 1 (Autumn 2000). <socialchass.ncsu.edu/jouvert/v5i1> (accessed 12 May 2005).

———. *Scattered Hegemonies: Postmodernity and Transnational Feminist Practices.* Minneapolis: University of Minnesota Press, 1996.

———. "Warrior Marks: Global Womanism's Neo-Colonial Discourse in a Multicultural Context." *Camera Obscura: A Journal of Feminism, Culture, and Media Studies* 39 (1996): 5–33.

Gruenbaum, Ellen. *The Female Circumcision Controversy: An Anthropological Perspective.* Philadelphia: University of Pennsylvania Press, 2001.

———. "The Islamic Movement, Development and Health Education: Recent Changes in the Health of Rural Women in Central Sudan." *Social Science and Medicine* 33, 6 (1991): 637–45.

Hale, Sondra. "A Question of Subjects: The Female Circumcision Controversy and the Politics of Knowledge." *Ufahamu* (Journal of the African Activist Association, University of California, Los Angeles) 22, 3 (1994): 26–35; in *Female Circumcision and the Politics of Knowledge: African Women in Imperialist Discourses,* ed. Obioma Nnaemeka. Westport, Conn.: Greenwood, 2005.

Hammond, Tim. "A Preliminary Poll of Men Circumcised in Infancy or Childhood." *British Journal of Urology* 83, suppl. 1 (January 1999): 85–92.

Hand, Eugene A. "Circumcision and Venereal Disease." *Archives of Dermatology and Syphigraphy* 60 (1949): 341–46.

Harris, Marvin. *Culture, Man, and Nature*. New York: Cromwell, 1971.

Hayes, Rose Oldfield. "Female Genital Mutilation, Fertility Control, Women's Roles, and the Patrilineage in Modern Sudan: A Functional Analysis." *American Ethnologist* 2, 4 (1975): 617–33.

Henninger, Joseph. *Eine eigenartige Beschneidungensform in Südwestarabien*. In *Arabica Varia*. Fribourg: Universitätsverlag, 1989.

Hernlund, Ylva. "Cutting Without Ritual and Ritual Without Cutting: Female 'Circumcision' and the Re-Ritualization of Initiation in the Gambia." In *Female "Circumcision" in Africa: Culture, Controversy, and Change*, ed. Bettina Shell-Duncan and Ylva Hernlund. Boulder, Colo.: Lynne Rienner, 2000.

Herzfeld, Michael. *Anthropology: Theoretical Practice in Culture and Society*. Malden, Mass.: Blackwell, 2001.

Hicks, Esther Kremhilde. *Infibulation: Female Mutilation in Islamic Northeast Africa*. Piscataway, N.J.: Transaction Publishers, 1996.

Hodges, Frederick. "The History of Phimosis from Antiquity to the Present." In *Male and Female Circumcision Among Jews, Christians, and Muslims: Religious, Medical, Social and Legal Debate*, ed. Aldeeb Abu-Sahlieh and Sami Awad. Warren Center, Pa.: Shangri-La Publications, 2001.

———. "A Short History of the Institutionalization of Involuntary Sexual Mutilation in the United States." In *Sexual Mutilations: A Human Tragedy*, ed. George C. Denniston and Marilyn Fayre Milos. New York: Plenum Press, 1997.

Hoffman, Lawrence A. *Covenant of Blood: Circumcision and Gender in Rabbinic Judaism*. Chicago: University of Chicago Press, 1996.

Hosken, Fran P. "At Last Excisor in Paris Imprisoned for 8 Years." *WIN News* 25, 2 (1999).

———. "The Epidemiology of Female Genital Mutilation." *Tropical Doctor* 8 (July 1987): 150–56.

———. *Female Sexual Mutilations: The Facts and Proposals for Action*. Lexington, Mass.: Women's International Network News, 1980.

———. *The Hosken Report: Genital and Sexual Mutilation of Females*. 4th ed. Lexington, Mass.: Women's International Network News, 1994.

Howard, Michael. *Contemporary Cultural Anthropology*. 3rd ed. Glenview, Calif.: Scott, Foresman, 1988.

Hundley, Tom. "Immigrants Bring Practice of Female Circumcision to Europe." *Knight-Ridder/Tribune News Service*, 7 June 2002, PK 2310.

Ibn Abd Al-Hakim. *The History of the Conquest of Egypt, North Africa and Spain, Known as the Futuh Misr*. Ed. Charles C. Torrey. New Haven Conn.: Yale University Press, 1922.

Ibn-al-Assal, Al-Safi Abu-al-Fada'il. *Al-majmu al-safawi* (Al Safawi Collections). Vol. 2. Cairo: n.p., 1908.

Ibn-Baz, Abd-al-Aziz. *Majmu'at fatawi* (Fatwa Collections). Vol. 4 of *Majmu'at fatawi*. Riyadh: Dar al-watan, 1995.

Ibn-Hanbal. *Musnad Ibn-Hanbal*. Vol. 4 of *Musnad Ibn-Hanbal*. Riyadh: Bayt al-afkar al-dawliyyah, 1998.

Ibn-Qudamah. *Al-Mughni*. Vol. 1 of *Al-Mughni*. Riyadh: Maktabat al-Riyad al-hadithah, n.d.

Ignatieff, Michael. *Human Rights as Politics and Idolatry.* Princeton, N.J.: Princeton University Press, 2001.

Institut National de la Statistique et de la Démographie (INSD) and Macro International Inc. *Enquête démographique et de santé, Burkina Faso 1998–1999.* Calverton, Md.: Macro International, 2000.

Inter-African Committee on Traditional Practices Affecting the Health of Women and Children (IAC). *Newsletter.* <http://wworks.com/~IAC/toc.htm> (accessed March 2002); also <http://www.iac-ciaf.org/> (accessed 12 May 2005).

Inter-African Committee (IAC), Summary Report on the IAC Regional Seminar on Traditional Practices Affecting the Health of Women and Children in Africa, held in Addis Ababa 6–10 April 1987. Addis Ababa: IAC-CIAF, 1987.

Izett, Susan and Nahid Toubia. *Learning About Social Change: A Research and Evaluation Guidebook Using Female Circumcision as a Case Study.* New York: Rainb♀, 1999.

Jad-al-Haq, Ali. *Khitan al-banat* (Female Circumcision). Vol. 9 of *Al-fatawi al-islamiyyah min dar al-ifta al-masriyyah.* Cairo: Wazarat al-awqaf, 1983.

———. *Al-khitan*, annex of *Al-Azhar*, October 1994. In Sami Awad Aldeeb Abu-Sahlieh, *Khitan al-dhukur wal-inath al-yahud wal-masihiyyin wal-muslimin, al-jadal al-dini.* Riyadh and Beirut: El-Rayyes, 2000. Annex 6.

Jaldesa, Guyo W., Ian Askew, Carolyne Njue, and Monica Wanjiru. *Female Genital Cutting Among the Somali of Kenya and Management of its Complications.* Nairobi: Frontiers in Reproductive Health Program, Population Council, February 2005.

James, Stanlie M. and Claire C. Robertson, eds. *Genital Cutting and Transnational Sisterhood: Disputing U.S. Polemics.* Urbana: University of Illinois Press, 2002.

Jones, Heidi, Nafissatou Diop, Ian Askew, and Inoussa Kaboré. "Female Genital Cutting and Its Negative Health Outcomes in Burkina Faso and Mali." *Studies in Family Planning* 39, 3 (1999): 219–30.

Junos, LeYoni. *Bodily Integrity for Both: The Obligation of Amnesty International to Recognize All Forms of Genital Mutilation of Males as Human Rights Violations.* 2nd ed. Amnesty International-Bermuda, 1 August 1998.

Karim, Mahmoud and Roshdi Ammar. *Female Circumcision and Sexual Desire.* Cairo: Ains Shams University Press, 1965.

Kassindja, Fauziya and Layli Miller Bashir. *Do They Hear When You Cry?* New York: Delacorte, 1998.

Kennedy, John G. "Circumcision and Excision in Egyptian Nubia." *Man* n.s. 5, 2 (1970): 175–90.

Koriech, O. M. "Penile Shaft Carcinoma in Pubic Circumcision" (Case Reports from Saudi Arabia). *British Journal of Urology* 60, 1 (July 1987): 77.

Koso-Thomas, Olayinka. *The Circumcision of Women: A Strategy for Eradication.* London: Zed Books, 1992.

———. "Tradition Against Health: The Struggle for Change." In *A Diplomacy of the Oppressed: New Directions in International Feminism*, ed. Georgina Ashworth. London: Zed Books, 1995.

Kratz, Corinne. *Affecting Performances: Movement and Experience in Okiek Women's Initiation.* Washington, D.C.: Smithsonian Institution Press, 1994.

Kreiss, J. K. and S. G. Hopkins. "The Association Between Circumcision Status and Human Immunodeficiency Virus Infection Among Homosexual Men." *Journal of Infectious Diseases* 168 (1993): 1404–8.

Laboratoire de Santé Communautaire (LSC). *Etude participative pour l'identifcation des stratégies communautaires de lutte contre la pratique de l'excision dans le Bazega*. Ouagadougou, Burkina Faso: Laboratoire de Santé Communautaire de la Ministère de la Santé, and Population Council, 1998.

Lam, Maivan Clech. "Feeling Foreign in Feminism." *Signs* 19, 4 (1994): 865–93.

Laumann, E. O. et al. "Circumcision in the United States: Prevalence, Prophylactic Effects, and Sexual Practice." *Journal of the American Medical Association* 277 (1997): 1052–57.

Leonard, Lori. "Adopting Female 'Circumcision' in Southern Chad: The Experience of Myabé." In *Female "Circumcision" in Africa: Culture, Controversy and Change*, ed. Bettina Shell-Duncan and Ylva Hernlund. Boulder, Colo.: Lynne Rienner, 2000.

Leslau, Wolf. *Coutumes et croyances des Falachas (Juifs d'Abyssinie)*. Paris: Institut d'Ethnographie, 1957.

Lewis, Joseph. *In the Name of Humanity*. 1949. Reprint New York: Eugenics Publishing Company, 1956.

Lightfoot-Klein, Hanny. *Prisoners of Ritual: An Odyssey into Female Genital Circumcision in Africa*. Binghamton, N.Y.: Harrington Park Press; New York: Haworth Press, 1989.

———. *Secret Wounds*. New York: Haworth Press, 2003.

———. *A Woman's Odyssey into Africa: Tracks Across a Life*. Binghamton, N.Y.: Harrington Park Press; New York: Haworth Press, 1992.

Machan, Tibor. "Human Rights Reaffirmed." *Philosophy* 69 (1994): 479–90.

Mackie, Gerry. "Ending Footbinding and Infibulation: A Convention Account." *American Sociological Review* 61 (1996): 999–1017.

Mackie, Gerry. "Female Genital Cutting: The Beginning of the End." In *Female "Circumcision" in Africa: Culture, Controversy and Change*, ed. Bettina Shell-Duncan and Ylva Hernlund. Boulder, Colo.: Lynne Rienner, 2000.

Maendeleo Ya Wanawake Organization (MYWO). "A Report on Harmful Traditional Practices That Affect the Health of Women and Their Children in Kenya." Nairobi: MYWO, 1992.

Maendeleo Ya Wanawake Organization (MYWO) and Program for Appropriate Technology in Health (PATH). *Qualitative Research Report on Female Circumcision in Four Districts in Kenya: Harmful Traditional Practices That Affect the Health of Women and Children*. Nairobi: MYWO and PATH, February 1993.

Magubane, Bernard and James Faris. "The Political Relevance of Anthropology." *Dialectical Anthropology* 9 (1985): 91–104.

Maimonides, Moses. "The Guide for the Perplexed." In *Sex Ethics in the Writings of Moses Maimonides*, ed. Fred Rosner. New York: Fred Bloch, 1974.

Makhlouf, Hassanayn Muhammad. *Hukm al-khitan*. Vol. 2 of *Al-fatawi al-islamiyyah min dar al-ifta' al-masriyyah*. Cairo: Wazarat al-awqaf, 1981.

Mamdani, Mahmood, ed. *Beyond Rights Talk and Culture Talk: Comparative Essays on the Politics of Rights and Culture*. Cape Town: David Phillip; New York: St. Martin's Press, 2000.

Mandara, Mairo. "Female Genital Cutting in Nigeria: Views of Nigerian Doctors on the Medicalization Debate." In *Female "Circumcision" in Africa: Culture, Controversy and Change*, ed. Bettina Shell-Duncan and Ylva Hernlund. Boulder, Colo.: Lynne Rienner, 2000.

Mark, Elizabeth Wyner, ed. *The Covenant of Circumcision: New Perspectives on an Ancient Jewish Rite.* Hanover, N.H.: University Press of New England for Brandeis University Press, 2003.

Masterson, Julie M. and Julie Hanson Swanson. *Female Genital Cutting: Breaking the Silence, Enabling Change.* Washington, D.C.: International Center for Research on Women and CDPA, 2000.

McCullough, Marie. "Manual Addresses Circumcised Females' Problems." *Philadelphia Inquirer*, 27 May 1999. <Sudanese@list.msu.edu> (accessed 2 December 2002).

McMillen, S. I. M. *None of These Diseases.* 15th ed., rev. David E. Stern. Grand Rapids, Mich.: Revell, 1995.

Ministry of Economic and National Planning, Institute for Resources Development, Republic of the Sudan. *Sudan Demographic and Health Survey* (DHS), 1989–1990. Calverton, Md.: Macro International, May 1991.

Mohamud, Asha. *Conceptual Framework. Passing from Childhood to Adulthood: Modified Ceremonies for Girls in Kisii and Meru.* Washington, D.C.: PATH, October 1995.

Mohamud, Asha, Stella Abwao, and E. Omwega. *Community Perspectives on Female Genital Mutilation: A Qualitative Research Report in Nyamira District.* Nairobi: PATH and Seventh Day Adventist Rural Health Services, 1995.

Mohamud, Asha, Samson Radeny, Nancy Yinger, Zipporah Kittony, and Karin Ringheim. "Protecting and Empowering Girls: Confronting the Roots of Female Genital Cutting in Kenya." In *Responding to Cairo: Case Studies of Changing Practices in Reproductive Health and Family Planning*, ed. Nicole Haberland and Diana Measham. New York: Population Council, 2002.

Mohamud, Asha, Karin Ringheim, Susan Bloodworth, and Kristina Gryboski. "Girls at Risk: Community Approaches to End Female Genital Mutilation and Treating Women Injured by the Practice." In *Reproductive Health and Rights: Reaching the Hardly Reached.* Washington, D.C. PATH, 2002.

Mohanty, Chandra T. "Under Western Eyes: Feminist Scholarship and Colonial Discourses." *Feminist Review* 30 (1988): 61–88. In *Third World Women and the Politics of Feminism*, ed. Chandra Mohanty, Ann Russo, and Lourdes Torres. Bloomington: Indiana University Press, 1991.

Mohanty, Chandra T., Ann Russo, and Lourdes Torres, eds. *Third World Women and the Politics of Feminism.* Bloomington: Indiana University Press, 1991.

Montagu, Ashley. "Mutilated Humanity." Paper presented at the International Symposium on Female Circumcision, San Francisco, California, 30 April-3 May 1991; published in *The Humanist* 55, 4 (July-August 1995).

Morsy, Soheir A. "Safeguarding Women's Bodies: The White Man's Burden Medicalized." *Medical Anthropology Quarterly* n.s. 5, 1 (1991): 19–23.

Mottin-Sylla, Marie Helene. *L'Excision au Sénégal: informer pour agir.* Etudes et Recherches 137. Dakar: ENDA Tiers-Monde, 1990.

Muller, Christa. "(I)NTACT and Female Genital Mutilation in Germany." In *Sexual Mutilations: A Human Tragedy*, ed. George C. Denniston and Marilyn Fayre Milos. New York: Plenum Press, 1997.

Nassar, Allam. *Khitan al-banat*, Vol. 6 of *Al-fatawi al-islamiyyah min dar al-ifta' al-masriyyah*. Cairo: Wazarat al-awqaf, 1982.

Nassif, Issam-al-Dine Hafni. Forward to Joseph Lewis, *Al-khitan dalalah isra'iliyyah mu'dhiyah* (Circumcision is a harmful Jewish mistake), trans. Issam-al-Dine Hanfi Nassif. Cairo: Matabi' dar al-sha'b, 1971.

National Organization of Immigrant and Visible Minority Women of Canada. *Female Genital Mutilation: Workshop Manual*. Ottawa, Canada: National Organization of Immigrant and Visible Minority Women of Canada, 1998.

National Council for Population and Development and Central Bureau of Statistics, Kenya. *Kenya Demographic and Health Survey, 1998 (DHS 1998)*. Calverton, Md.: National Council for Population and Development and Central Bureau of Statistics, Kenya, and Macro International, 1999.

National Population Council. *Egypt Demographic and Health Survey 1995*. Cairo: National Population Council, September 1996.

Ndiaye, Malick et al. *L'Excision dans la région de Kolda*. Dakar: Environment and Development Action, 1993.

Neusner, Jacob, trans. *The Talmud of Babylonia*. Atlanta: Scholars Press, 1993.

Newman, Constance J. and David Nelson. "Counseling and Advocacy to Abandon Female Genital Cutting." PRIME II (Provider Training and Community Outreach to Eliminate Harmful Practices), RR34. Chapel Hill, N.C.: PRIME II Project, IntraHealth International, 2003.

Nhlaop, Thandabantu. "The African Customary Law of Marriage and the Rights Conundrum." In *Beyond Rights Talk and Culture Talk: Comparative Essays on the Politics of Rights and Culture*, ed. Mahmood Mamdani. Cape Town: David Phillips, 2000.

Ntiri, Daphne W. "Circumcision and Health Among Rural Women of Southern Somalia as Part of a Family Life Survey." *Health Care for Women International* 14, 3 (1993): 215–26.

Njue, Carolyne and Ian Askew. *Medicalization of Female Genital Cutting Among Abagusii in Nyanza Province, Kenya*. Nairobi: Frontiers in Reproductive Health, Population Council, December 2004.

Nnaemeka, Obioma, ed. *Female Circumcision and the Politics of Knowledge: African Women in Imperialist Discourses*. Westport, Conn.: Praeger, 2005.

O'Barr, Jean. *Third World Women: Factors in Their Changing Status*. Raleigh, N.C.: Duke University Center for International Studies Working Paper 2, 1976.

Obermeyer, Carla. "Female Genital Surgeries: The Known, the Unknown, and the Unknowable." *Medical Anthropology Quarterly* 13, 1 (1999): 79–106.

Obiora, Leslye Amede. "Bridges and Barricades: Rethinking Polemics and Intransigence in the Campaign Against Female Circumcision." *Case Western Reserve Law Review* 47 (1997): 275–378. In *Global Critical Race Feminism*, ed. Adrien Katherine Wing. New York: New York University Press, 2000. 260–74.

Obiora, Leslye Amede. "The Deficits of the Anti-Circumcision Campaign." In *Female Circumcision and the Politics of Knowledge: African Women in Imperialist Discourses*, ed. Obioma Nnaemeka. Westport, Conn.: Greenwood, 2005.

———. "Female Excision: Cultural Concerns and Feminist Legal Theory." In *International Encyclopedia of the Social and Behavioral Sciences*, ed. Neil J. Smelser and Paul B. Baltes. Oxford: Elsevier Science, 2001.

———. "The Full Belly Quotient: Renegotiating a Rite of Passage." *Women's Rights Law Reporter* 24, 3 (2003): 181. In *Female Genital Cutting in the World*, ed. Ylva Hernlund et al. London: Routledge, forthcoming.

———. "Reconstituted Consonants: The Reach of a 'Common Core' Analogy in Human Rights." *Hastings International and Comparative Law Review* 21, 4 (1998): 921–55.

———. "Supri, supri, supri, Oyibo? An Analysis of Gender Mainstreaming Deficits." *Signs* 29, 2 (Winter 2004): 649–62.

O'Hara, K. and J. O'Hara. "The Effect of Male Circumcision on the Sexual Enjoyment of the Female Partner." *British Journal of Urology* 83, suppl. 1 (January 1999): 79–84.

Okin, Susan Moller. *Is Multiculturalism Bad for Women?* Princeton, N.J.: Princeton University Press, 1999.

Olenja, Joyce. "Evaluation Report on Eliminating the Practice of Female Genital Mutilation: Awareness Raising and Community Change in Four Districts of Kenya." Report to PATH and MYWO, October 2000.

Ouédraogo, Ousmane et al. *La pratique de l'excision: données qualitatives collectées dans 19 provinces sur 15 groupes ethniques auprès de clientes et prestataires de services des formations sanitaires*. Ouagadougou, Burkina Faso: Population Council, 1996.

Palmer, David. *Descent into Discourse: The Reification of Language and the Writing of History*. Philadelphia: Temple University Press, 1990.

Paravisin-Gerbert, Lizabeth. "Decolonizing Feminism: The Homegrown Roots of Caribbean Women's Movement." In *Daughters of Caliban: Caribbean Women in the Twentieth Century*, ed. Consuelo Lopez Springfield. Bloomington: Indiana University Press, 1997.

Petchesky, Rosalind. Introduction to Rosalind Petchesky and Karen Judd, eds., *Negotiating Reproductive Rights: Women's Perspectives Across Countries and Cultures*. London: Zed Books, 1998.

Petchesky, Rosalind and Karen Judd, eds. *Negotiating Reproductive Rights: Women's Perspectives Across Countries and Cultures*. London: Zed Books, 1998.

Philo. *The Special Laws*. Vol. 7 of *Philo in Ten Volumes*. Books I and II. Trans. F. H. Colson. Cambridge, Mass.: Harvard University Press, 1984.

Philo. *Questions and Answers on Genesis*. Book III. Trans. Ralph Marcus. Cambridge, Mass.: Harvard University Press, 1979.

Piot, Charles. *Remotely Global: Village Modernity in West Africa*. Chicago: University of Chicago Press, 1999.

Pollack, Miriam. "Circumcision: A Jewish Feminist Perspective." In *Jewish Women Speak Out: Expanding the Boundaries of Psychology*, ed. Kayla Weiner and Arinna Moon. Seattle: Canopy Press, 1995.

———. "Redefining the Sacred." In *Sexual Mutilations: A Human Tragedy*, ed. George C. Denniston and Marilyn Fayre Milos. New York: Plenum Press, 1997.

Population Council. "FGC Excisors Persist Despite Entreaties." In *Female "Circumcision" in Africa: Culture, Controversy and Change*, ed. Bettina Shell-Duncan and Ylva Hernlund. Boulder, Colo.: Lynne Rienner, 2000.

————. *Using Operations Research to Strengthen Programmes for Encouraging Abandonment of Female Genital Cutting.* Nairobi: Population Council, 2002.

Population Council and Centre National de Recherche Scientifique et Technologique (CNRST). *Evaluation de la stratégie de reconversion des exciseuses pour l'éradication des mutilations génitales féminines au Mali.* Bamako, Mali: Population Council, 1998.

Prescott, James W. "Genital Pain vs. Genital Pleasure: Why the One and Not the Other?" *Truth Seeker* 1 (July-August 1989): 14–21.

Program for Appropriate Technology in Health (PATH) and Maendeleo Ya Wanawake Organization (MYWO). *Evaluating Efforts to Eliminate the Practice of FGM: Raising Awareness and Changing Harmful Norms in Kenya.* Washington, D.C.: PATH, 2000. Available from <www.path.org>, accessed 17 April 2005.

Program for Appropriate Technology in Health (PATH) and Seventh Day Adventist Church (SDA). *Quantitative Research Report on Health Workers' Knowledge and Attitudes about Female Circumcision in Nyamira District, Kenya.* Nairobi: PATH, 1996.

Rahman, Anika and Nahid Toubia. *Female Genital Mutilation: A Guide to Laws and Policies Worldwide.* London: Zed Books 1998, 2000.

Ras-Work, Berhane. *Activity Report 1997: Inter-African Committee on Traditional Practices Affecting the Health of Women and Children.* Addis Ababa and Geneva: IAC, 1997.

Ravich, Abraham R. A. "Prophylaxis for Cancer of the Prostate, Penis and Cervix by Circumcision." *New York State Journal of Medicine* 51 (1951): 1519–20.

Ravich, Abraham. *Preventing VD and Cancer by Circumcision.* New York: Philosophical Library, 1973.

————. "The Relationship of Circumcision to Cancer of the Prostate." *Journal of Urology* 48 (1942): 298–99.

Rich, Adrienne. "Feminism." In *Words of Women,* ed. Ann Stibbs. London: Bloomsbury, 1993.

Richards, Audrey. *Chisungu: A Girl's Initiation Ceremony Among the Bemba of Zambia.* London: Routledge, 1982.

Rickwood, A. M. K. "Medical Indications for Circumcision." *British Journal of Urology* 83, suppl. 1 (January 1999): 45–51.

Ritter, Thomas J. *Say No to Circumcision.* Aptos, Calif.: Hourglass, 1992.

Rizq, Samyah Sulayman. *Nahwa istratijiyyah i'lamiyyah li-muwajahat al-khitan.* Cairo: Maktabat al-anglo al-masriyyah, 1994.

Romberg, Rosemary. "Circumcision and the Christian Parent." <www.noharmm.org/christianparent.htm> (accessed 12 May 2005).

————. *Circumcision, the Painful Dilemma.* South Hadley, Mass.: Bergin and Garvey, 1985.

Rubin, Gayle. "The Traffic in Women: Notes on the 'Political Economy' of Sex." In *Toward an Anthropology of Women,* ed. Rayna Reiter. New York: Monthly Review Press, 1975.

Salim, Muhammad Ibrahim. *Dalil al-hayran fi hukm al-khifad wal-khitan kama yarah al-fuqaha wal-atibba.* Cairo: Maktabat al-Qur'an, 1994.

Sault, Nicole, ed. *Many Mirrors: Body Image and Social Relations.* New Brunswick, N.J.: Rutgers University Press, 1994.

Savell, Kristin Louise. Wrestling with Contradictions: Human Rights and Traditional Practices Affecting Women. *McGill Law Journal* 41, 4 (1996): 781–817.

Schuler, Margaret, ed. *Freedom from Violence: Women's Strategies from Around the World.* New York: United Nations Development Fund for Women, 1992.

———, ed. *From Basic Needs to Basic Rights.* Washington, D.C.: Institute of Women, Law, and Development, 1995.

Seif El Dawla, Aida, Amal Abdel Hadi, and Nadia Abdel Wahab. "Women's Wit over Men's: Trade-Offs and Strategic Accommodations in Egyptian Women's Reproductive Lives." In *Negotiating Reproductive Rights: Women's Perspectives Across Countries and Cultures*, ed. Rosalind Petchesky and Karen Judd. New York: Zed Books, 1998.

Sen, Amartya. *Development as Freedom.* New York: Anchor Books, 1999.

Shaltout, Mahmoud. *Al-fatawi.* 10th ed. Cairo and Beirut: Dar al-shourouq, 1980.

Shanafelt, Robert. "Idols of Our Tribes? Relativism, Truth and Falsity in Ethnographic Fieldwork and Cross-cultural Interaction." *Critique of Anthropology* 22, 1 (2002): 7–31.

Shell-Duncan, Bettina. "The Medicalization of Female 'Circumcision': Harm Reduction or Promotion of a Dangerous Practice?" *Social Science and Medicine* 52 (2001): 1013–28.

Shell-Duncan, Bettina and Ylva Hernlund, eds. *Female "Circumcision" in Africa: Culture, Controversy, and Change.* Boulder, Colo.: Lynne Rienner, 2000.

Shell-Duncan, Bettina, Walter Obungu Obiero, and Leunita Auko Muruli. "Women Without Choices: The Debate over Medicalization of Female Genital Cutting and Its Impact on a Northern Kenyan Community." In *Female "Circumcision" in Africa: Culture, Controversy and Change*, ed. Bettina Shell-Duncan and Ylva Hernlund. Boulder, Colo.: Lynne Rienner, 2000.

Shweder, Richard. "What About Female Genital Mutilation?" and "Why Understanding Culture Matters in the First Place." In *Engaging Cultural Differences: The Multicultural Challenge in Liberal Democracies*, ed. Richard Shweder and Martha Minow. New York: Russell Sage, 2002.

Sperlich, Betty Katz. "Cutting Edge." *Nursing Times* 93, 9, 19 February 1997.

Spock, Benjamin. "Letter to Editor." *Moneysworth* 5, 5, 29 March 1976: 12.

*Strabon. *Géographie de Strabon*, trans. Amédée Tardieu. Vol. 3. Paris: Hachette, 1909.

Strathern, Marilyn. "An Awkward Relationship: The Case of Feminism and Anthropology." *Signs* 12 (1986): 278–92.

Strathern, Marilyn. *The Gender of the Gift: Problems with Women and Problems with Society in Melanesia.* Berkeley: University of California Press, 1988.

Stengers, Jean and Anne Van Neck. *Histoire d'une grande peur: la masturbation.* Brussels: Éditions de l'Université de Bruxelles, 1984.

Tadros, Mariz. "Breaking the Silence: An Egyptian Experience." *Hadithi* (Rainb ♀) 2 (2000).

Tapsoba, Placide et al. "FGM: What Are the Determinants to Behavior Change? Findings from Various Appraisal Techniques in Bazega, Burkina Faso, and Navrongo,

Ghana." Paper presented at the annual meeting of the American Public Health Association, Washington D.C., 1998.

Thesiger, Wilfred. *Arabian Sands*. London: Longmans, 1959.

Tostan and Population Council. *Breakthrough in Senegal: A Report on the Process Used to End Female Genital Cutting in 31 Villages*. Dakar: Population Council and US-AID, 1999.

Toubia, Nahid. *Female Genital Mutilation: A Call for Global Action*. New York: Rainb ♀, 1993, 1995; also Women, Ink.

Toubia, Nahid and Susan Izett. *Female Genital Mutilation, an Overview*. Geneva, Switzerland: WHO, 1998.

Turner, Terence. "Social Body and Embodied Subject: The Production of Bodies, Actors, and Society Among the Kayapo." *Cultural Anthropology* 10, 2 (1995): 143–70.

United Nations Economic and Social Council. Report of the United Nations seminar on traditional practices affecting the health of women and children, Ouagadougou, Burkina Faso, 29 April-3 May 1991. 12 June 1991. E/CN.4/Sub.2/1991/48.

United Nations Economic and Social Council. Report of the United Nations conference on traditional practices affecting the health of women and children. 1997. E/CN.4/sub.2./1997/10.

United States Department of Justice, Board of Immigration Appeals. Matter of Kasinga; Gender Asylum Decision. Interim Decision 3278 (BIA), In Re Fauziya Kasinga, Applicant, File A73 476 695-Elizabeth, decided June 13, 1996. <www.usdoj .gov.eoir/vll.intdec.vol21.3278.pdf> (accessed 21 April 2005).

United States Department of State, Bureau of Democracy, Human Rights and Labor, Office of Asylum Affairs. *Female Genital Mutilation in Guinea*. Washington, D.C.: Department of State, Bureau of Democracy, Human Rights and Labor, Office of Asylum Affairs, 27 January 1997.

United States Department of State, Bureau of Democracy, Human Rights, and Labor. *Togo Country Report on Human Rights Practices for 1996*. Washington, D.C.: Department of State, Bureau of Democracy, Human Rights and Labor, 30 January 1997. <http://www.state.gov/www/global/human_rights/1996_hrp_report/togo .html> (accessed 12 May 2005).

United States Department of State, Office of the Senior Coordinator for International Women's Issues. *Sudan: Report on Female Genital Mutilation (FGM) or Female Genital Cutting (FGC)*. Washington, D.C.: U.S. Department of State, 2001. <http://www.state.gov/g/wi/rls/rep/crfgm/10110.htm> (accessed 12 May 2005).

Van Howe, Robert S. "Neonatal Circumcision and HIV Infection." In *Male and Female Circumcision Among Jews, Christians and Muslims: Religious, Medical, Social and Legal Debate*, ed. Aldeeb Abu-Sahlieh and Sami Awad. Warren Center, Pa.: Shangri-La Publications, 2001.

———. "Why Does Neonatal Circumcision Persist in the United States?" In *Sexual Mutilations: A Human Tragedy*, ed. George C. Denniston and Marilyn Fayre Milos. New York: Plenum Press, 1997.

Walker, Alice and Pratibha Parmar. *Warrior Marks: Female Genital Mutilation and the Sexual Binding of Women.* New York: Harcourt, Brace, 1993.

Wallerstein, Edward. *Circumcision: An American Health Fallacy.* New York: Springer Publishing, 1980.

———. "Female Circumcision." *Encyclopedia Americana,* 6: 735. Danbury, Conn.: Grolier, 1984.

Walley, Christine J. "Searching for 'Voices': Feminism, Anthropology, and the Global Debates over Female Genital Operations." *Cultural Anthropology* 12, 3 (1997): 405–38.

Warren, John P. "Norm UK and the Medical Case Against Circumcision, a British Perspective." In *Sexual Mutilations: A Human Tragedy,* ed. George C. Denniston and Marilyn Fayre Milos. New York: Plenum Press, 1997.

Warsame, Mohamed. "Medical and Social Aspects of Female Circumcision in Somalia." Paper presented at the International Seminar on Female Circumcision: Strategies to Bring About Change, held in Mogadishu, Somalia, sponsored by the Italian Association for Women in Development (AIDOS) and the Somali Women's Democratic Organization (SWDO), 1988. Rome: Italian Association for Women in Development, 1989.

Whitfield, H. N., J. D. Frank, G. Williams, and J. A. Vale, eds. Special Supplement on Circumcision. *British Journal of Urology* 83, suppl. 1 (January 1999).

Williams, Melissa. "The Uneasy Alliance of Group Representation and Deliberative Democracy." In *Citizenship in Diverse Societies,* ed. Will Kymlicka and Wayne Norman. Oxford: Oxford University Press, 2000.

Williams, Preston. "A Personal Perspective on the Elimination of Female Circumcision." *Case Western Reserve Law Journal* 47, 2 (1997): 491–99.

Wiswell, T. E. and J. W. Bass. "Decreased Incidence of Urinary Tract Infections in Circumcised Male Infants." *Pediatrics* 75 (1985): 901–3.

Wolbarst, Abraham L. "Circumcision and Penile Cancer." *Lancet* 1 (1932): 150–53.

World Health Organization (WHO). *Female Genital Mutilation. A Joint WHO/ UNICEF/UNFPA Statement.* Geneva: WHO, 1997.

———. *Female Genital Mutilation: An Overview.* Geneva: WHO, 1998.

———. *Female Genital Mutilation Information Kit.* Geneva: WHO, 1996.

———. *Female Genital Mutilation Programmes to Date: What Works and What Doesn't: A Review.* Geneva: WHO, 1999.

———. *Female Genital Mutilation: The Prevention and the Management of the Health Complications: Policy Guidelines for Nurses and Midwives.* Geneva: WHO, 2001.

———. "Female Genital Mutilation: Report of a World Health Organization Technical Working Group, 17–19 July 1995." Geneva: WHO, 1996.

World Health Organization (WHO). *Female Genital Mutilation: The Practice.* Geneva: WHO, July 1994.

———. *Mutilations sexuelles féminines: dossier d'information.* Geneva: WHO, 1994.

World Health Organization (WHO), Regional Office for the Eastern Mediterranean. "Traditional Practices Affecting the Health of Women and Children: Female Circumcision, Childhood Marriage, Nutritional Taboos etc." Report of a seminar, Khartoum, 10–15 February 1979.

Yoder, P. Stanley and Mary Mahy. *Female Genital Cutting in Guinea: Qualitative and Quantitative Research Strategies.* Calverton, Md.: Opinion Research Center Macro, 2001.

Yoder, P. Stanley, Papa Ousmane Camara, and Baba Soumaoro. *Female Genital Cutting and Coming of Age in Guinea.* Calverton, Md.: Macro International; Conakry, Guinea: Université de Conakry and 1999.

Zenie-Ziegler, Wedad. *La Face voilée des femmes d'Egypte.* Paris: Mercure de France, 1985. In *Sexual Mutilations: A Human Tragedy*, ed. George C. Denniston and Marilyn Fayre Milos. New York: Plenum Press, 1997.

Zwang, Gérard. "Functional and Erotic Consequences of Sexual Mutilations." In *Sexual Mutilations: A Human Tragedy*, ed. George C. Denniston and Marilyn Fayre Milos. New York: Plenum Press, 1997.

Contributors

Raqiya Dualeh Abdalla is President of the Somali Family Care Network, which provides technical assistance to community-based organizations of ethnic Somalis in the United States and works with refugee women from the Horn of Africa on issues related to reproductive and sexual health and health care. Abdalla has held several important policy-making posts in government, nongovernmental organizations, and international institutions. In Somalia, she was a vice minister of health and vice president of the Somali Women's Democratic Organization. She served as senior program advisor to the United Nations Development Programme in the Sudan for five years. Abdalla initiated the first campaign to combat the practice of female genital mutilation in Somalia. Her ground-breaking 1982 book, *Sisters in Affliction*, was very influential, especially when it was translated into the Somali language. She holds a B.A. in Social Sciences from the College of Education in Somalia and a Master's in Public Policy and Women in Development from the Institute of Social Studies, The Hague.

Amal Abdel Hadi, a physician and human rights activist, directs the New Woman Research Center and Foundation in Cairo, Egypt. With Nadia Abdel Wabah, she edited *The Feminist Movement in the Arab World*. Abdel Hadi is a long-time member of the Egyptian Female Genital Mutilation Task Force and coordinated the Women's Program at the Cairo Institute of Human Rights Studies. With Seham Abdel-Salam, she also carried out a study of the attitudes of Egyptian physicians toward female circumcision. Abdel Hadi is a member of the Coalition for Sexual and Bodily Rights in Muslim Societies, an international coalition of nongovernmental organizations to promote the recognition of women's sexual, bodily, and reproductive rights as human rights and the realization of the Beijing Platform for Action on its tenth anniversary in 2005. She has written widely on Islamic law, human rights, and women's reproductive health.

Rogaia Mustafa Abusharaf is a senior research associate at the Pembroke Center for Teaching and Research on Women at Brown University. She has been a fellow at the Royal Anthropology Institute, Durham University, and at the Carr Center for Human Rights Policy at the John F. Kennedy School of Government, the Center for the Study of World Religions at the Divinity School, the François-Xavier Bagnoud Center for Health and Human Rights at the School of Public Health, and the W. E. B. Du Bois Institute for African and African American Research, all at Harvard University. She has held teaching appointments at Connecticut College, Brown University, Tufts University, Wellesley College, and Durham University. A native of the Sudan, Abusharaf was educated at the Cairo University School of Economics and Political Sciences in Egypt and earned a Ph.D. in Anthropology at the University of Connecticut. Her first book focused on recent migrations to the U.S. and Canada. Abusharaf is currently doing research on refugee women in the Sudan, focusing especially on rape as an instrument of forced migration in Darfur and on Arabization and Islamization among displaced southern Sudanese women in Khartoum.

Shahira Ahmed is Program Coordinator at the Program on International Health and Human Rights, François-Xavier Bagnoud Center for Health and Human Rights, School of Public Health, Harvard University. Among various projects, she coordinates the work of the UNAIDS Global Reference Group on HIV/AIDS and Human Rights, providing expert guidance to UNAIDS on applying rights-based approaches to key and emerging HIV/AIDS issues. Previously, she was a research coordinator at the Women and Public Policy Program at the John F. Kennedy School of Government at Harvard University, where she worked in the Women Waging Peace initiative, which aims to connect women in conflict areas to one another and to policy shapers worldwide. Ahmed provides technical advice on addressing the health and humanitarian situation in the Sudan, her home country, and has also researched, written, and spoken on the cultural aspects and implications of female circumcision. She has a Master's in Public Health degree with an International Health concentration from Boston University School of Public Health.

Sami Awad Aldeeb Abu-Sahlieh is head of Arab and Islamic Law at the Swiss Institute of Comparative Law in Lausanne. A Christian Arab of Palestinian origin, he now has Swiss citizenship (where his official surname is Aldeeb). He holds a doctorate in law from the University of Fribourg and a degree in political science from the Graduate Institute of International Studies in Geneva. Aldeeb has written many books and articles on Arab and Islamic law, on male and female circumcision in the Islamic, Christian, and Jewish traditions, and on Muslims in Europe. He is best known for his articulate and deeply informed opposition to male as well as female circumcision. Aldeeb is also active in international efforts to secure a just peace in Israel/ Palestine.

Ian Askew has over twenty years of international experience in the field of reproductive health, including fifteen years living and working in sub- Saharan Africa. He holds a Ph.D. in Sociology from Exeter University and previously served as deputy director of its Institute of Population Studies. He also studied geography at York University in Toronto. Askew is currently a se- nior associate with the Population Council and heads its office in Nairobi. He is also associate director for Africa for the Population Council's research program, Frontiers in Reproductive Health. Since 1994, this USAID-funded program has supported and undertaken operations research studies of fe- male genital cutting, HIV/AIDS prevention, and integrated maternal and child health programs in several African countries. Askew has published nu- merous articles coauthored with Jane Njeri Chege, Guyo W. Jaldesa, Heidi Jones, Baker Ndugga Maggwa, and Carolyne Njue, as well as Nafissatou J. Diop.

Nafissatou Jocelyne Diop is a program associate for Frontiers in Reproduc- tive Health, an operations research program conducted by the Population Council with support from USAID. Based in the Population Council's Sene- gal Regional Office for West and Central Africa, Diop implements and mon- itors operations research studies in family planning and reproductive health programs and services in West Africa, especially studies of female genital mutilation and youth. She played a key role in evaluations of Tostan's Village Empowerment Program and its replication in other countries. Diop was ed- ucated in France, where she earned a Master's degree in Sociology at the Uni- versity of Nanterre, Paris, focusing on the socioeconomics of development; she earned a Ph.D. in Demography at the University of Montreal, with a dis- sertation on adolescent fertility.

Hamid El Bashir is currently program coordinator for UNICEF in Romania. After joining UNICEF in 1995, he worked in the Sudan, Bangladesh, and the Caucasus countries (Armenia, Georgia, and Azerbaijan) as a Child Protec- tion officer and advisor. His commitment to development, social change, hu- man rights, and peace is also expressed in his writing. El Bashir has written two books on the civil war in the Nuba Mountains in Sudan, published in Arabic in Khartoum, as well as articles in English about famine and coping strategies in the Darfur region of Sudan and de-agrarianization in Africa.

A native of the Sudan, he earned a Ph.D. in Anthropology from the University of Connecticut.

Fadwa El Guindi taught anthropology at the University of California, Los Angeles, until her retirement, and currently teaches anthropology at the University of Southern California. In addition to her long-term field research among Nubians in Egypt, she has studied life cycle rituals and gender in Arab and Islamic culture, in the contemporary Islamic movement, and among Arab and Muslim Americans. Her most recent book, *Veil: Modesty, Privacy, and Resistance,* has attracted wide notice among feminists. By presenting life crisis rituals from a native's point of view, her previous book, *Zapotec: The Myth of Ritual,* represented an innovation in ethnographic methodology. El Guindi has conducted and produced several visual ethnographies, including "El Segou': Egyptian Brith Ritual," "El Moulid: Egyptian Religious Festival," and "Ghurbal." She directs El Nil Research, a visual anthropology center with emphasis on Arab culture, Arab-American culture, and Islam, which is located in Los Angeles.

Audrey Macklin is on the Law Faculty at the University of Toronto. Her main interests include migration and citizenship, law and culture, and gender. Macklin has served as a member of Canada's Immigration and Refugee Board, where she adjudicated asylum claims and participated in revising and applying guidelines on gender-related persecution and refugee status. In 1999, Macklin was a member of a fact-finding mission investigating links between the oil industry and violations of humanitarian and international human rights law in the Sudan. In 2002, she participated in a mission to Israel and Palestine with a group of Canadian women of Jewish, Arab, and Muslin backgrounds to document the experiences of Palestinian and Israeli Jewish feminist activists under the second Intifada and reoccupation. Macklin took law degrees at Yale and Toronto after earning a B.S. in Alberta.

Asha Mohamud was formerly a senior program officer with the Program for Appropriate Technology in Health (PATH), where she supervised field staff in programs to eradicate female genital mutilation and evaluate their effectiveness and directed the International Programs Department of Advocates for Youth. A physician, pediatrician, and reproductive health specialist, she earned her medical degree from the Somali National University and an M.P.H. from the School of Public Health at the University of California, Los Angeles. In her home country, Somalia, she served as deputy director of the

Family Health and Family Planning Program at the Ministry of Health, overseeing the national Maternal and Child Health and Family Planning health
centers. Mohamud is currently director of the African Youth Alliance Project
for PATH. Based in Uganda, this cooperative project, a partnership with
Pathfinder and UNFPA, addresses adolescent AIDS prevention and care in
four African countries.

Leslye Amede Obiora teaches at the University of Arizona College of Law.
With law degrees from the University of Nigeria, Yale, and Stanford, she spe-
cializes in human rights, public international law, jurisprudence and gender
and has written numerous influential articles on feminism, legal theory, and
culture. At the time she commented on the essays collected in this volume,
she was Visiting Gladstein Distinguished Professor of Human Rights at the
University of Connecticut. Her activist background includes founding the
Indigent Patients' Free Medical Care Center and the Institute for Research on
African Women, Children, and Culture (IRAWCC).

Charles Piot is Creed Black Associate Professor of Cultural Anthropology
and African and African American Studies at Duke University. His research
has focused on the political economy and history of rural Africa; his most recent book is *Remotely Global: Village Modernity in West Africa*. One of his
current projects examines the ways human rights discourse, democratization,
development, and charismatic Christianity are articulating with West
African political cultures. Piot is also tracking global discourses about female
genital cutting from Western courtrooms and media into the capitals and
villages of West Africa.

Samson Radeny was formerly a senior program officer with the Program for
Appropriate Technology in Health (PATH), where he was in charge of the
culture, gender, and health programs. Currently regional program director
(East and Southern Africa) for Medical Assistance Program International,
he is responsible for the conceptualization, direction, and evaluation of
behavior-change and training programs in the region. Born in Kenya, he
holds a Ph.D. in Sociology. Radeny is a member of the Global Health Council, a member of the Center for the Study of Adolescence, and board chair of
the Child to Child Organization in Kenya. Among his noteworthy projects
are a reproductive health education program with Boy Scouts focusing on
the prevention of HIV infection and changing attitudes toward FGM and a
study of first-time sexual experiences among adolescents in Kenya. He has

also published in collaboration with other contributors to this volume, including Ian Askew and Asha Mohamud.

Karin Ringheim, a sociologist, was formerly a senior program officer with the Program for Appropriate Technology in Health (PATH). Her work at PATH focused on evaluation system and on projects addressing HIV/AIDS, gender, and human rights. Ringheim holds graduate degrees in Sociology, Health Education, and Epidemiology. She previously worked for the World Health Organization in Geneva and for the Office of Population at USAID in Washington, D.C., where she managed operations research. Her commitment to gender equity led her to convene and cochair the Men and Reproductive Health Committee of the USAID Interagency Gender Working Group. In her current work as Research and Analysis Director for the Global Health Council, she is involved in a qualitative study on the role of faith-based organizations in HIV prevention, care, and support in six countries.

Index

Acknowledgments

This book is dedicated to Elizabeth Weed, who recognized the importance of African women's agency in addressing female circumcision and acknowledged their voices as the authoritative sources on this issue. Only by attending to women as subjects can the violence of representation be redressed, just as the practice of female circumcision can only be eradicated by women themselves.

We would like to thank the Rockefeller Foundation, Bellagio Program, for supporting the conference in Italy which most contributors attended; Elizabeth Barboza, of the Pembroke Center at Brown University, for managing the international conference; and Karen Colvard, of the Harry Frank Guggenheim Foundation, for participating in the Bellagio conference and providing constructive suggestions.

For helping to make this book, we thank Grey Osterud, our editor, who helped pull together these disparate contributions; at the University of Pennsylvania Press, Patricia Smith, Eric Halpern, Walda Metcalf, and the three anonymous readers who provided guidance along the way, and especially Peter Agree, who despite the delays and difficulties that remain in this era of seemingly instant international communication, finally brought this project to fruition.

Special thanks extend to those people who participated in the international conference but could not contribute to this volume. Asma Abdel Halim, who has worked in the field in Senegal, Burkina Faso, Gambia, and Egypt and whose essay, "Claiming Our Bodies," first framed female circumcision as a women's rights and human rights issue, played a key role in formulating the questions this book addresses, as well as inspiring other African activists to act as advocates internationally. Manal Abdelhalim, of the Mwtawinat Group in Khartoum, spoke at the conference about Sudanese women's efforts to eradicate the practice. Connie Kamara also shared her work in Guinea with the conference participants.

Finally, I acknowledge Amna Mahgoub, who might otherwise remain anonymous, who inspired women in her family and neighborhood network to abandon female circumcision entirely, exemplifying the everyday struggles and achievements of African women to improve their lives.